A Legacy of Caring

A HISTORY OF THE CHILDREN'S AID SOCIETY OF TORONTO

A Legacy of Caring

A HISTORY OF THE CHILDREN'S AID SOCIETY OF TORONTO

JOHN MCCULLAGH

THE DUNDURN GROUP
TORONTO · OXFORD

Copy-Editor: Lloyd Davis
Design: Jennifer Scott
Printer: Transcontinental

National Library of Canada Cataloguing in Publication Data

McCullagh, John
      A legacy of caring : the Children's Aid Society of Toronto / John McCullagh.

Includes bibliographical references and index.
ISBN 1-55002-335-7

1. Children's Aid Society of Toronto–History. I. Title.

HV746.T6M33 2002   362.7'06'0713541   C2002-901066-7

1   2   3   4   5   06   05   04   03   02

We acknowledge the support of the **Canada Council for the Arts** and the **Ontario Arts Council** for our publishing program. We also acknowledge the financial support of the **Government of Canada** through the **Book Publishing Industry Development Program** and **The Association for the Export of Canadian Books**, and the **Government of Ontario** through the **Ontario Book Publishers Tax Credit** program.

Dundurn Press
8 Market Street
Suite 200
Toronto, Ontario, Canada
M5E 1M6

Dundurn Press
73 Lime Walk
Headington, Oxford,
England
OX3 7AD

Dundurn Press
2250 Military Road
Tonawanda NY
U.S.A. 14150

Dedicated to the present and former board members,
staff, foster parents and volunteers of the
Children's Aid Society of Toronto and the
Infants' Home and Infirmary.

TABLE OF CONTENTS

The deaths of Shanay Johnson and Jennifer Koval's'kyj-England
Child Welfare Reform

ACKNOWLEDGMENTS

This history of the Children's Aid Society of Toronto is the product of the cooperative efforts of many people without whose support and input it could not have been written.

The society's Staff Alumni Association — and, in particular, former president Paul Michaelis, current president Maureen Duffy and members Tony Diniz, Jean Fuerd, Terry MacFarlane, Mona Robinson, Jessie Watters and Dave Wright — conceived the idea of publishing a history of the agency and saw it through to completion.

A generous grant from the Children's Aid Foundation supported the research, much of which was undertaken by Dr. Gail Aitken and Dr. Don Bellamy. Over the course of several years, they combed through agency and government archival materials, academic theses and books, journals and articles (both published and unpublished), many of which were located by George Wharton and his colleagues at the City of Toronto Archives. Doctors Aitken and Bellamy also conducted lengthy interviews with a large number of the society's current and former board members, foster parents, staff and volunteers, analyzed their research and organized it into the first draft of this book.

An advisory committee consisting of Gail Aitken, Don Bellamy, Tony Diniz, Maureen Duffy, Sheilagh Johnson, Bruce Leslie, Melanie Persaud and Bruce Rivers provided me with invaluable support and direction as well as feedback on the style and content of the manuscript. Bev Lepischak gave useful advice from the perspective of a social work professional not directly connected to the society and its work.

Conversations with a large number of witnesses to the work of the society over the past fifty years form a significant part of the source material for this book, particularly from Chapter 4 onward. The names of a fair number of these witnesses appear in the text, while the information provided by others helped put the agency's day-to-day work in the historical context of the times. All were unfailingly responsive to Gail Aitken's, Don Bellamy's or my inquiries. Their names are: Ethel Allen, Doug Barr, Joyce Barretto, Joan Berndt, Carolyn Buck, Mollie Christie, Joyce Cohen, Anne Coulter, Nancy Dale, Jack Darville, Tony Diniz, Kim Dorian, Sheila Dowdell, Kathy Duncan, Jill Evertman, Nancy Falconer, Mel Finlay, Jean Fuerd, Doug Gardner, Brian Greggains, Joyce Greggains, Leyland Gudge, Janet Haddock, Peter Hagerdoorn, Valerie Hartling, Farrell Haynes, Don Hepburn, Dorothy Herberg, Maggie Hunter, Carol Irwin, James Joyce, Sheliagh Johnson, Russell Joliffe, Betty Kashima, Linda Kiss, Margaret Leitenberger, Donna Leslie, Mary Lewis, John Liston, Joanne Maltby, Ruth Manke, Mardy Marlow, Sheila McDermott, Hanna McDonough, Marcellina Mian, Paul Michaelis, Lori Morina, Sandy Moshenko, Susan Oley, Jim Patterson, Shirley Pearse, Marilyn Pearson, Marjorie Perkins, Richard Phillips, Brenda Pickup, Joan Poole, Ron Poole, Steve Raiken, Kenn Richard, Sharron Richards, Bruce Rivers, Mona Robinson, Agnes Roy, Sandra Scarth, Ron Smith, Sybil Smith, Mary Speers, Paul Steinhauer, Debbie Stillemunkes, Betty Stubbins, Jim Thompson, Ed Watson, Jessie Watters, Lois Wicks, Bob Witterick, Valerie Witterick, Gordon Wolfe, Wilma Wrabko and Dave Wright. I extend my apologies to anyone who, through my own oversight, I may have omitted from this list.

I would like to thank all the people at Dundurn Press who helped produce this book, in particular the company's president, Kirk Howard, copy editor Lloyd Davis and graphic designers Jennifer Scott and John Lee.

Finally, I owe a personal debt to my partner Arnold Brodkin for enduring my long hours at the computer.

JOHN McCULLAGH
Toronto,
October 2001

Foreword

It has often been said that the work of child welfare is a calling. It touches your heart, your spirit and your thoughts like few other experiences in life. Perhaps it is the immensity of the children's suffering and their resilience in overcoming adversity that underlies this phenomenon. Perhaps it is the complexity of the human condition and the journey to understand child maltreatment or to help parents stop the hurt and find a better way to care for their children. It may be the impact of an investigation, a complex court proceeding or an adoption-matching process between a child and adoptive parents. Whatever it is, the result is profound.

Four years ago, a group of committed staff alumni, including the then president of the Alumni Association, Paul Michaelis, along with committee members Tony Diniz, Jean Fuerd, Terry MacFarlane, Mona Robinson, Jessie Watters and David Wright, conceived the idea of a book to chronicle the history and development of child welfare service in Toronto at the Children's Aid Society of Toronto. With the generous funding support of the Children's Aid Foundation, the thorough research of Dr. Gail Aitken and Dr. Don Bellamy and the analysis and expert writing skills provided by John McCullagh, the dream of a book about the Children's Aid Society of Toronto and its exceptional history has finally been realized.

This book tells the story of child welfare in Toronto. Specifically, it recounts the history of two separate agencies concerned with the welfare of children: the Infants' Home and Infirmary, established in 1875, and the Children's Aid Society, incorporated in 1891. These agencies merged in 1951 to create one of the largest and most progressive child welfare organizations in Canada. This history extends to

1998 and ends with an analysis of what the future holds with the turn of the millennium. Through captions, pictures, excerpts and narrative, McCullagh weaves a powerful account of social policy development and the evolution of child welfare practice and legislation over the past 125 years.

Throughout the long history of the Children's Aid Society of Toronto and that of the Infants' Home, board members, staff, foster parents and volunteers have largely worked in obscurity. Theirs, however, is the legacy of more than 125 years of caring for Toronto's children in need and it is to them that this book is dedicated.

BRUCE RIVERS
Executive Director, Children's Aid Society of Toronto
Toronto, October 2001

CHAPTER 1

The Infants' Home,
1875–1890

The development of social services in nineteenth-century Toronto

Since the earliest days of European settlement in the late eighteenth century, orphaned, abandoned and neglected children were features of life in Upper Canada, as Ontario was known before Confederation. Apprenticeship and indenture were the main legal provisions for dealing with these youngsters, embodied in the Orphans Act of 1779 and the Apprentices and Minors Act of 1851. (In 1827, a Guardianship Act had provided for court-appointed guardians for fatherless children, although it would be another twenty-eight years before custody of a child could be awarded to a mother.)

The reality, however, was that most of those young people in need were simply taken in by neighbours without formality. Although this could be construed as an act of humanitarian kindness, such unregulated foster families undoubtedly believed that the young person's help around the house or on the farm would eventually more than offset the cost of their care.

By the mid-nineteenth century, many communities had begun to experience rapid growth and urbanization, and none more so than Toronto. Having become the provincial capital at Confederation, by the 1870s the city was Ontario's major commercial and manufacturing centre. Its population grew from about 60,000 in the 1850s to almost 200,000 in 1891, when the Children's Aid Society (CAS) was founded. In that year, it is estimated that there were about 15,250 children under five years of age in Toronto.

During the Victorian era, the majority of people in Toronto were Protestant Christians of British and Irish background. Others could trace their ancestry back to the United Empire Loyalists — colonists who had remained loyal to the Crown after the American Revolution — and other migrants from the United States. Some newcomers arrived, but Canada lost more people to emigration in those days than it gained through immigration.

Life in Toronto in this era was a comfortable experience for the middle class but was not easy for working people, most of whom spent the majority of their waking hours on the job, six days a week. Poor lighting, overcrowding and unsanitary conditions characterized most workplaces. Factory machines were unguarded, and fire escapes and ventilation systems were nonexistent. Although these factories and businesses in the burgeoning city provided jobs for many, unemployment and poverty were widespread, with crime, panhandling, alcoholism and prostitution the outcome.

Working-class children under the age of eight were assigned domestic chores such as housecleaning, fetching fuel and water and babysitting. Schooling often took second place. Enforcement of Ontario's compulsory education laws in the later years of the century was inadequate, while truancy and its accomplice, child labour, became commonplace.

Working-class children under the age of eight were assigned domestic chores such as housecleaning, fetching fuel and water and babysitting. Schooling often took second place. Enforcement of Ontario's compulsory education laws in the later years of the century was inadequate, while truancy and its accomplice, child labour, became commonplace.

According to historian G.P. de T. Glazebrook, girls under fourteen years of age and boys under twelve were officially barred from factory work — except in food canning, which was seasonal — while ten years was the minimum age for work in stores. However, collusion between employers, families and government inspectors meant that the law was often ignored. In 1882, a survey of nearly 44,000 workers found that 5 percent of them were children between the ages of five and fourteen. As will be described in Chapter 2, newsboys, regarded as running their own businesses, became a special focus of concern under the leadership of John Joseph Kelso, who was to go on to found Ontario's children's aid movement.

Living conditions for many of these families were harsh. They often had no alternative but to rent rundown and unsanitary houses, which contributed to serious health problems and high death rates from such contagious diseases as cholera, typhus and typhoid fever. Tuberculosis was responsible for as many as a third of deaths.

In 1875, thirty percent of all infants under one year of age died. While some of these deaths resulted from burns, scalding, drowning or other accidents, the main reason was infection, often transmitted by nursing mothers as well as through unpasteurized milk.

In Ontario, there was no equivalent to the British poor laws that provided help for the needy. Public action to address the circumstances of destitute families was held back because of an attitude, developed during the province's pioneer days, that valued those who were self-supporting, respectable and hard-working.

Some care, far from sufficient, was available at such houses of refuge as Toronto's House of Industry and House of Providence — workhouses where the residents received board in return for their labour. Jails sheltered the destitute elderly along with criminals and vagrants. For the most part, though, the poor were expected to fend for themselves or depend upon their families or private philanthropy for assistance.

Historians Andrew Jones and Leonard Rutman describe how the consequences of urbanization and industrialization nevertheless forced people to reconsider these predominant views about poverty:

> The mass movement of population to new industrial cities such as Toronto created problems of housing, health and employment. Family ties were perceived as weakening and individuals were left without resources to cope with distressing circumstances. The plight of the sick, the poor and the handicapped became more apparent in a closely settled city than in the country. Also, their problems impinged more directly on the lives of the more affluent city dwellers.
>
> As early as the 1830s, it was recognized that public aid could not be wholly withheld from the sick poor because of the danger posed by the outbreak of cholera. The developments in public health during the century were given impetus by the recognition that disease was no respecter of boundaries and that the slum dweller's illness was not his purely private misfortune that could be safely ignored by his wealthier neighbours.

In 1875, thirty percent of all infants under one year of age died. While some of these deaths resulted from burns, scalding, drowning or other accidents, the main reason was infection, often transmitted by nursing mothers as well as through unpasteurized milk.

"The developments in public health during the century were given impetus by the recognition that disease was no respecter of boundaries and that the slum dweller's illness was not his purely private misfortune that could be safely ignored by his wealthier neighbours."
—Andrew Jones and Leonard Rutman

Working alongside the Board of Inspectors of Prisons, Asylums and Public Charities, churches, fraternal organizations and private charitable societies established a wide range of institutions such as inner-city missions, orphanages, reformatories and hospitals, as well as programs to aid prisoners, encourage temperance, prevent cruelty to children and animals and maintain the moral and religious well-being of young women.

Between the mid-19th century and the First World War, more than a dozen institutions to protect children were established in Toronto.

"Women from prominent families played a major initiating role in these private charitable ventures [to protect children]. They usually espoused strong moral, evangelical and humanitarian aims and were committed to the values of respectability, Christian morality, established authority and personal responsibility."

— G.P. de T. Glazebrook

The Charity Aid Act of 1874 established a funding formula for government assistance. The act also required agencies receiving government funds to submit to inspection by provincial officials and to meet standards set by the province.

By mid-century, there was a budding acceptance of a sense of public responsibility for the relief of distress as well as the maintenance of social order and stability. In 1859, the province established the Board of Inspectors of Prisons, Asylums and Public Charities to develop governmental social welfare services. Working alongside the board, churches, fraternal organizations and private charitable societies established a wide range of institutions such as inner-city missions, orphanages, reformatories and hospitals, as well as programs to aid prisoners, encourage temperance, prevent cruelty to children and animals and maintain the moral and religious well-being of young women.

Institutions for children began to emerge under these auspices, first for those who were physically or developmentally handicapped, then for orphans, and finally for young offenders. Between mid-century and the First World War, more than a dozen institutions to protect children were established in Toronto. They included the Roman Catholic Orphans' Asylum of St. Paul's, founded prior to 1850; the Protestant Orphans' Home and Female Aid Society, set up in 1851 and known subsequently as the Protestant Children's Home and, since 1971, as Family Day Care Services; the Girls' Home (1856); the Boys' Home (1859); the Infants' Home (1875); the Rescue Home for Fallen Girls (1888); the Toronto Children's Aid Society (1891); the St. Vincent de Paul Children's Aid Society, now known as the Catholic Children's Aid Society (1894); and the Jewish Day Nursery and Orphanage (1909). There was also an orphanage connected with the House of Providence; in 1877, it cared for 223 children.

Glazebrook writes that "Women from prominent families played a major initiating role in these private charitable ventures. They usually espoused strong moral, evangelical and humanitarian aims and were committed to the values of respectability, Christian morality, established authority and personal responsibility."

Although these agencies were initiated under private sponsorship, it was not long before they were making demands for provincial government funds. This pressure resulted in the passing in 1874 of the Charity Aid Act, which established a funding formula for government assistance. The act also required agencies receiving government funds to submit to inspection by provincial officials and to meet standards set by the province.

The act had the effect of dramatically increasing the number of private agencies in Ontario that were involved in social welfare work. According to Jones and Rutman, within two decades of the law's enactment, the number of hospitals receiving government aid rose from ten to thirty-two, orphanages doubled from fourteen to twenty-eight and houses of refuge increased more than ninefold to thirty-two. By the 1890s, government-supported private agencies were an established feature of social welfare provision.

Baby farms

"Baby farming," the practice of taking as boarders children under two years of age who had been abandoned, orphaned or born to unmarried mothers, was very prevalent in nineteenth-century Toronto. Until the founding of the Infants' Home in 1875, there was no alternative for women who could not look after their own children.

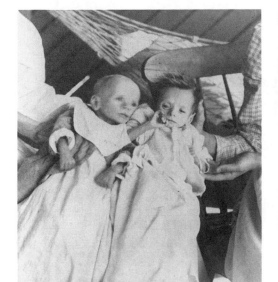

While some of these homes provided adequate care, others did not. Many of the children who boarded in them were neglected and ill treated. If the mother could not afford the fee, the babies were often underfed and given laudanum, an addictive opium derivative, to keep them quiet.

Sometimes, babies were traded for a fee between various care providers. Many infants who survived this treatment were subsequently abandoned and often died. If they were lucky, they might be informally adopted or bound into indentured service.

If the mother could not afford the fee demanded by the care providers, the babies were often underfed and given laudanum, an addictive opium derivative, to keep them quiet.

According to newspaper reporters who investigated baby farms, many of the children had "bodies that might be transparent if held against the light" and "features scarcely to be discerned through the layer of dirt which covered each face."

The concern about conditions in baby farms meant that, for many years, children's agencies had no interest in developing foster care facilities as an alternative to institutional care. It was in this climate that a group of socially prominent women, alarmed about high infant mortality and the spread of disease, joined together in 1875 to establish the Infants' Home.

The founding of the Infants' Home

Since the 1850s, Fenton Cameron, a Toronto physician, and his wife, Ann, had been trying to persuade influential friends, and the Burnside Lying-in Hospital, to open a home for destitute mothers and their babies. (The Burnside Lying-in Hospital was an Anglican institution that had been founded in the 1850s as a place where unwed mothers could give birth to their babies. In 1878, it amalgamated with Toronto General Hospital.)

It took twenty-five years, but, thanks to their efforts, the Infants' Home opened its doors in a cold, drafty, rented house at 11 Caer Howell Street — known today as Elm Street — on September 1, 1875. The home's purpose was described at a meeting of the managers of the Burnside Hospital earlier that year:

> To establish a nursery in connection with the hospital for the two-fold benefit of preserving the life of the infant and keeping the mother's in a state of comfortable assurance that, while she was nursing another child, her own would be properly and kindly treated. The fact of children dying so frequently has originated the idea of thus saving them.

Care and attention was to be expended "[t]o render the system as perfect as possible, deeming it a Christian duty to care for these children, whose feebleness and misfortune makes them worthy of compassion and whose preservation is an advantage because they may be useful in the country's service."

Charlotte Ridout, one of the managers of the Burnside hospital, was named the first president and held that position until 1900. During that time, the organization grew from a cottage of six or eight rooms to a 150-bed institution. As a result of her efforts, the city and the province made grants and the agency received many legacies and donations. Ann Cameron became the vice president and Fenton Cameron the home's visiting physician. A working board of twenty managers, all women, took turns visiting the home each day to supervise the care of the infants. They were also expected to solicit funds by canvassing from door to door.

Miscellaneous.

INFANTS' HOME.

The committee of the Infants' Home beg to announce that this Institution is now opened at No. 11 Caer Howell-street, and that contributions of money, fuel, furniture, clothing, and provisions of all descriptions are earnestly solicited and will be gratefully received by the MATRON at

NO. II CAER HOWELL-ST.

In twenty-five years, the Infants' Home grew from a cottage of six or eight rooms to a 150-bed institution.

A working board of twenty managers, all women, took turns visiting the home each day to supervise the care of the infants. They were also expected to solicit funds by canvassing from door to door.

Mayor William Howland, who dominated municipal politics in the 1880s and was deeply involved in improving the circumstances of the city's poor, chaired an advisory committee of three businessmen to assist the board of managers in financial matters. A committee of physicians provided medical expertise in the care of the children living in the home, all of whom were under two years of age, many sickly and dying.

The board of managers never seemed to have been daunted by any of the numerous difficulties that arose, including lack of funds, inadequate legislation, poorly trained staff and continuous epidemics among the children. For many years, they struggled with considerable public opposition to a home in which single mothers and their children were properly cared for — opposition rooted in the prevailing belief that "the weak moral values" of unmarried mothers could lead them to earn a living through prostitution.

In the agency's early days, many children from baby farms were admitted after payments from their mothers had ceased or the mother became alarmed at the kind of care her child was receiving. The 1879 annual report describes how "Wan, pinched children were brought to the home in [great] numbers, some half dead from the baby farms of the city, others suffering from the want and privation of the mothers."

Not all those who sought assistance from the Infants' Home were single mothers. Many admissions arose from disruptions to family life caused by death or because there were too many mouths to feed.

One of the first children admitted was the son of an immigrant widower whose wife's death had left him with a young baby to care for. At first, he boarded the child in a baby farm, but had to remove him after four months because the child was being neglected. In a letter of appreciation to the Infants' Home, he wrote:

> The baby had never been strong and was wore away [in the baby farm] to a perfect skeleton. So I applied to the lady president of the Infants' Home and the baby was kindly admitted. I visited him daily, expecting his death at each visit. By kindness, careful nursing and good nourishment, coupled with perfect cleanliness, my poor baby is now in perfect health and strength and as healthy looking as you could wish to see.

For many years, the board of managers struggled with considerable public opposition to a home in which single mothers and their children were properly cared for — opposition rooted in the prevailing belief that "the weak moral values" of unmarried mothers could lead them to earn a living through prostitution.

"The baby had never been strong and was wore away [in the baby farm] to a perfect skeleton. So I applied to the lady president of the Infants' Home and the baby was kindly admitted. I visited him daily, expecting his death at each visit. By kindness, careful nursing and good nourishment, coupled with perfect cleanliness, my poor baby is now in perfect health and strength and as healthy looking as you could wish to see."

Letter of appreciation from an early client

The Infants' Home admitted many foundlings — children abandoned at birth. The home's managers often named them after the streets where they were found, such as the infant who was given the name Matthew Yonge.

In 1882, a residence was built at 21 St. Mary Street, on the site of an old reservoir rented from the city for $1 a year. A fundraising drive had secured $14,000 for the new building.

Jessie Watters, the agency's casework consultant, and recipient of the Ontario Association of Children's Aid Societies' Outstanding Achievement Award, pictured here in 1996.

The Infants' Home also admitted many foundlings — children abandoned at birth. The home's managers often named them after the streets where they were found, such as a baby girl who was given the name Adelaide Street. Matthew Yonge was left on the doormat of the Infants' Home when it was located on Yonge Street. John Dufferin was found at the Dufferin Gate of the exhibition grounds, while Jane Western was left inside the door of the city's Western Hospital.

Meeting the needs of these children was the motivating factor that led to the establishment of the home. The founders knew that, in the absence of an institution that would admit infants, such children would continue to be abandoned and left to die or be boarded out in unsatisfactory baby farms.

The house on Caer Howell Street was, however, far too small to meet the heavy demand for admission and so on April 3, 1876, the home moved to a large mansion at 678 Yonge Street, which had been loaned to the organization rent-free in exchange for a promise to maintain it in a state of good repair. That house, in turn, quickly proved inadequate, which led to the decision in 1882 to erect a residence at 21 St. Mary Street, on the site of an old reservoir which was to be rented from the city for one dollar per year. A fundraising drive secured $14,000 for the new building.

Jessie Watters, who worked at the Children's Aid Society of Toronto from the 1940s until the 1970s, recalls a legend about the site:

> When workmen were draining the reservoir they came across the bodies of several infants. It was thought that these were children whose unmarried mothers had thrown them into the reservoir to conceal their births, due to the unyielding Victorian condemnation of child bearing outside marriage.

Although it was purpose-built, the agency's new home began to show its deficiencies at an early date. Because of trouble with the drains, the walls were constantly damp, which also meant that there were regular infestations of such vermin as rats and cockroaches. These invasions compromised the health of children who were already vulnerable and contributed to the epidemics to which the home was subject. It is not surprising, therefore, that in 1885 one of the home's doctors reported that

"Several children are suffering from inflamed eyes and eruptions of the face due to draughts in the nurseries which strike the infants as they lie on the floor asleep."

The residents and staff were constantly complaining about the drabness of the building's appearance, both inside and out. According to Vera Moberly, later to become the chief executive of the Infants' Home:

> It was a red-brick building, three stories in height, the very picture of an institution. The garden, which consisted largely of cinders, was enclosed by a high board fence surmounted by barbed wire. The lower windows were protected by netting and the doors were always kept locked.
>
> The ground floor was occupied by offices, the second floor by the dining room and day nurseries and the third by dormitories … [where] children whose mothers were [also living in] the institution slept in their mother's beds.
>
> The only place for exercise for the mothers was in the corridors, where, because of the draughts, they were advised to wear their shawls. All the radiators were constantly covered with drying diapers.

"The only place for exercise for the mothers [at the Infants' Home] was in the corridors, where, because of the draughts, they were advised to wear their shawls. All the radiators were constantly covered with drying diapers."

— Vera Moberly

Staffing

A "lady superintendent" was in charge of the day-to-day running of the house, supported by an assistant known as the matron. At first, the superintendent's salary was set at $10 a month. Over the years, it gradually increased and reached $50 a month by 1912. Among the superintendent's responsibilities, she was to "[m]ake herself personally acquainted with the mothers, with a view to encouraging them to lead a new life that they may look upon her as a friend to be confided in."

At first, the mothers did most of the work of the home in return for food, clothing and shelter for themselves and their children. Some of these mothers, often admitted to the home precisely because of their skills as cooks or needlewomen, were hired as paid employees. Over the course of time, however, the home hired two untrained

At first, the salaery of the superintendent of the Infants' Home was set at $10 a month. Over the years, it gradually increased and reached $50 a month by 1912.

nurses, a laundress, a seamstress and a caretaker. According to Moberly, "Petty jcal-
ousies among the staff were frequent and disrupting and there were continual changes
in personnel. On several occasions, the superintendent and matron were called before
the board in an effort to straighten out their quarrels."

Medical care

The children's medical care was a constant worry. Many were seriously ill, often close
to death, and had been admitted to the Infants' Home because, at that time, Toronto's
Hospital for Sick Children did not treat children under two years of age. The condition of the children in the shelter was aggravated by epidemics of whooping cough,
measles, chicken pox, diphtheria and scarlet fever that constantly swept the home. In
1880, there was an epidemic of malaria. Such outbreaks meant that the institution
was often closed to admissions, sometimes for several months at a time.

The condition of the children in the shelter was aggravated by epidemics of whooping cough, measles, chicken pox, diphtheria and scarlet fever that constantly swept the home.

During some of the epidemics, all of the children became ill and many died.
Malnutrition was the greatest cause of death. Others included tuberculosis, respi-
ratory diseases, congenital syphilis and the effects of the laudanum dispensed in
many baby farms.

The agency's managers paid serious heed to the prevalence of these epidemics
and high rates of child mortality at the Infants' Home. The workload was so heavy
that, in March 1877, they decided it was necessary to appoint two additional doctors. A further two were added in October of that year. These doctors, who volunteered their time, were among the best pediatricians in the city, and they worked
hard to save the lives of the children. The Infants' Home also allowed these doctors
to bring in students specializing in pediatric medicine. It thus became the first institution in the city to provide opportunities for students to gain experience in the
practical skills of their profession.

The Infants' Home's doctors, who volunteered their time, were among the best pediatricians in the city, and they worked hard to save the lives of the children. The agency also allowed them to bring in students specializing in pediatric medicine. It thus became the first institution in the city to provide opportunities for students to gain experience in the practical skills of their profession.

At about this time, after a string of upsetting incidents, the appointment of a
trained resident nurse was discussed. On one occasion, the person in charge of an
infant fainted and fell on the child, breaking his leg. Another time, the night nurse
fed the babies milk spiked with whiskey to keep them quiet. But a trained nurse was

not appointed, because the board of managers thought that an untrained superintendent could not work with a qualified professional. It was not until 1911 that the board, "feeling that the time has come when this home should be placed upon the footing of a hospital," appointed a trained nurse, Isobel Wilson, as superintendent.

Despite the board of managers' hesitance to hire a trained nurse, it had, in 1877, changed the agency's name to the Infants' Home and Infirmary because it had decided that the organization should not be merely a refuge for destitute children but also a hospital for infants. It proved difficult to attain this goal for several years, but in 1888, with the death rate among the children still high, funds were raised to add an annex to the west of the main building to serve as isolation quarters during periods of infection.

The board of managers had, in 1877, changed the agency's name to the Infants' Home and Infirmary because it had decided that the organization should not be merely a refuge for destitute children but also a hospital for infants.

Admissions and discharges

Early on, the Infants' Home could accommodate about forty-five infants and mothers at one time, but high infant mortality led to a similarly high rate of turnover. In all, 160 children were admitted during the first year of operation, of whom seventy-one died — an alarming death rate of 44 percent. Although the organization was able to reduce this percentage significantly in subsequent years, not until the introduction of foster family care in 1919 was the Infants' Home able to reduce the death rate of children in its care to the provincial average.

Not until the introduction of foster family care in 1919 was the Infants' Home able to reduce the death rate of children in its care to the provincial average.

Until then, the agency's managers gave serious attention to the prevalence of epidemics in the home and its high rates of child mortality. The agency's physicians played an important role by examining every child and mother seeking admission and recommending who should be received into the home. The annual report of 1877 cites one example:

> Dear Madam, there is a family named Thomas living on Albert Street, the mother of whom is in very bad health and must go to the hospital. Three of the children are to go to the Boy's Home, the youngest I have promised to aid. May I request that you will

"Dear Madam, there is a family named Thomas living on Albert Street, the mother of whom is in very bad health and must go to the hospital. Three of the children are to go to the Boy's Home, the youngest I have promised to aid. May I request that you will receive the little one in the Infants' Home? He is sadly in want of food, proper clothing and a bath."
— Infants' Home physician of a mother and her baby

Should an unmarried woman become pregnant a second time, readmission was always denied because, according to the values of the period, the mother was judged immoral. If it was discovered after admission that the child was not the first one born out of wedlock, both mother and baby were discharged immediately without any inquiry as to where they would go.

receive the little one in the Infants' Home? He is sadly in want of food, proper clothing and a bath.

Although foundlings were admitted as a matter of course, the process of admission for a mother with an infant was an ordeal. There was no certainty they would be accepted by the home — and often no alternative if they were not. According to Moberly:

> The mother had to appear [before a committee of the board of managers] to tell her story and produce her marriage certificate and give details concerning her husband and relatives. If she was unmarried, she was asked about her family, immigration [status], residence, employment and religion and had to obtain a certificate from a doctor stating that the child was her first. Whenever the committee had any doubt as to the veracity of the story, they might delay admission until they were satisfied.

Should an unmarried woman become pregnant a second time, readmission was always denied because, according to the values of the period, the mother was judged immoral. If it was discovered after admission that the child was not the first one born out of wedlock, both mother and baby were discharged immediately without any inquiry as to where they would go.

Overcrowding at the home was another frequent reason for admission to be denied. At least a thousand infants were turned away in the first five years of operation. The experience of a mother and her infant Lucy in 1878, described in that year's annual report, was not unusual.

> When admitted, the baby's father was dying of consumption in the hospital, the mother went out washing. Some charitable people gave her assistance and she took her baby out. Some time after, her husband died, and she reapplied again for the readmission of her child, but the home was overcrowded to such an extent that the

managers were compelled to refuse admission, although the child was dying and the case a very distressing one.

While rationing the home's resources could be upsetting, it was also treated dispassionately, as two further examples from the 1878 report testify:

> Fred was admitted for a few days with his mother. As the home was overcrowded, they were both sent away. It was believed she had friends who could help her.
>
> As the home was too crowded, after a few days Sarah was sent back to her mother as she was earning good wages and was able to provide for her elsewhere.

These examples bring into focus the paucity of other community resources for infants at the end of the nineteenth century.

Of the sixty-five children who were admitted in 1878, eighty-six percent were less than a year old. Of those, three-quarters were under the age of three months. What happened to them? According to that year's annual report, "Nine infants were adopted, four were sent to the Girls' Home, three to the House of Providence, 26 left for other institutions with their mothers and seven went to live with relatives. Twenty-three died. As for the mothers, a total of 44 were sent to their relatives or [referred for domestic service] and three were [expelled for breaking house rules]."

Breast-feeding

At a time when breast-feeding was considered unfashionable among the privileged, the managers stuck tenaciously to their view that it, as well as wet nursing (breast-feeding another woman's child in her absence), was essential to the saving of infant lives. The story of Walter's short life from the 1878 annual report is an example of how many bottle-fed babies fared in those times:

The origins of this baptismal font are unknown. It belonged to Vera Moberley and was used to baptize children at the Infants' Home.

"Nine infants were adopted, four were sent to the Girls' Home, three to the House of Providence, 26 left for other institutions with their mothers and seven went to live with relatives. Twenty-three died. As for the mothers, a total of 44 were sent to their relatives or [referred for domestic service] and three were [expelled for breaking house rules]."

— *1878 discharge statistics*

At a time when breast-feeding was considered unfashionable among the privileged, the managers of the Infants' Home stuck tenaciously to their view that it, as well as wet nursing (breast-feeding another woman's child in her absence), was essential to the saving of infant lives.

Infants' Home and Infirmary Formula Recipe

1/2 lb [230 g]   Oswego Cornstarch
(Oswego is found better than other brands)
4 qt [3.9 L]   New milk (our own cow's)
2 qt [1.9 L]   Water
3/4 lb [340 g]   Bright coffee sugar

Mother a wet nurse. The child had been [living at a baby farm] before coming to the home and as usual with bottle-fed children, was weak and wasted when admitted. Only lived a few weeks.

It was because of these experiences that the agency's medical report of 1879 stated that "Experience has been gained in the [bottle] feeding of infants. All of the patent foods have proved unsatisfactory and, with the exception of condensed milk, have been dispensed with."

The importance that the Infants' Home placed on breast-feeding "at nature's font" was the reason the board of managers insisted that a mother must enter the home along with her baby. Mothers were required to stay at least four months and, if possible, to nurse and feed another child who was orphaned or whose mother's whereabouts were unknown. Over time, the women became increasingly unwilling to act as wet nurses and the practice was dropped, although the insistence on a mother nursing her own child was maintained. But, this meant that some babies did require bottle feeding. The home had developed its own recipe for infant formula:

1/2 lb [230 g]   Oswego Cornstarch
(Oswego is found better than other brands)
4 qt [3.9 L]   New milk (our own cow's)
2 qt [1.9 L]   Water
3/4 lb [340 g]   Bright coffee sugar

Boil milk and water together and add cornstarch already moistened with a little cold milk and sweetened with the bright coffee sugar, the whole to be boiled by steam heat over a brisk fire for 1/2 hour. To be fed hot — never cold. The reason for using steam heat is to avoid the possibility of the mixture ever acquiring a burnt taste.

As the recipe illustrates, the agency owned its own cow. This was later supplemented by milk from the city dairies. Sir John Ross Robertson, the publisher of the

Toronto *Telegram* and a major benefactor of the Hospital for Sick Children, donated pasteurized milk for six months in the 1880s in an effort to convince the mothers of its worth.

Life at the Infants' Home

The children who lived in the home were dressed in mouse-grey flannel rompers with scarlet bands at the neck and cuffs. Their days were spent largely in the day nursery, where they ate their meals and slept on the floor for their afternoon nap. In good weather, they played outdoors in the sand pit.

The care of each child was left largely to its mother or wet nurse. The women were provided with striped blue and white uniforms, covered by a large apron. Their hair had to be worn drawn into a tight bun and covered by a white mob cap.

Cooking facilities were inadequate and meals on the scanty side. They might include a breakfast of oatmeal porridge, a lunch of meat and vegetables and a supper of bread and butter along with cheese or fruit. Tea was the regular beverage and occasional treats of ice cream were made available in the summer.

Only spasmodic attempts were made to introduce recreation, although morning and evening prayers were held each day, along with Sunday evening service and Wednesday Bible classes.

Given the adverse social attitudes toward unmarried mothers, this regime was well intentioned but, at the same time, demeaning. The women were not allowed to leave the grounds "owing to the general class of women in the home," and keys were not given to staff except for special emergencies. The mothers were physically isolated from their families and friends, who were often unaware of their circumstances. Although visitors were allowed on Sundays, and later on Thursday afternoons as well, all mail was censored and might be withheld.

Mothers were often summoned before the board of managers for swearing, quarrelling or insubordination. Many were asked to leave on account of such behaviour. Others simply ran away.

The care of each child was left largely to its mother or wet nurse. The women were provided with striped blue and white uniforms, covered by a large apron. Their hair had to be worn drawn into a tight bun and covered by a white mob cap.

Mothers were often summoned before the board of managers for swearing, quarrelling or insubordination. Many were asked to leave on account of such behaviour. Others simply ran away.

Not only did these women have to live by these strict rules but they also had to endure the ever-present threat of losing their babies to infectious diseases or because they were induced to allow them to be adopted.

Each woman was informed that her good conduct was necessary for the managers to recommend her to a family who might eventually employ her as a domestic servant. Although many of the mothers accepted such opportunities for work, especially when they were allowed to have their children with them, others opted for employment in factories and stores.

Although mothers who worked outside could board their infants at the home, the rule that non-working mothers had to stay for a fixed period of time, even if they did not have a living child, caused strong dissatisfaction among the residents.

Although mothers who worked outside could board their infants at the home, the rule that non-working mothers had to stay for a fixed period of time, even if they did not have a living child, caused strong dissatisfaction among the residents. Strict application of this rule eventually led to a lower rate of admission and consequent budgetary problems, because the home's per capita revenue was reduced. It took years for the board of managers to recognize that this policy had failed and to rescind it.

Advocacy and community development

The board of managers was progressive in its thinking and keenly interested in any approach that would improve the lives of the city's children. The managers took a very broad interest in community problems, engaging in what today we would regard as advocacy and community development work.

The board of managers was progressive in its thinking and keenly interested in any approach that would improve the lives of the city's children. The managers took a very broad interest in community problems, engaging in what today we would regard as advocacy and community development work.

One example was their success in getting the city to pass a bylaw in 1887 that required children's boarding homes to be registered. This made it illegal to retain more than one infant (exceptions were made for twins, but not for other siblings) under twelve months of age in boarding homes unless the home was registered, the care providers were legal guardians of the children, or the home was receiving aid from — and therefore subject to inspection by — the province. As a result of these efforts, the province passed the Maternity Boarding Home Act of 1898, making the licensing of children's boarding homes mandatory across Ontario.

Another initiative undertaken by the Infants' Home was the key role it played in the adoption of children. In this era, adoptions were managed through an Indenture of Adoption. This signed agreement was not binding, and was all too often entered into with the impression that the child could be returned if the plan did not work out. Any problems of adjustment were attributed to bad background coming out in the child.

The agency did much to make adoption a less hazardous undertaking by developing procedural rules as early as 1876. One of the requirements was related to the obtaining of good references.

> Those wishing to adopt children must bring a certificate to the board from a clergyman or some well-known resident in the neighbourhood where they live stating that they are able to bring up a child properly. If these references are considered satisfactory, they will be allowed to come and make their selection.

The Infants' Home handled all adoptions in Toronto until 1891, when the CAS was founded and began to share the responsibility. However, it would be another thirty years before the province recognized that adoption was an important public responsibility and regulated it under the Adoption Act, 1921.

Funding

The budget of the Infants' Home in 1875, its first year of operation, was $2,558. By 1919, it had reached $35,000. Throughout those years, the agency depended mainly on voluntary contributions, raised by the board of managers, to finance its operations. Donations were made in cash and in kind — including food, clothing and household wares.

This method of fundraising was maintained until 1919, when the home joined the newly formed Federation for Community Service, one of the earliest united charitable fund drives in Canada.

"Those wishing to adopt children must bring a certificate to the board from a clergyman or some well-known resident in the neighbourhood where they live stating that they are able to bring up a child properly. If these references are considered satisfactory, they will be allowed to come and make their selection."

— Procedural rule for adoption, 1876

Meanwhile, Mayor Howland arranged for the city to pay an annual stipend of $250 to the home, in return for which the mayor had the right to admit any seriously neglected infants who came to his attention. The city also paid for the care of foundlings admitted to the home.

The province initially contributed a grant of $150 a year. In return, it tried to enforce the admission of the children of prison inmates and patients of mental hospitals, without any further payment but under the threat of withdrawal of the grant.

These government grants increased over the years. By 1919, the city was contributing $3,270 annually and the province $1,383. That same year, the Infants' Home hired the nurse and social worker Vera Moberly as its first executive secretary. She was to go on to a long and distinguished career as the organization's chief executive, taking it into the modern era.

CHAPTER 2

A Society to Protect Children, 1891–1919

John Joseph Kelso

John Joseph Kelso did more than any other person in nineteenth-century Canada to improve the lives of poor and needy children. Perceptive and energetic, a persuasive speaker and a convincing writer, he brought their experiences and requirements to the attention of a largely apathetic public.

Kelso — or J.J., as he became known — founded and became the first president of the Children's Aid Society of Toronto, then went on to establish similar societies across Ontario and in much of the rest of the country. For forty-one years, he was the provincial government's Superintendent of Neglected and Dependent Children, responsible for ensuring that systems were in place to protect young people from exploitation and neglect.

Born in Ireland on March 31, 1864, Kelso came to Canada in 1874 at the age of ten. His father, George, and his mother, Anna, had been left penniless after a fire destroyed their starch manufacturing business, and they decided to try their luck in Toronto. Unfortunately, George found he could not support his family of six girls and three boys on his earnings from a low-paying clerical position. They suffered from hunger and cold.

J.J. — George and Anna's youngest child — was deeply affected by the family's disgrace at their circumstances. This spurred him, at age eleven, to skip school and get a job at a local bookstore. The ensuing years often found him as a messenger for the Dominion Telegraph Company or as a cash boy at Timothy Eaton's department store.

Kelso's success as a reporter led eventually to a job at The Globe, *where he exposed the circumstances under which the poor, particularly poor children, lived.*

In downtown Toronto, many poor children, most of them boys, engaged in street trades to help support their families. They worked long hours as bootblacks or sold newspapers, shoelaces, pencils and other small items. Sometimes they were their families' sole support in times of illness or unemployment.

The newspapers were complicit in supporting child labour because, without the newsboys, they would have been hard-pressed to distribute their product.

In 1884, when he was twenty years old, he enrolled at Jarvis Collegiate Institute to complete his education and, with the help of private tutoring, graduated in one year. He found work as a printer's apprentice, but soon started to dream of becoming a journalist. Eventually, he landed a job as a proofreader at *The World*, a racy, colourful newspaper aimed at Toronto's factory workers and clerks. In his spare time, he wrote articles for the paper — without pay — and became expert at reading and writing shorthand. This led to a promotion to crime reporter.

Kelso's success on that beat led eventually to a job at *The Globe*, a paper whose news coverage was soberer in tone than *The World*'s and which was more in tune with his aspirations. At *The Globe*, he exposed the circumstances under which the poor — and poor children, in particular — lived.

Kelso's campaign against child labour

As a crime reporter, Kelso had spent most of his working days in and around Toronto's downtown, where many poor children, most of them boys, engaged in street trades to help support their families. They worked long hours as bootblacks or sold newspapers, shoelaces, pencils and other small items. Sometimes they were their families' sole support in times of illness or unemployment.

An 1887 survey found that at least 700 Toronto youngsters were engaged in this kind of work. The newsboys were the most numerous and the most prominent. The papers were complicit in supporting child labour because, without the newsboys, they would have been hard-pressed to distribute their product. Boys who were not living with their families were paid ten cents a day for a bed and meals at lodgings, or just over a dollar for full weekly room and board. Some privately run agencies, such as the Newsboys' Lodging and Industrial Home, also gave shelter to a limited number of boys.

Even though these children had important roles in business and the family economy, reformers found little good to say about the youthful vendors on city streets. Their lives and living conditions were all too often thought to be conducive to rootlessness and criminal activity. Reformers were concerned that the young vendors might eventually become violent, untrustworthy adults who would become dependent on public resources.

Kelso and like-minded associates set about tackling the problem. In 1889, they were successful in having the Toronto Police Commission enact a bylaw that required street vendors under the age of sixteen to be licensed by the police. These licences were conditional on the child not acquiring a criminal record, steering clear of thieves, and spending at least two hours a day in school. Boys under the age of eight and girls of any age were barred from street vending. Children who broke the rules could be fined or sent to jail or an industrial school. (Industrial schools, first established in the mid-1880s, were the forerunners of Ontario's young offender institutions.) Employers could also be fined heavily for violations.

In response, the newspapers, as the most affected vested interest, labelled Kelso the "enemy of the newsboy" and — because of the bylaw's stipulation that newsboys wear identification tags — "Tagger Kelso." As was always the case throughout his life, J.J. was impervious to such criticism.

Newspapers called called Kelso the "enemy of the newsboy" because he and like-minded associates helped enact a bylaw that required street vendors under the age of sixteen to be licensed by the police.

The Humane Society of Toronto is established

Kelso was now in the public eye. W.F. Maclean, the editor of *The World*, had received a letter from John Kidston MacDonald, a prosperous businessman prominent in charitable activities, in which he complained about the lack of a society for the prevention of cruelty to animals — in particular, the overburdened delivery and street railway horses. This letter was forwarded to Kelso as something else for him to write about. He took the suggestion in earnest and, in response to his articles, money started to roll in for the establishment of such an organization.

Kelso, however, began to envision a society oriented toward the prevention of all types of cruelty, including the mistreatment of children. According to Jones and Rutman, Kelso was strongly influenced in this direction by a personal experience.

> Walking along Yonge Street late one night in November 1886, he
> came across two sobbing children, a brother and a sister. They told

him that their father had promised them a severe beating unless they could beg at least 25 cents that night. So far their tally was only 15 cents. J.J. took pity on them and searched for three hours to find a charitable institution to take them in for the night. The parents were charged the next morning with neglect but the case was dismissed by the judge on the basis that there were insufficient grounds for prosecution.

Kelso called for a non-denominational humane society with a broad set of objectives that would protect both children and animals.

Shortly afterward, the secretary of the Canadian Institute, where reform issues were often discussed, casually asked Kelso to speak. J.J. took advantage of the opportunity and, on February 19, 1887, delivered a paper whose title was "The Necessity of a Society for the Prevention of Cruelty in Toronto." He called for a non-denominational humane society with a broad set of objectives that would include the protection of both children and animals. Among its aims was the safeguarding of children from abusive and neglectful parents, the appointment of a full-time police officer to investigate complaints, and the establishment of a refuge for destitute children. His ideas were received enthusiastically.

Encouraged, Kelso began to set up the Humane Society of Toronto and was elected, at age twenty-three, as its organizing secretary. Mayor William Howland was named honorary president. For the next two years (in his spare time, for, like all such positions in those days, it was a volunteer job), Kelso collaborated with the police to protect both children and animals. Reformers were pleased with the society, while critics mocked it. The Toronto journal *Life Magazine*, for example, referred to Kelso in a May 1888 article as "The Secretary of the Humane Society, the General Reformation Society and the Interfere with Everybody's Business Society."

"The Secretary of the Humane Society, the General Reformation Society and the Interfere with Everybody's Business Society."
— Critics from the Toronto journal
Life Magazine *mock Kelso's efforts*

Undaunted, Kelso, under the auspices of the Humane Society, promoted free, tax-supported children's playgrounds. Another initiative was the Fresh Air Fund, which received a small municipal grant to provide excursions to the Toronto Island and the lakeside parks. In the first five years, 30,000 children benefited from it. Christmas entertainments and gifts were also arranged. To make happy Christmas celebrations for poor children, the society also organized a Santa Claus Fund that sponsored a party on Christmas Eve for hundreds of children.

Eventually, the *Toronto Star* took over the Fresh Air and Santa Claus funds. The good these funds did, however, gave only temporary relief to poor children who participated. More reform was obviously needed. Initially, this took the form of legislative change.

Under the auspices of the Humane Society, Kelso formed the Fresh Air Fund to provide excursions to Toronto Island and the Santa Claus Fund, which sponsored a Christmas Eve party. Eventually, the Toronto Star *took over these funds.*

Children's Protection Act, 1888

Existing legislation to protect children was notably lacking. With the help of a lawyer friend, Kelso drafted a model law for the consideration of Ontario Premier Sir Oliver Mowat, who was also the province's attorney general. With Mowat's backing, the legislature passed the Children's Protection Act in 1888.

The act established a legal basis for interceding in the lives of children who were being harmed by parental "neglect, crime, drunkenness or other vices," were "growing up [in] harmful, idle or dissolute" circumstances, or who were "orphans found begging." The act also provided for children under the age of sixteen who were found associating with thieves or prostitutes to be charged. In all these situations, the youngsters could be sent away to an industrial school or placed in the care of a charitable agency, where they would be required to stay until they reached the age of eighteen.

The act was important because it recognized, for the first time, public responsibility to care for neglected children in institutions that met their special needs. As historian Clifford J. Williams writes,

The Children's Protection Act of 1888 was important because it recognized, for the first time, public responsibility to care for neglected children in institutions that met their special needs.

> [It also] allowed charitable organizations to place children in foster homes as an alternative to institutions and permitted some intervention between a child and unsatisfactory parents. But this latter idea was still far from popular acceptance. It seemed to most citizens a dangerous invasion of personal rights when the state presumed to regulate the way in which parents treated their own offspring and even delegated power to strangers to abduct the child from the family home. Cruelty to children was deplorable but the rights of parents and citizens were precious.

"[The Children's Protection Act] allowed charitable organizations to place children in foster homes as an alternative to institutions and permitted some intervention between a child and unsatisfactory parents. But this latter idea was still far from popular acceptance. It seemed to most citizens a dangerous invasion of personal rights when the state presumed to regulate the way in which parents treated their own offspring and even delegated power to strangers to abduct the child from the family home. Cruelty to children was deplorable but the rights of parents and citizens were precious."
— Clifford J. Williams

Hostility toward the new act quickly developed as opponents argued that, on constitutional grounds, such provincial legislation could have no authority to deal with offences under the federal Criminal Code. As a result — and because juvenile offences such as petty theft were relatively minor — the act was not enforced. Nevertheless, it was the foundation for all subsequent legislation to protect children.

Though the Children's Protection Act had failed, pressure for reform continued to be applied, thanks in part to the leadership of Mayor Howland. One outcome was the appointment, in 1890, of a prison reform commission before which Kelso appeared to present his ideas about the needs of children. Despite the success of the Humane Society, he talked of his belief that neglected, delinquent and homeless children could be better served if their needs were separated from those of animals.

The origins of the children's aid movement

The movement that Kelso joined, known variously as "child rescue," "child saving" or "children's aid," originated in the United States.

The movement that Kelso joined, known variously as "child rescue," "child saving" or "children's aid," originated in the United States. In 1853, the philanthropist and social reformer Charles Loring Brace established the first children's aid society in New York City. Its aim was to send children who were living on the streets to work for and be cared for by farm families in the American west.

New York's Children's Aid Society was followed by the establishment of similar organizations in Philadelphia, Boston and other cities on the U.S. east coast and in the Midwest. The scheme was copied by English child rescue organizations such as Dr. Barnardo's, which sent large numbers of youngsters to Canada as immigrant workers.

The children's aid society that originated in New York did not offer assistance to children living in families. In 1875, however, the publicity given to an abused and neglected New York City child, Mary Ellen, caused many to recognize the need for agencies to intervene in situations in which children were being ill treated. The case had a strong impact in Canada and paralleled the advances that were beginning to be made in Ontario.

The children's aid society founded by Brace did not offer assistance to children living in families. In 1875, however, the publicity given to an abused and neglected New York City child, Mary Ellen, caused many to recognize the need for agencies to intervene in situations in which children were being ill treated. The case had a strong impact in Canada and paralleled the advances that were beginning to be made in Ontario.

The founding of the Children's Aid Society of Toronto

In the wake of J.J. Kelso's success in gaining support for the idea of a children's aid society, he organized a meeting on July 21, 1891, chaired by Mayor Howland, to bring his ideas together. The seventy-five people who were present that evening at the YMCA on McGill Street passed the following resolution:

> Resolved that this meeting, realizing the importance of united work in behalf of neglected children, do approve of the formation in Toronto of a "Children's Aid Society and Fresh Air Fund" to deal with all matters affecting the moral and physical welfare of children, especially those who, through lack of parental care or other causes, are in danger of growing up to swell the criminal class.

Incorporated as the Toronto Children's Aid Society, the agency would provide a short-term shelter for neglected children and promote decent schools for the poor, separate treatment of young offenders, and more boys' clubs and playgrounds.

The twenty-seven-year-old Kelso was named president of the new society's board of management, which was elected at this meeting. (Until 1951, the society's board of directors was known as the board of management because, in its early days, the agency's board members were directly involved in running the day-to-day operations of the organization.) Like the boards of many charitable organizations at that time, most of the members came from socially prominent families; but, unlike those other boards, which were made up either of all women or all men, the CAS's board comprised ten men and ten women. The men dealt with financial matters, while the women concentrated on organizing the shelter.

In February 1892, after only seven months in office, Kelso resigned the position of president, citing pressures of work — he was still a busy reporter at *The Globe*. There may, however, have been another reason: his temperament suited him better to initiating reforms than to managing the ongoing work that resulted from them.

The Toronto Children's Aid Society would have a short-term shelter for neglected children and promote decent schools for the poor, separate treatment of young offenders and more boys' clubs and playgrounds.

Like other boards of charitable organizations at that time, most members of the CAS board came from socially prominent families. However, unlike other boards whose members comprised either all women or all men, the CAS board included ten men and ten women. The men dealt with financial matters while the women concentrated on organizing the shelter.

Kelso was succeeded by John Kidson MacDonald, the businessman who had identified the need for a Humane Society. He was to remain president of the Toronto CAS for the next twenty-eight years.

John Kidson MacDonald

John Kidson MacDonald was born in Scotland in 1837. At the age of eight, he came with his family to Upper Canada, where they settled on a farm in Weston, a small village in York Township, northwest of Toronto.

A talent for business led him to found the Confederation Life Assurance Company, and from 1871 until his death he was a key figure in the company's management, becoming its first full-time president in 1912. A man of great energy, determination and dedication, he was actively involved in the development of several voluntary organizations, of which the Children's Aid Society was only one.

MacDonald's influence over the day-to-day work of the Toronto CAS was pervasive. In 1892, one of his first acts as the agency's president was to request that all committee reports be written and not given verbally, as had been the custom. It was characteristic of MacDonald's businesslike approach. He rarely missed the monthly board meetings, and sat on all standing committees, while appointing dozens of subcommittees — which he also chaired, more often than not.

Leading by example, MacDonald's many contributions of talent, time and money persuaded others, including several governors general and members of City Council, to make contributions of their own.

From 1892, MacDonald made the offices of Confederation Life at 12 Richmond Street East available to the society, which made use of them for more than fifty years. (This remains the only building that survives from the early history of both the Infants' Home and the CAS.) The house at 33 Charles Street East, where MacDonald's family lived for many years, was sold to the society after his death in 1927 and used until 1951 as its children's shelter. In that year — as we will see in Chapter 5 — the house was demolished to make way for a new operational centre for the society's work.

The Children's Charter

With the founding of the Toronto CAS, the public and politicians alike had become well aware of the need for effective child welfare legislation. Within two years, the government introduced a bill, known as the "Children's Charter," that ushered in the modern era of child welfare legislation.

The charter — known officially as the Act for the Prevention of Cruelty to and Better Protection of Children, 1893 (and later shortened to the Children's Protection Act) — provided for the establishment of children's aid societies across the province. Approved by the provincial government and run by local community boards, CASs were empowered to protect children from abandonment, mistreatment and neglect and, when necessary, to place them as wards in foster homes or institutions. The courts were always to consider the best interests of the child and could refuse the parents custody, if need be. Although the act was amended on several occasions, it remained the legal basis for child welfare work in Ontario for more than sixty years.

The Toronto CAS was the first society to be recognized under the 1893 act, at which time it changed its name to the Children's Aid Society of Toronto.

In 1893, the government introduced a bill, known as the "Children's Charter", that ushered in the modern era of child welfare legislation.

Kelso as superintendent of neglected and dependent children

The Children's Protection Act called for the appointment of a superintendent of neglected and dependent children, and Premier Mowat was quick to appoint J.J. Kelso (who was a natural choice, given his expertise in child protection) to the post. Kelso immediately began travelling to communities across the province to organize children's aid societies — within six months of the Toronto society's establishment, Ottawa, Peterborough, London and Guelph had all followed suit. By 1906, there were fifty-six societies in Ontario, a number that has remained relatively stable ever since.

Kelso also often addressed public meetings several times a week, speaking of the need for compassion in dealing with needy youngsters. He was his own public relations expert, keeping the press well supplied with articles, and soon the newspapers were supporting his cause.

By 1906, there were fifty-six children's aid societies in Ontario, a number that has remained relatively stable ever since.

So far, Kelso was the only government employee working in the field of child welfare. As a result, his perceptions and beliefs shaped the system for many years. As Beth Hoen, Phillipa Wild and Vicki Bales write:

> He believed that if children were neglected it was owing to weakness or vice on the part of the parents who therefore should forfeit their custodial rights. Children in such cases, he believed, were best served by being removed from their homes and placed elsewhere, usually in a foster home, often in a rural community. Such placements were compatible with the widely held belief that rural surroundings provided a healthier environment for young people; they also provided a pool of farm labour for a still largely agrarian economy.

Throughout the Kelso era, the parents of children that CASs placed with foster parents usually were not told where their children were living. Although the public generally supported this, it did not deter the occasional newspaper report about societies supposedly infringing on the rights of parents or breaking up families.

One consequence of these beliefs was that, throughout the Kelso era, the parents of children that CASs placed with foster parents usually were not told where their children were living. Although the public generally supported this value, it did not deter the occasional newspaper report about societies supposedly infringing on the rights of parents or breaking up families.

Jones and Rutman believe that, despite his successes as superintendent — Ontario's point man in child welfare — Kelso was never completely reconciled to his role as government official. They suggest that "He was well suited to the task of promoting and encouraging the formation of children's aid societies but routine administration and the need to observe bureaucratic procedures and guidelines were not to his liking. He preferred the image of 'children's friend' to that of 'government official.' He remained committed to the view that child saving was the responsibility of private citizens. Government, he believed, should assist, but never supplant, voluntary organizations."

The children's shelter

Each CAS in cities of over 10,000 inhabitants was required to establish and maintain a temporary receiving home for the young people in its care. Thus, one of the first acts of the new CAS of Toronto was to establish a children's shelter. It opened without fanfare in May 1892 in a six-room, two-and-a-half-story house at 32 Centre Avenue.

This property, however, quickly proved inadequate and the shelter moved in June 1894 to larger premises at 135 Adelaide Street East. That building — the former rectory of the Anglican cathedral of St. James — also proved to be imperfect as well as rundown. As a result, the society decided in 1902 to purchase (for $9,000) and renovate a large building at 229 Simcoe Street. It occupied the land between Simcoe Street and University Avenue and had a frontage of more than 40 metres.

Although it was a distinct improvement over the previous buildings, the Simcoe Street shelter in its turn became so overcrowded that an extension was added in 1908. Like the Infants' Home, it too was closed periodically because of epidemics of contagious diseases. Hoping to reduce the spread of infection throughout the institution, in 1912 the board built a separate receiving centre in the playground to the south at a cost of $3,600. Upon admission, children were quarantined there for fourteen days before they were moved into the main building.

The shelter cared for children who were four years of age or older. An informal agreement with the Infants' Home called for that agency to look after children under four. However, according to Russell Jolliffe, the author of an earlier history of the society, cooperation between the two organizations was not always cordial.

> There was no legal relationship stating that the Infants' Home would accept children under a specific age. It seemed to depend on the good will of the Infants' Home board and whether beds were available.

In its first four years of operation, more than 1,000 children were admitted to the society's shelter — 443 of them in 1896 alone. The number of annual admis-

The children's shelter opened without fanfare in May 1892 in a six-room, two-and-a-half-story house at 32 Centre Avenue.

The society purchased 229 Simcoe Street for $9,000 in 1902. It occupied the land between Simcoe Street and University Avenue and had a frontage of more than 40 metres.

sions increased significantly over the years, reaching 1,280 by 1919. At first, children were made wards of the society by board resolution instead of through court proceedings, but this changed in 1896, after J.J. Kelso intervened in what was the first recorded instance of conflict between him and the society he founded.

Generally, as many children were discharged as admitted to the shelter, but the turnover was high because the children did not stay long. The board expected that a stay of ten days to a month, at a maximum, would be sufficient time for the society to make plans for their future.

Generally, as many children were discharged as were admitted to the shelter, but the turnover was high because the children did not stay long. The board expected that a stay of ten days to a month, at a maximum, would be long enough for the society to make plans for their future, "[e]ither by compelling parents to do their duty to their offspring or [by] securing for homeless children, or those whom the courts decide should be removed from parental control, admittance to one of the public institutions provided for such cases."

This meant that the agency had to plan expeditiously for the children's discharge. Many were returned to their parents or sent to live with relatives or family friends, while others were adopted, cared for in foster homes or sent to work for families as servants.

The society's early annual reports regularly gave examples of the circumstances of the children admitted to its care, as in these examples from 1897:

> Case no. 1495 is a little girl, three years old, whose mother had got into bad ways and would not stay home. The father professed to love the child but did nothing to show his affection. The case was brought before the magistrate who gave the mother a chance to reform. When it was found that the mother did not improve, the case was again brought before the magistrate and the child was made a ward of the society and [was soon placed] in a good home.
>
> Case no. 2111 is the son of a widow who became incapacitated through rheumatism and was fast losing control of the boy. When shown that there was a good chance for him in [a foster home] in the Northwest [Territories], she consented to surrender him to the society.
>
> Case no. 2432 is the son of a widower who married a second time. The stepmother of this boy and his older brothers and sisters

soon gained the upper hand in the household and was so unkind and cruel to them that they were driven from the home. As the father seemed quite unequal to ruling his own household, he was advised to hand the boy over to the society for placing in Manitoba. This he did and [after a short stay in the shelter] the boy is doing finely in his new home.

A few physically handicapped children — as well as those "of weak intellect" — who were admitted to the agency's care were sent to institutions, as was the case with a developmentally handicapped girl who was placed in the asylum at Orillia. Most such children, however, remained at the shelter for a long time. The responsibility for planning for them would for many years remain a contentious issue between the society and the provincial government. The society's view was that handicapped children should not be its responsibility, "as foster homes cannot be found for such children."

Life at the shelter

The overall operation of the shelter was entrusted to a male superintendent, although a female nurse known as the matron ran it on a day-to-day basis. Members of the board of management's shelter committee were expected to take turns visiting the shelter daily and to spell off the matron at intervals.

The board took great pains to write a set of rules that would govern the shelter's operation. Besides the keeping of appropriate records, they specified bedtimes, mealtimes and the activities the children were required to engage in, including daily and Sunday religious observances.

The shelter had its own school and kindergarten class, run by teachers seconded by the board of education. It also had a dental clinic. Physicians visited regularly to check on the children's health.

Although the young people were obviously well cared for physically, their emotional and social needs were barely understood. Parents, for example, were allowed

SCENES IN OUR DINING ROOM.

Although the young people in the shelter were obviously well cared for physically, their emotional and social needs were barely understood. Parents, for example, were allowed to visit for only fifteen minutes twice a week, and only if the shelter committee consented.

One of the earliest advocacy tasks that the agency undertook resulted in the passing in 1894 of the federal Act Respecting the Arrest, Trial and Imprisonment of Youthful Offenders. It set out, for the first time, procedures for dealing with young offenders separately from adults.

to visit for only fifteen minutes twice a week, and only if the shelter committee consented. The only time a child was allowed to leave the shelter was to go to hospital in the event of a serious illness — or when it was time to return to the family home or to be placed in a foster home or elsewhere.

The shelter quickly became a large institutional operation that accommodated between sixty and eighty children. It was described as immaculately clean — the children did most of the cleaning — with the beds a gleaming white, giving it more the appearance of a hospital than of a home. To some observers, however, it looked like a jail, what with its iron bars on the windows and the high fence that surrounded the property to prevent the children from running away.

"It is less expensive to save children than to punish criminals"

The society's earliest motto — "It is less expensive to save children than to punish criminals" — underlies the idea that, for many years, the society saw its purpose as the prevention of crime and to provide a detention home for young offenders.

J.J. Kelso himself had campaigned against the inadequacy of legislation to deal with young offenders, many of whom were thrown into jails amongst hardened adult criminals. Thus it was no accident that one of the earliest advocacy tasks that the agency undertook resulted in the passing in 1894 of the federal Act Respecting the Arrest, Trial and Imprisonment of Youthful Offenders. This law set out, for the first time, procedures for dealing with young offenders separately from adults — although the establishment of juvenile courts would have to await the Juvenile Delinquents Act of 1908. (Even then, the establishment of juvenile courts was not mandatory, and Toronto did not get one until 1911.)

Kelso was a leader in the campaign for the Juvenile Delinquents Act, which treated a young offender "not as a criminal but as a misdirected and misguided child and one needing aid, encouragement and assistance." For almost eighty years, this philosophy was to govern the treatment of young people who broke federal, provincial and municipal laws. It diverted children away from the criminal justice system by providing for them to be supervised in their own homes by probation officers or placed in foster homes or other specialized institutions. Under no circumstances were they to be placed amongst adult offenders.

In Toronto, many youngsters in trouble with the law were placed in the CAS's shelter, which acted as a detention home for young offenders. Those who the courts decided required a longer period of incarceration were eventually transferred to industrial schools or placed in children's aid society foster homes.

In 1896, there were 175 young offenders in the shelter, accounting for 40 percent of all residents. By 1914, however, 745 of the 1,445 children in the shelter were young offenders, and their numbers as a percentage of all children cared for in the shelter continued to increase — by 1919, they represented over 66 percent (841 out of 1,280) of all children in residence that year.

At first, these juvenile delinquents, as they were usually called, lived alongside — although in separate rooms from — those who had been admitted because they were in need of protection. However, because of the increase in the number of young offenders the society was required to care for, it became evident to the board that there was a need for a separate building to house them. As Jolliffe writes:

> [In 1915, the agency approached the city] about the matter, pointing out that the children's aid society was not bound to care for juvenile delinquents. The city asked the society to continue the care of these children since it was unable to do so because of the [First World] War. So, in February 1916, the board rented 226 Simcoe Street, [up the street] from the shelter, for two years as a detention home. In the following month, they hired a man and his wife to be in charge of the children. This home was for boys only, the girls remaining in the shelter. At the end of the two-year period, the city still refused to accept responsibility for juvenile delinquents.

In 1919, likely as a result of pressure from the society, legislation was enacted that made municipalities responsible for the care of young offenders, thereby compelling the city to make its own arrangements. As a result, the detention home was finally able to close its doors in March 1920.

In Toronto, many youngsters in trouble with the law were placed in the CAS's shelter, which acted as a detention home for young offenders.

In 1919, likely as a result of pressure from the society, legislation was enacted that made municipalities responsible for the care of young offenders, thereby compelling the city to make its own arrangements.

AT HAPPILAND CAMP.

Photo reprinted with permission of City of Toronto Archives, SC1, Series B, 1910 Annual Report, Page 21.

Summer camp

After many years of having children with a whole range of challenges living year-round at the shelter, the society moved to provide them with a more extended summer holiday experience than the Fresh Air Fund was able to do.

In 1910, an Orillia couple, Mr. and Ms. William Thomson, set up Camp Happiland on the shores of nearby Lake Couchiching and invited the society to send the shelter children there for a holiday. Every year until 1928, it became a regular feature of summer life for these children, who travelled by train to Orillia, where Thompson would meet them in his motor launch and ferry them to the scenic site. Once there, they spent their days bathing, boating and enjoying the physical and mental benefits of the country air. At night, they would sleep in tents until permanent sleeping quarters were erected in 1917.

In 1911, the society itself mounted a search for land closer to the city to provide a place where "weakly children and tired mothers" could have a holiday experience together. Seven hectares near the lakeshore in Halton County were purchased for $8,000 and became known as the Bronte Fresh Air Camp. According to Jolliffe,

> A pavilion to serve as a dining room and kitchen were erected and tents were used for sleeping accommodation. Parts of the grounds were used as a farm and a team of horses and farm equipment were purchased in 1915. This was probably done in expectation that the camp would be self-sustaining for it was later recorded that enough potatoes and vegetables were grown to supply itself, Camp Happiland and the shelter.

In 1914, forty-two mothers and 140 children spent 2,155 days at the camp. It continued to provide twelve-day holidays to mothers and children until 1920, when, due to financial, administrative and transportation difficulties, its operation was given over to the Neighbourhood Workers' Association. This was the beginning of Bolton Camp, one of the longest-running children's summer camps in Canada. (The society retained ownership of the site until 1943.)

Substitute family care

From the very beginning, the Children's Aid Society of Toronto placed children with substitute families. In this way, it differed from the Infants' Home, which did not begin to do so until the 1920s. The society's preference to place the young people in its care with substitute families in an age when most other children's agencies preferred orphanages and other institutions was largely the result of J.J. Kelso's strongly held belief that institutions were inappropriate places for neglected and abused children. Not only was institutional care expensive but, more importantly, children in care "crave for a real home, a real mother and a real, instead of artificial, system of work and play."

Once a suitable substitute family had been selected for an individual child, the society might enter into a contract with them under which it would make annual payments on behalf of the child until he or she reached the age of eighteen years. Given its limited revenues, however, and because children were still regarded as an economic asset, the agency's preferred approach was to negotiate placement of children in "free" homes. This relieved the agency from any responsibility to reimburse the family for the child's care. Another form of placement was a non-binding indenture, whereby the child became part of the family.

Whatever the label, however, the status of these placements was referred to interchangeably as both foster care and adoption. (As will be described in the next chapter, the modern concept of adoption was not formalized in Ontario until 1921).

The typical substitute family home was a farm in rural Ontario — or even as far away as Manitoba or the Northwest Territories. Lacking agency escorts, the society enlisted the help of railway conductors to look after the children on their way to their placements. Once they had settled into their new homes, they were expected to work on the farm or around the house. This could result in a disregard for the children's legal right to education and thus condemn them to limited opportunities for advancement in their future lives.

Most children remained in their placements until they reached the age of eighteen, or in some cases, twenty-one. Once the girls turned twelve or the boys reached the age of fourteen, however, they were expected to be self-supporting. For

From the very beginning, the Children's Aid Society of Toronto placed children with substitute families. In this way, it differed from the Infants' Home, which did not begin to do so until the 1920s.

J.J. Kelso believed that institutions were inappropriate places for neglected and abused children. Not only was institutional care expensive but, more importantly, children in care "crave for a real home, a real mother and a real, instead of artificial, system of work and play."

The typical substitute family home was a farm in rural Ontario, or even as far away as Manitoba or the Northwest Territories. Once they had settled into their new homes, the children were expected to work on the farm or around the house.

"I arrived safely in my new home and I like it very much. I am glad you sent me out here and my Uncle and Auntie are very kind to me … I help Auntie to milk and feed the calves. We have five calves. I milk one cow but I will milk two when I get more used to it."

— a society ward writing in 1897

many, this meant working as farm labourers or as domestic servants for several years at subsistence wages.

From today's perspective, this integration of caring for children in need of protection with employing them as household and farm help is disturbing. It was, however, consistent with Kelso's long-held belief:

> The chief cure we have for the average neglected child is to transfer him from an urban to a rural district … a child of a poor family in a city is so cramped and hindered and restricted in his development that artificial means have to be supplied for legitimate play activities.

Nevertheless, however good their care, these children were usually placed far away from family members, often even from siblings who might be placed in foster homes in distant communities. They undoubtedly suffered from the trauma of separation and the transition from an urban to a rural way of life.

Those placed outside Ontario never received visits from society workers or government inspectors to monitor their progress. Without a doubt, some were mistreated, but many appreciated their placements, as young Fred wrote in a letter quoted in the agency's 1897 annual report:

> I arrived safely in my new home and I like it very much. I am glad you sent me out here and my Uncle and Auntie are very kind to me … I help Auntie to milk and feed the calves. We have five calves. I milk one cow but I will milk two when I get more used to it.

Several years later, in 1919, the annual report reproduced a letter from Harold, a much older youth, in which he writes to William Duncan, the superintendent of the shelter:

> It has been a long time since I wrote to you but I am still living and in the best of health and strength … I can do anything on the farm now … I will soon be ploughing for next spring. We have all our fall

wheat ready now, 150 acres [60 hectares]. There is nothing like experience ... I am glad now that I was taken to the CAS. Mr. Duncan, you have been just like a father to every one of us and certainly used us good and I hope the boys will all appreciate it as I do.

Children placed within Ontario would receive a supervisory visit at least once a year, either from a home visitor from Kelso's office or from the local children's aid society. The visitors, who might be volunteers as often as paid employees, usually worked hard to avoid having the children recognize them as government or agency representatives. This reflected the era's belief that a strict separation of young people from their parents was in the best interests of children in care. However, it also reveals the prevailing lack of awareness of the needs of children adjusting to a new family and surroundings and in dealing with their personal histories, as illustrated by an item from the society's 1904 annual report:

> Mrs. Harvie [J.J. Kelso's first salaried assistant] continues her good work among the children for the Ontario Department of Neglected and Dependent Children and many are the homes all over Ontario where she is heartily welcomed by both foster parents and children.
> In many cases, the children know her only as a looked-for and welcome friend of the foster parents, for when children have been adopted into homes when too young to remember anything of their past lives it is her care that she shall not say or do anything while making her visit which will inform them that she is an official visitor.

These home visitors saw themselves as counsellors and friends, but there is no doubt that the quality of supervision they provided was perfunctory by modern standards, as the following reports about children in the care of the CAS of Toronto in 1919 suggest:

> Her foster parents have become very much attached to Jean, who is now eight years old and in splendid health. She is taking music

"It has been a long time since I wrote to you but I am still living and in the best of health and strength ... I can do anything on the farm now ... I will soon be ploughing for next spring. We have all our fall wheat ready now, 150 acres [60 hectares]. There is nothing like experience ... I am glad now that I was taken to the CAS. Mr Duncan, you have been just like a father to every one of us and certainly used us good and I hope the boys will all appreciate it as I do."
— a society ward writing in 1919

The belief of the time was that strict separation of young people from their parents was in the best interests of children in care.

lessons on the piano and doing well. Everything is quite satisfactory here and I consider this child well placed.

A good farm home for Willie, aged 13. He is bright and doing well at school. Foster mother complained to me that the boy was disobedient and if left alone for any time would shirk any work left for him to do. I called at the school and had a talk with the boy, who seems to be a very bright, cheerful lad. He promised me that he would try and do better in the future. Would advise leaving him where he is as long as they will help him, for he is certainly in good company and making progress.

Eve, who is 15 now, is a good, healthy and well-developed girl. Foster mother says the only trouble is she will not always tell the truth … They are fond of her and want to do all they can for her. These are good respectable people … I am satisfied that they are doing all they can for her and that, if she remains with them and is willing to be guided by them, that she will grow up to be a good, useful woman.

The prevailing attitude seems to have been that foster parents were motivated by altruism, removing any requirement for close supervision — for which there were, in any event, no standards.

The society was never short of foster homes, because the needs of farm families exceeded the supply of available children. It did, however, have to compete with other agencies, most notably British child rescue societies such as Dr. Barnardo's. According to Clifford J. Williams, between the 1880s and the First World War, these British agencies were settling annually about 2,500 immigrant children in Ontario homes — nearly ten times the number placed by CASs. At the turn of the century, the Toronto society was placing almost fifty children a year in foster homes; by 1919, that number had almost doubled to ninety-three.

The CAS of Toronto was rigorous in its approval process for those interested in becoming foster parents, as this report from the society's 1897 annual report testifies:

The society was never short of foster homes because the needs of farm families exceeded the supply of available children.

The society receives a very large number of letters of inquiry for children and this is due to the kindness of the editors of nearly all the Toronto and Winnipeg weekly papers in inserting in their columns frequent letters from the [society] descriptive of children available for adoption.

The nature of the application forms which inquirers are required to fill out will be evident when it is said that, while hundreds inquire, the number who formally apply — when they become aware of what responsibilities the society requires them to assume — only adds up to scores. Even of these, many are rejected by the president and secretary, whose duty it is to pass on them.

"The nature of the application forms which inquirers interested in becoming foster parents are required to fill out will be evident when it is said that, while hundreds inquire, the number who formally apply — when they become aware of what responsibilities the society requires them to assume — only adds up to scores. Even of these, many are rejected by the president and secretary, whose duty it is to pass on them."

— Foster home procedures, 1897

Managing the work

According to Williams, "During the first twenty or thirty years, children's aid work was a relatively uncomplicated business of apprehending neglected or abused children referred by police, charities, churches and other organizations and individuals. After a short stay in a shelter, the child was brought before a judge and, if circumstances of neglect or abuse were substantiated, the court usually assigned the child to the society's care for an indefinite period. The child was then placed more or less permanently with foster parents."

As has already been indicated, some of that work, including home visiting and foster home supervision, was carried out partly by volunteers. Likewise, the members of the board of management — all of whom, apart from the secretary, were volunteers — involved themselves in the day-to-day management of the society's business. For example, John MacDonald, the president, personally reviewed every application from those offering to become foster parents, and carefully examined every document and reference before he would allow a child to be placed in such a home.

This did not, however, render the society impervious to constant criticism that it employed paid staff rather than volunteers to carry out its work. The board

The society was subjected to constant criticism that it employed paid staff rather than carrying out all of its work with volunteers.

The agency's first paid employee was Stuart Coleman. He held the executive position of secretary at an annual salary of $500. His job was to keep the society's records and to find and arrange placement in foster homes for the children living in the shelter.

The agent made home visits, usually early in the morning before the police court sat or in the late afternoon and early evening after it had adjourned for the day. The workload was so heavy that it was not long before the agency had to hire an assistant to help the agent with his tasks.

worked hard to justify this decision, based on the volume and complexity of the work that was required to fulfil the society's mandate.

The agency's first paid employee was Stuart Coleman. He held the executive position of secretary at an annual salary of $500. His job was to keep the society's records and to find and arrange placement in foster homes for the children living in the shelter.

Beginning in 1894, the secretary was supported by a staff member initially known as the "agent" but later renamed the inspector. For several years, John Graham held this position at a salary of $1,000 a year. His responsibilities were to attend the police court (a municipal court that dealt with minor offences) daily to help the magistrate determine how to deal with the young offenders brought before him. He was also responsible for investigating reports of neglect or cruelty toward children. This involved making home visits — usually early in the morning before the court sat or in the late afternoon and early evening after it had adjourned for the day. The workload was so heavy that it was not long before the agency had to hire an assistant to help the agent/inspector with his tasks.

In 1906, the society hired, at an annual salary of $800, William Duncan into the newly combined position of secretary, inspector and superintendent of the shelter. This gave him senior management responsibilities, although the agency's overall direction remained under the firm control of president John MacDonald. Duncan's wife — the first names of female employees were rarely recorded — was taken on as the matron of the shelter at $400 a year, assisted by several nurses and housekeeping staff.

Mr. and Ms. Duncan carried on in these capacities until the agency hired its first executive director in 1923 — a tenure of seventeen years. At that point, Ms. Duncan retired and her husband was made honorary secretary of the board, a position he held until his death in 1926.

In 1907, the board approved the appointment of Ms. V.C. Hamilton as a "lady visitor," at an annual salary of $400. By 1911, the number of salaried visitors had increased to three. Two of them — Ms. G. Shepphard and Ms. A. Trimble — became long-time employees of the agency, retiring in 1926 and 1936 respectively.

Although they had no professional training, these visitors were the first social workers employed by the CAS of Toronto. MacDonald described their jobs as "[going out to] see what child life in the city is without waiting for complaints or police action. The women with love of the Saviour and children in their hearts will find entrance into homes where it is not possible for men to get in."

Between them, they investigated about a thousand cases every year. Each harried visitor was assigned a district of the city, and, along with a few volunteers, was expected to do child protection work with children in their own homes, to make admission and discharge decisions and, in such time as remained, to visit the wards of the society placed in foster homes in their area.

While these home visitors were appalled by the conditions under which many of their clients lived, they saw their raison d'être as child protection rather than the alleviation of the conditions that gave rise to children being in need of protection. Social reform was left to the churches, private charities and, notably, settlement houses such as Central Neighbourhood House. The society's workers, however, were progressive in that they saw working with families in the community as an alternative to taking children into the agency's care. Indeed, as early as 1894, the annual report indicated that admitting children to the shelter was secondary to working with families in their own homes:

> The management and officers [of the society] are keenly alive to the fact that the parents are the natural guardians of their children, though it is sometimes a difficult task to make them realize their true responsibility. Hence, the first effort in all cases, where it is deemed proper that the society should interfere, is to bring about such changes in the parents and the home as render the separation of children from their parents unnecessary.

The annual reports of the society regularly gave examples of the casework undertaken by the visitors:

In 1907, the first "lady visitor" was paid $400 per year. Although the visitors had no professional training, they were the first social workers employed by the CAS of Toronto.

By 1911, the three visitors investigated about a thousand cases annually. Each was assigned a district of the city, and, along with a few volunteers, was expected to do child protection work with children in their own homes, to make admission and discharge decisions and, in such time as remained, to visit the wards of the society placed in foster homes in their area.

As early as 1894, the annual report indicated that admitting children to the shelter was secondary to working with families in their own homes.

In one of the poorest homes in the centre of the city, four little children were found by visitor. Children and house in deplorable condition. The mother was in hospital and the father not taking care of them. Clothing was borrowed for the baby who was placed in the Infants' Home and the others brought to the [CAS] shelter. Home conditions improved under the supervision of the [visitor] and the children given back to the parents.

A fine little girl whose father was overseas [on active service during the First World War] was deserted by her mother. She was taken in charge by the children's aid society and later sent to the father, who stayed in England [after the war].

Two little girls were found living in two rooms with father who was very careless and did not provide sufficient food or clothing for them. The mother had been dead for some months. The girls were brought to shelter, one of them needing medical attention which she received at once. The father was given some time to prepare a home for the children but he failed to do this, so children were made wards of the society and already one has been placed in a home where she gets every care.

Two fine little children were found living with their mother who was living an immoral life and the father serving a term at jail farm. The children were made wards of the society and in a very short time placed in good foster homes where they are loved very much.

In this era, parents whose children had been apprehended by CAS workers enjoyed few legal rights; meanwhile, children in the society's care had no legal rights at all — the assumption was that the agency's fiduciary responsibility toward them ensured it would act in their best interests.

Funding the work

Initially, the society had almost no money for its work, and at the end of its first year the books recorded a deficit of almost $200. In 1896, its receipts amounted to $6,575, all but $95 of which was spent on maintaining the shelter and caring for the children who lived there, as well as staff salaries and day-to-day administrative expenses.

Throughout the period covered by this chapter, the only provincial aid the society received was to reimburse it for all or most of the salary and expenses of the superintendent of the shelter. In 1906, J.J. Kelso offered the agency a grant of two cents a day for each child living in the shelter, but this was refused by the board on the grounds that it would invite government interference. The board also feared that government grants "might possibly stop the flow of voluntary contributions" toward the society's work.

In 1912, the inconsistency of government support for child welfare led to the formation of a provincial association of CASs that became known as the Ontario Association of Children's Aid Societies. Although its establishment brought no immediate increase in government funding for the work of its member agencies, this organization did go on to play an important role in strengthening child welfare legislation, practice and administration.

Meanwhile, under the Children's Protection Act, municipalities were required to contribute "a reasonable sum" — not less than $1 a week — for each child from their jurisdiction who was in the care of a CAS. In Toronto, the city and the society entered into an agreement to substitute these payments for an annual grant. Reflecting this important role as funder, the city gained the right in 1900 to be represented on the society's board of management.

The financial arrangement the society made with the city was a mixed blessing. While it gave the agency some financial stability and enabled forward planning, it also shortchanged the society because the grant never kept pace with expenses. In 1896, the grant amounted to $3,000, representing almost 50 percent of the agency's expenditures. By 1909, when it was raised to $4,000 (at which level it remained until 1919), it covered only about 25 percent of outlays, which that year amounted to $15,000. This included the cost of running the detention home on behalf of the city.

Initially, the society had almost no money for its work. In 1892, at the end of its first year of operation, the books recorded a deficit of almost $200.

In 1906, J.J. Kelso offered the agency a grant of two cents a day for each child living in the shelter, but this was refused by the board on the grounds that it would invite government interference.

In 1912, the inconsistency of government support for child welfare led to the formation of a provincial association of CASs that became known as the Ontario Association of Children's Aid Societies.

The financial arrangement the society made with the city for an annual grant was a mixed blessing. While it gave the agency some financial stability and enabled forward planning, it also shortchanged the society because the grant never kept pace with expenses.

In its early years, the society depended
heavily on donations from the public.

*By 1918, with expenditures approaching $32,000
annually, the society faced a deficit of almost
$8,000.*

Fortunately, however, the society was quickly becoming a favourite charity, thanks in part to the more than 200 collection boxes that were strategically placed in private homes and business offices, on bank and post office counters, in hotels and in the hallways of foster homes. They would often bring in more than $700 annually for the society's work. In addition to cash, agency supporters also contributed food, clothing, bedding, furniture, books and toys.

The agency supplemented this income by selling annual and life memberships in the society, through Sunday school collections and through yearly Thanksgiving donations organized in city schools. It also benefited from a number of bequests of several hundred dollars each.

These various sources of income, however, were not enough to manage the society's business. In 1914, the Social Service Commission, a citizens' committee that advised the city on social welfare matters, persuaded the municipality to bring its financial support more in line with the CAS's needs. The outcome was that the city agreed to help the agency care for its wards with municipal grants on a per capita/per diem basis.

The agency and the city disagreed constantly, however, on which cases merited such compensation. In an attempt to resolve such disputes, the society eventually took the city to court. Unfortunately for the society, the judges sided with the city's interpretation of its fiscal responsibilities toward the agency. In the meantime, the agency's financial situation was rapidly deteriorating. By 1918, with expenditures approaching $32,000 annually, the society faced a deficit of almost $8,000.

It was at this time that the Federation for Community Service was being formed, and many saw membership in such a united community appeal as the solution to the society's financial problems. However, in January 1919, after a presentation from the president of the federation — who was careful to explain that the organization would not interfere in the running of the society — the board of management voted against membership.

As a result of this decision, the agency was hindered in carrying out its work and in developing new approaches to child welfare. As Jolliffe writes, "The board lacked the leadership [necessary for] giving direction in the changing field of philanthropy. It clung tenaciously to the old ideas of private charity and scorned the financial assistance from provincial and municipal governments to which it was entitled."

The result was that the society was unable to hire enough staff to fulfil its mandate capably. By the end of the First World War, with the city's population approaching 500,000, the Children's Aid Society of Toronto still employed only three salaried field workers. The sheer magnitude of their responsibilities, coupled with their lack of training, jeopardized the effectiveness of their work.

By the end of the First World War, with the city's population approaching 500,000, the society still employed only three salaried field workers. The sheer magnitude of their responsibilities, coupled with their lack of training, jeopardized the effectiveness of their work.

Conflict and concern

Matters came to a head during and after the First World War, when many community leaders and ordinary citizens were starting to rethink the suitability of established systems as a result of the upheavals the war had caused. Among the issues that aroused concern were the needs of children and families, many of whom were the orphans and widows of soldiers killed in the war or of those who had died in the influenza epidemic of 1918.

After the First World War, many community leaders and ordinary citizens were beginning to rethink the suitability of established systems.

These matters were foremost in the minds of members of the new profession of social work, who, along with those who worked at City Hall, were becoming increasingly concerned about what they regarded as the inefficient operation of the CAS of Toronto. Their unease was shared by J.J. Kelso, who had been the founding president of the society but who was now responsible for overseeing its operation on behalf of the provincial government.

Although supportive of the work of Mr. and Ms. Duncan, who ran the shelter, Kelso was antagonistic toward the society's board — and particularly so toward its long-time president, John MacDonald, whom Kelso believed was responsible for the agency's doing only the bare minimum required to meet its obligations under the Children's Protection Act. Jolliffe suggests that Kelso also came into conflict with the CAS of Toronto because he had become too personally involved in the affairs of the agency he had founded, and that MacDonald had come to resent his interference — and, by extension, that of the government. Certainly, Kelso was a man of strongly held views who tended to impose his own standards on others. It

In March 1916, Kelso expressed his concerns about the operations of the CAS of Toronto via an open letter to the mayor which was published in the local newspapers.

Before the city's board of control, the society's president, John MacDonald, claimed that Kelso had not visited the agency in five years and therefore did not know what he was talking about.

did not help that his role as provincial superintendent was ill defined, particularly in relation to local CASs.

In March 1916, Kelso expressed his concerns about the operations of the CAS of Toronto via an open letter to the mayor which was published in the local newspapers. He wrote that "friendly mediation" had failed to bring about necessary changes in the operation of the society. It was behind the times in dealing with the children who came to its attention, and too few of those in its care were being placed in foster homes. Young offenders were not receiving remedial treatment. The shelter was like a jail, with "sixty children in close confinement in the middle of the city." The children were locked up with no opportunity for constructive activities or outdoor exercise. They slept on beds without mattresses or pillows. The building was overrun by vermin.

Kelso's criticisms were supported by the city's representative on the agency's board of management and by the local chapter of the National Council of Women, who asked for a reorganization of the society because the children, they alleged, were suffering from malnutrition.

MacDonald was incensed at these charges and reacted angrily, suggesting that they were exaggerated. This simply confirmed for many the case against the society and strengthened support for an investigation before the city's board of control. MacDonald, defending the society before that board, claimed that Kelso had not visited the agency in five years and therefore did not know what he was talking about. He was able to convince the board of control that the concerns were overstated, resulting in a City Council resolution of confidence in the society.

The disagreement between Kelso and MacDonald, both of whom were strong-willed men, centred on methods and philosophies rather than on goals. Nevertheless, according to Jones and Rutman, it strained the relationship between Kelso and the society he had founded:

> Looking back in retrospect on the altercation with the Toronto
> society, Kelso recognized the damage it had done to his standing
> in the movement and to his relationship with his old colleagues,
> but he felt the action was unavoidable. "This whole affair was one

of the sorrows of my life," he wrote. "But looking back, I cannot see
that I could have done otherwise since I owed a supreme duty to
the children of Toronto and to the social movement for which I
was to a large extent responsible."

Although Kelso felt he had lost the battle with MacDonald, his views ultimately prevailed, for the incident was to lead to a complete reorganization of the
society and the way it was managed.

CHAPTER 3

The Growth of Professionalism, 1920–1939

Life in early-twentieth-century Toronto

By the early 1900s, Toronto's economy was booming. While Montreal was still the country's major metropolis, Toronto was beginning to rival its dominance. The city's banks, investment houses and insurance companies financed not only the development of large-scale forestry and mining in northern Ontario but also the settlement of the Canadian west. The mail-order catalogue of Eaton's department store found its way into almost every home. The newly tapped hydroelectric power of Niagara Falls provided the energy that fuelled Toronto's burgeoning factories.

While an established group of prominent upper-income families ran these businesses and dominated the local cultural, religious and social organizations, the industries also contributed to a substantial growth in the mercantile, or middle, class of people. The number of unemployed and poor, however, continued to grow; this phenomenon was the result of an increasing displacement of agricultural workers as Ontario continued to industrialize and become more urban.

It was also the effect of immigration. In the years before the First World War, many English, Scottish and, to a lesser extent, Protestant Irish immigrants settled in Toronto. A second wave of newcomers arrived in the 1920s, although their numbers did not climb as high as those during the pre-war period. By 1931, immigrants made up more than 30 percent of Toronto's 600,000 inhabitants, the largest percentage of any city in the country. They were still mainly from the British Isles, helping to maintain Toronto's profile as a Protestant, Anglo-Celtic city. However, a

By 1931, immigrants made up more than 30 percent of Toronto's 600,000 inhabitants, the largest percentage of any city in the country.

great many Catholic and Jewish people also came, as did Germans, Italians, Poles, Scandinavians and Ukrainians.

For many of these newcomers, employment was harder to get than it was for Canadian-born people, and not only because of language and perceived skill barriers. Discrimination was much in evidence. Anti-Semitism was prevalent, while "No Irish need apply" notices appeared in many want ads and decorated the windows of rooms available for rent.

During the 1920s, women outnumbered men by a large margin, mainly as a result of the deaths of soldiers during the First World War.

During this era, women outnumbered men by a large margin, mainly as a result of the deaths of soldiers during the war. The nuclear family often comprised three generations: children, parents and grandparents. Fathers were assumed to be the providers, while mothers usually remained at home to care for their families. Divorce was rare, and remarriages and those reconstituted families that existed were usually the result of the death of a previous spouse.

Women, generally speaking, either had families or careers, but not both.

Women, generally speaking, either had families or careers, but not both. Although attitudes began to change as a result of the upheaval of the war years, a working mother, unless she was a widow, was stigmatized as having no husband — or an unreliable, improvident one. As jobs became scarce during the Great Depression, married women, and particularly women with children, were excluded from the work force.

A more accepting attitude toward unmarried mothers was slowly taking hold, but most were still made to feel that having a baby out of wedlock was shameful. They were usually still sent away to give birth in secret at the home of a distant relative or in an institution such as the Infants' Home.

A more accepting attitude toward unmarried mothers was slowly taking hold, but most were still made to feel that having a baby out of wedlock was shameful. They were usually still sent away to give birth in secret at the home of a distant relative or in an institution such as the Infants' Home.

Wages for labourers, factory workers, clerks and those in service industries were generally low, while the hours were long. As a consequence, a number of slum neighbourhoods sprung up, of which none was more notorious than The Ward, located north of Queen Street between Bay Street and University Avenue. There, families lived in houses and tenements that were dilapidated, overcrowded and expensive to rent. Water supplies were often contaminated and waste disposal unsanitary. These conditions often gave rise to family stress that led, in turn, to child abuse and neglect.

The affluence of the 1920s allowed governments to introduce old age pensions and mothers' allowances to help those who were less well off. (The stigma attached to children born out of wedlock, however, prevented mothers' allowances being extended to unwed mothers who wished to keep their babies.) A Soldier's Aid Commission offered financial assistance to veterans of the war and supported their families thorough its own child welfare service. Nevertheless, the prevailing attitude was that personal success or misfortune was a function of individual character, and that government welfare should be restricted to the "deserving" poor.

These values were subsequently challenged, but not overcome, as a result of the Great Depression of the 1930s. Although the hardships it produced did not affect Toronto as badly as other Canadian centres, the numbers of transient people — including whole families and single women — looking for work in the city became very visible. Many people, including some social workers, perceived male transience as related to a desire to escape family responsibilities during difficult times. Arrests of the homeless for vagrancy continued.

Many families were in dire straits because of unemployment or job cuts, not only in terms of hourly wages — the average per capita income was less than a dollar a day — but also in weekly work hours. No comprehensive government programs of unemployment insurance or social welfare existed. The government's primary response was to create jobs through municipal public works, an initiative that was later supplemented by a limited public relief program under which benefits — taking the form of vouchers that could be exchanged for food or secondhand clothes in specified stores or depots — were carefully controlled and scrutinized. Missions operated soup kitchens, but many people remained malnourished.

Governments and most of the population that were not destitute thought that charitable organizations would take care of the truly needy. Families in crisis, they believed, could always look to agencies such as the Infants' Home or the CAS of Toronto for assistance. Others approached both organizations looking for children to board, in the hopes of increasing their meagre incomes.

The Depression, however, was also a difficult time for social agencies. The families and children with whom they worked suffered from stark privation, anxiety and worry. These conditions, in turn, often led to family arguments, alcoholism and crime, with their sequels of desertion and imprisonment. Such circumstances were a detriment to family life and the conditions in which children were brought

The prevailing attitude was that personal success or misfortune was a function of individual character, and that government welfare should be restricted to the "deserving" poor.

During the Depression of the 1930s, governments and most of the population that were not destitute thought that charitable organizations would take care of the truly needy. Families in crisis, they believed, could always look to agencies such as the Infants' Home or the CAS of Toronto for assistance.

The Depression, however, was also a difficult time for social agencies. It was a detriment to family life and the conditions in which children were brought up. The agencies did what they could, but public and private funds for their work decreased even while their caseloads increased.

up. The agencies did what they could, but public and private funds for their work decreased even while their caseloads increased.

Vera Moberly

Vera Moberly was intrigued by the notion of foster care, particularly because of a series of epidemics in Toronto that had caused life-threatening diseases and death among children housed in various institutions across the city, including the Children's Aid Society and the Infants' Home.

A generation younger than J.J. Kelso, Jessie Vera Moberly is another of the early heroes of child welfare in this country. From 1919 until her death in 1945, she was executive director — or executive secretary, as the position was officially known — of the Infants' Home. It was in this capacity that she pioneered the modern system of foster family care.

Vera Moberly was born in Fort William, Ontario (part of what is now the city of Thunder Bay), but was educated in Scotland. On her return to Canada as a young adult, she spent time with her father Frank — a government surveyor — on many of his trips across the country. During these journeys she travelled through several aboriginal communities, and it was as a result of these experiences that she developed a deep understanding of human need as well as an interest in social welfare.

Having trained as a nurse, in 1917 Moberly attended a lecture on the subject of foster care given at the University of Toronto by a doctor from Boston. Dr. Charles Hastings, the medical officer of health for the City of Toronto, accompanied her to the lecture. In 1902, Hastings and his wife had lost their three-year-old child to typhoid fever which had arisen from contaminated milk from a local dairy. As a result of this tragedy, he committed himself to the health and welfare of children and worked tirelessly to that end.

Moberly and Hastings were intrigued by the notion of foster care, particularly because of a series of epidemics in Toronto that had caused life-threatening diseases and death among children housed in various institutions across the city, including the Children's Aid Society and the Infants' Home. They believed that if they could move these children out of the institutions into the homes of foster families, they would be less likely to suffer the illnesses and death that, it seemed, were endemic to institutional care. Their theory proved correct after they persuaded the superintendent of the Infants' Home to place two babies in foster homes as an experiment. Both babies flourished in these family settings.

Institutional care to boarding home care

When Moberly took over as head of the Infants' Home in 1919, two areas caused her deep concern: the continual illness among the children the agency was caring for and the difficulty of raising sufficient funds to operate the organization in the way she believed appropriate.

There had been four epidemics at the home that year. Seventy-three of the 183 babies who were being cared for died. Moberly described the babies being looked after by the Infants' Home as "wan, apathetic, colourless in appearance, suffering from rickets and many [other] diseases."

One of Moberly's first initiatives was to go to Boston and New York to study the techniques of foster family care that had so impressed her and Charles Hastings and that child welfare agencies in those cities were starting to use. She returned to Toronto determined to replicate at the Infants' Home the success of these American agencies.

To do so would take knowledge, courage and vision. The public would have to be persuaded that children could be boarded in foster homes and appropriately supervised so that no harm would come to them. It would be no mean task: her ideas were opposed even by some of the board members of the Infants' Home, enough so that they resigned.

The approach to foster care that Moberly believed in also differed from that being provided by the CAS. As described in Chapter 2, children's aid society foster care often meant placement or indentured service in a rural community far from home, with minimal, if any, ongoing support or supervision by the society. These types of foster homes became known as "free homes."

Moberly envisioned a different method, one that came to be labelled "boarding home" care. The sole motivation for becoming a boarding home foster parent would be to provide a substitute family for needy children — rather than to gain an additional pair of hands to help around the home or on the farm. These foster par-

Moberly envisioned a different foster care technique, one that came to be labelled "boarding home" care. The sole motivation for becoming a boarding home foster parent would be to provide a substitute family for needy children — rather than to gain an additional pair of hands to help around the home or on the farm.

In 1920, the Infants' Home distributed leaflets and set up a booth at the Canadian National Exhibition to publicize its work and describe what was being done in other cities to care for children in foster families.

By 1927, the Infants' Home had recruited 634 foster homes. On an average day, 180 foster families were looking after children in the agency's care.

"With what fear and trepidation we placed those first one or two babies. How [we] watched over them to be sure they would receive kindness and good care! How amazing the results! They made such progress in six weeks that we could hardly believe they were the same babies. Those were the first children in Canada to be placed by an institution in boarding homes."

— Vera Moberly in 1939, writing about twenty years' experience in foster care

ents would be recruited mainly from within the city so that children could retain contact with their own families, if appropriate. Expenses would be reimbursed. Most importantly, children in boarding home care would be carefully supervised and the foster parents well supported by trained professionals.

In 1920, the Infants' Home distributed leaflets and set up a booth at the Canadian National Exhibition to publicize its work and describe what was being done in other cities to care for children in foster families. The response was overwhelmingly positive; many people inquired about fostering, while others contributed money — one donation was for $10,000. Through these and other initiatives, by 1927 the Infants' Home had recruited 634 foster homes. On an average day, 180 foster families were looking after children in the agency's care.

In 1939, reflecting on her twenty years of experience in foster care, Moberly wrote:

> With what fear and trepidation we placed those first one or two babies. How [we] watched over them to be sure they would receive kindness and good care! How amazing the results! They made such progress in six weeks that we could hardly believe they were the same babies. Those were the first children in Canada to be placed by an institution in boarding homes.
>
> Now, children of all types and with whatever problems can find homes to meet their particular needs. Instead of regimenting underprivileged children into one pattern of behaviour in institutions, they are having the normal family life with father, mother, sister and brother, school and sports, just like any other children.

The agency's 1928 annual report tells the story of Jimmy, an unhappy child with impaired vision, who was one of thousands of children who benefited from the introduction of foster care. Deserted by his mother at the age of three months, he was placed with foster parents who, although living in frugal circumstances, delighted in meeting his every need. In no time at all his general disposition and health began to improve.

The child is now a year and nine months old. What he is receiving in the way of affection, understanding and guiding can never be reckoned in dollars and cents. A few months ago, he learned to walk. For some time, he was very timid about taking even one step alone. He had to be taught confidence in getting about and what patient hours were spent by Mrs F. in accomplishing this! The F.'s want to keep Jimmie until he goes to the school for the blind. They do not like to think of that distant time.

If children were still in care by the time they reached their fourth birthday — the Infant's Home's upper age limit — they were technically transferred to the care of the Children's Aid Society. (Some children, if it was determined that they required long-term care, were transferred to the society soon after their third birthday.) However, these children continued to live in the same foster home so that continuity of care was maintained. Over the years, hundreds of foster homes were transferred in this way between the Infants' Home and the CAS of Toronto.

Along with the expansion of service into boarding home care came an increase in the Infants' Home's staff and a gradual change in focus from nursing care to social work. Some recent social work graduates of the newly established social service program at the University of Toronto were hired, one of them being Audrey Hastings — the daughter of Charles Hastings, the city's medical officer of health with whom Moberly had worked so closely. In the mid-1920s, these social workers were paid $1,500 a year if they were professionally qualified, or $720 if they lacked credentials.

These staff and foster parents introduced modern methods of child care. Together they took part in regular discussion groups for support and training and received instruction from pediatricians and child psychologists. A manual was published that provided invaluable information for a foster mother caring for a young baby.

Moberly impressed upon the staff how important she believed it was to understand and focus on the root causes of a client's problems. During the Depression years of the 1930s, for example, she helped several staff, through the attitudes she modelled, to be less critical toward the unemployed.

"The child is now a year and nine months old. What he is receiving in the way of affection, understanding and guiding can never be reckoned in dollars and cents."
— Infants' Home Annual Report, 1928, describing one of thousands of children who benefitted from the introduction of foster care.

Social work graduates were paid $1,500 a year if they were professionally qualified, or $720 if they lacked credentials.

In the 1920s, Infants' Home staff and foster parents introduced modern methods of child care. Together they took part in regular discussion groups for support and training and received instruction from pediatricians and child psychologists. A manual was published that provided invaluable information for a foster mother caring for a young baby.

Another outgrowth of this openness to new ideas was the establishment of regular well-baby clinics, staffed by Dr. Doris Moneypenny, whom Moberly hired in 1930 as the agency's first full-time medical doctor. In addition, she arranged for regular developmental evaluations of children in foster care in cooperation with Dr. W.E. Blatz of the department of psychology at the University of Toronto.

The closing of the Infants' Home shelter

When she arrived at the Infants' Home, Moberly found the board and staff discouraged by the circumstances under which they had to care for the children. Several nurses had resigned, both because of unclear job expectations and deficiencies in the building at 21 St. Mary Street, which Moberly described as "[c]umbersome and poorly equipped. Washing done by hand. No kitchen for properly looking after the dozens of bottle feedings for the babies. No sterilizer. Scant medical and surgical supplies. Work [in the home] done by some 30 disgruntled mothers who were there against their wills. A housekeeper whose main interest in the mothers was that they be strong and willing to work so as to keep the building clean."

Moberly made many changes to address these problems. She did away with the requirement that mothers stay and work in the home for several months after giving birth. Regular medical clinics were established. An electric washing machine was installed as well as a refrigerator and sterilizer for the babies' feedings, which were to be carefully prepared according to the doctors' prescriptions. The home's sanitary conditions were improved and all children with the slightest suspicion of illnesses were isolated. As a result of these efforts, the home never had another epidemic.

Moberly's objective was to close the shelter entirely. She believed that by closing it and placing all the children in foster care, the infant mortality rate could be virtually eliminated.

Moberly's objective, however, was to close the shelter entirely. The year she took over as executive secretary, the mortality rate of the infants in the shelter was an alarmingly high 46 percent. She believed that by closing it and placing all the children in foster care, such deaths could be virtually eliminated.

She set about the task with vigour. By the end of 1921, most of the babies had been placed in foster homes, with the exception of those living in the shelter with their unmarried mothers. The agency then experimented with placing a few of those mothers along with their babies in what became known as "nursing foster homes." It proved a workable plan and it allowed the agency to close the shelter in 1926. From that point onward, the death rate of children in the agency's care never increased above one percent. Moberly's faith in her vision had been justified.

With all children in foster family care, the Infants' Home and Infirmary was now solely a child placement agency (protection work in the community was the responsibility of the Children's Aid Society). The shelter at 21 St. Mary Street, which was no longer needed, was sold to the Basilian Fathers for $50,000; with the proceeds, a building at 34 Grosvenor Street was purchased, renovated and furnished. It housed the agency's offices and clinics for the next twenty-five years.

One of the earliest ads for homes for children.

Stable funding for the Infants' Home

Before Vera Moberly arrived, the Infants' Home had depended largely on charitable donations and a small municipal grant to fund its activities. Her achievement was to negotiate membership of the agency in the Federation for Community Service. The role of the federation, founded by the Rotary Club of Toronto in 1918, was to raise and distribute funds on behalf of its member agencies. It also assisted its members in managing their organizations efficiently.

Membership in the federation was an important development for the Infants' Home. Using 1920 as an example, the federation's grant of $19,892 represented almost 65 percent of the agency's revenue of $31,221. This amount far outstripped the city's contribution of $3,627 and the provincial grant of $1,437. Legacies, donations and client fees made up the rest of that year's income. Expenditures in 1920 totalled $35,436. The $4,215 deficit was absorbed through the home's investment and endowment funds, which totalled more than $50,000.

Membership in the Federation for Community Service was an important development for the Infants' Home because in 1920, its grant represented almost 65 percent of the agency's revenue.

Moberly had very quickly achieved her second priority of placing the agency on a more stable financial footing. By 1939, the annual grant from the federation had increased to almost $47,000, the city was contributing more than $27,000 and the province about $5,700. The CAS of Toronto reimbursed the Infants' Home close to $22,000 for caring for its wards under the age of four. Donations and income from investments enabled the agency to handily meet that year's expenses of $116,750.

Reform at the CAS

As a result of the vote of confidence in its operations by the city's board of control in 1916 — referred to in Chapter 2 — the board of management of the Children's Aid Society of Toronto felt no need to make any changes to address the concerns of its critics. Indeed, John MacDonald, the society's president, proudly proclaimed that nothing had changed at the agency for several years, and, by implication, nothing needed to change.

To its critics, the CAS of Toronto seemed more like a closed, self-serving clique than a public agency responsive to the needs of the community's children.

To its critics, however, the society continued to seem more like a closed, self-serving clique than a public agency responsive to the needs of the community's children. Some in the community wanted to go as far as to pack an annual meeting, vote against the board and install a new one. Others, believing that more could be accomplished by working from within the agency, thought a better approach would be to vote some progressive members onto the board.

The latter approach prevailed and, in 1919 and 1920, led to an infusion of new board members, all of them active in modernizing community welfare. They included Professor J.A. Dale from the University of Toronto, John Appleton of the Winnipeg CAS, F.N. Stapleford of the newly formed Neighbourhood Workers' Association, Agnes MacPherson, a professionally trained social worker, social reformer Charlotte Whitton, and Bob Mills, head of social welfare for the City of Toronto.

These new, progressive members brought vitality to the board, helped professionalize the delivery of services, created positive links with other agencies in the community and restored the society's public image.

John Kidson MacDonald resigns

One outcome of these changes was the resignation, in 1920, of John Kidson MacDonald as the society's president, although he remained a board member with the courtesy title of honorary president until his death seven years later.

While J.J. Kelso had organized the society, he served as its president for only a few months. It was MacDonald who had provided the agency with direction and focus during its first three decades. The work of consolidation and growth was formidable, as were the challenges presented by epidemics, financial crises, war and societal change. Firm leadership had been needed, and MacDonald had provided it.

Many of the social issues debated in those early years have a familiar ring. The society was accused of breaking up families and of leaving children in institutional care for too long. The lack of foster homes, the problems associated with placing young offenders and children in need of protection in the same shelter, and the ever-increasing need for funds seemed insoluble.

MacDonald was involved, in one way or another, in wrestling with all of these questions. He was criticized frequently, but he was quick to defend himself and the society. Although in his later years his colleagues on the board would describe him as "splendid, strong, fearless and unwavering," his critics would probably have substituted stubborn for unwavering. Whichever way his legacy is viewed, the second president of the CAS of Toronto was clearly a towering figure in its history.

John MacDonald, the second president of the CAS of Toronto.

Bob Mills

To help stabilize the society and redefine its functions, the board of management recognized that a full-time executive director was needed. In 1923, Bob Mills, one of the reforming members brought onto the board in 1920, was appointed to the new position of managing director.

Mills came to this position from his job as director of the social welfare division in the city's department of health. He was, in effect, the executive assistant to

Many of the social issues debated in these years have a familiar ring. The society was accused of breaking up families and of leaving children in institutional care for too long. The lack of foster homes, the problems associated with placing young offenders and children in need of protection in the same shelter, and the ever-increasing need for funds seemed insoluble.

Charles Hastings, the pioneering medical officer of health with whom Vera Moberly had collaborated to promote the concept of boarding home foster care.

A statistician by profession, Mills brought order and consistency to the management of the society. He was an uncannily observant man — painstaking and careful in his habits, slow and deliberate in his thoughts and speech. These were qualities the agency needed as it reformed its operations in the face of crisis and complaint.

Mills believed that every child had the right to responsible parenting and that he or she should receive it from his or her own family as long as it was safe for the child and the community. If it was not, the child should be placed with a substitute family. To this end, it was the responsibility of the Children's Aid Society, in partnership with governments and the community, to provide the necessary legal safeguards, appropriate facilities, skilled staff and foster parents, backed up by necessary financial support from both private and public funds.

Under Mills' guidance over a period of twenty-seven years, the CAS of Toronto emerged as one of North America's outstanding child welfare agencies. His enlightened policies and untiring efforts on behalf of children and families did much to shape the society as we know it today.

"From a jail to a home"

Photo reprinted with permission of City of Toronto Archives, SC1, Item 2.

Mills's first concern was to address the criticism that the shelter had become more like a jail than a home for needy children. He threw open the front doors and removed the bars from the windows. The building was repainted and refurnished. Fire escapes and smoke partitions were installed. The heating system was overhauled. A new main entrance was built on University Avenue, which by this time had become a much grander thoroughfare than Simcoe Street.

From an institution housing an average of forty-five children, the shelter was returned to its original purpose as a temporary receiving home. Within ten years, the number of children resident at any one time was reduced to fifteen, while the average stay decreased from eighteen months to less than two weeks. Increasingly, the young residents began to be sent to the neighbouring Orde Street Public

Mills believed that every child had the right to responsible parenting and that he or she should receive it from his or her own family as long as it was safe for the child and the community. If it was not, the child should be placed with a substitute family.

School rather than the shelter classroom. Recreation activities were introduced, including outings to parks, theatres and exhibitions. Two evenings a week, social work students from the University of Toronto visited to play games with the children and to read them stories.

Administrative restructuring

From its earliest days, the Children's Aid Society of Toronto had worked with families in their own homes to investigate complaints of child abuse and neglect and, whenever possible, to avert the need for these children to be admitted to the agency shelter. The principal focus of CAS work, however, was to care for "dependent" children — those who were public wards or who needed temporary care away from home.

With Bob Mills's arrival as managing director, this focus changed. Content to leave the day-to-day running of the shelter to the matron, Mills focused his energies on the development of "field work for the prevention of cruelty and neglect of children, for the conservation of family life and the placing out and supervision of children in family homes."

To this end, he reorganized service delivery in 1923 into three work units: the shelter, a child-placing department and a family work — or protection — department. The number of staff who ran the shelter remained fairly constant over the years and was surprisingly small by today's standards: a matron, three nurses, a cook and a housekeeper. However, the introduction of boarding home foster care, described later in this chapter, and the development of social casework methods of working with children and families required considerable additions to the number of field staff. (Social casework was introduced into the CAS of Toronto in the 1920s by Helen Lawrence, the agency's first social work supervisor.)

By 1928, these field staff included twelve social workers, two supervisors, a psychologist and a half-time physician. Eleven years later, in 1939, the numbers had increased to include a supervisor and nine workers in protection, and a supervisor and twenty-three workers in child placement. There was also a full-time physician

Increasingly, the young residents at the shelter began to be sent to the neighbouring Orde Street Public School rather than the shelter classroom. Recreation activities were introduced, including outings to parks, theatres and exhibitions. Two evenings a week, social work students from the University of Toronto visited to play games with the children and to read them stories.

Mills reorganized service delivery in 1923 into three work units: the shelter, a child-placing department and a family work — or protection — department.

By 1939, the staff had grown to include a supervisor and nine workers in protection and a supervisor and twenty-three workers in child placement. There was also a full-time physician and a psychologist. Two workers in the clothing room made sure that children in care were adequately outfitted.

The society continued to depend, as did the Infants' Home, on volunteers to undertake work that, in a later age, would have been regarded as suitable only for paid staff. Volunteers kept the accounts, provided legal advice, managed the clinics and worked as case aides and clerical assistants. They also undertook the kind of assignments familiar to today's volunteers.

Then as now, volunteer work was seen to demonstrate that child welfare belonged not to a small isolated group of people but to the whole community.

The agency purchased the family home of its former president, John MacDonald, at 33 Charles Street East, for use as the children's shelter.

and a psychologist. Two workers in the clothing room made sure that children in care were adequately outfitted.

The society continued to depend, as did the Infants' Home, on volunteers to undertake work that, in a later age, would have been regarded as suitable only for paid staff. In the era before a unionized workforce, this raised no eyebrows. Volunteers kept the accounts, provided legal advice, managed the clinics and worked as case aides and clerical assistants.

They also undertook the kind of assignments familiar to today's volunteers. They sat on the board of management and its committees, raised funds, undertook public speaking engagements, drove workers to appointments, transported children to and from foster homes, knitted and sewed, and became special friends to children in care. Christmastime was a flurry of activity as volunteers chose, wrapped and distributed seasonal gifts for needy families and children in care.

Then as now, volunteer work was seen to demonstrate that child welfare belonged not to a small isolated group of people but to the whole community.

To support these staff and volunteers, office procedures had to be modernized. Case records were now typewritten instead of being completed by hand. An efficient system of accounting for children in various types of care was introduced. Financial records and statistics were completely overhauled. Fireproof storage was built for the protection of both casework and financial records. All this progress brought with it the need for additional accounting and clerical staff — by 1939, these included an office manager, eight stenographers, a bookkeeper and a switchboard operator.

The move to Charles and Isabella streets

This growth put the squeeze on the society's office space. From 1902 until 1924, the administrative office had been located in a single basement room of the shelter at 229 Simcoe Street. In the latter year, it took over the rooms on the first floor originally occupied by the superintendent and the matron. As the society's field work continued to grow and the number of children in the shelter decreased, additional rooms were taken over from time to time, but the office accommodation remained inadequate.

These pressing problems were solved in 1928, when the society decided that the Simcoe Street building no longer suited its purposes. It sold the property for $130,000 to the Canada Life Assurance Company, which built its corporate head offices on the site. With the proceeds, the agency purchased, for $40,000, the family home of its recently deceased former president, John MacDonald, at 33 Charles Street East, to be used as the children's shelter.

An adjacent house at 32 Isabella Street was bought to accommodate the society's administrative offices. This location was considered appropriate as it was close to the intersection of Yonge and Bloor streets, which was rapidly becoming an important commercial district. To provide additional space and "to make an appearance in keeping with the importance of the organization," a stone addition was added to the house and built to the street line.

In 1928, the society purchased property on Charles and Isabella streets. This location was considered appropriate as it was close to the intersection of Yonge and Bloor streets, which was rapidly becoming an important commercial district.

Protection work

The task of the society's protection workers was to "watch, advise and encourage" the parents on their caseloads so that children at potential risk could remain safely at home. If not, the workers had a duty to remove the children to a place of safety — likely the home of an extended family member, the society's shelter or a foster home.

The year 1928 provides a good example of the nature of this work. Staff in the family work department handled 1,320 cases involving 2,610 children. They made 4,654 home visits, conducted 1,331 office interviews, made 5,908 telephone calls, attended 197 conferences and wrote 1,153 letters. They worked on Saturdays as well as several overtime hours one or two evenings a week — some were also on a night patrol, about which Bob Mills wrote:

In 1928, staff in the family work department handled 1,320 cases involving 2,610 children. They made 4,654 home visits, conducted 1,331 office interviews, made 5,908 telephone calls, attended 197 conferences and wrote 1,153 letters. They worked on Saturdays as well as several overtime hours one or two evenings a week — some on a night patrol.

> On certain nights in the week, [CAS workers] drive through the most undesirable parts of the city, observing the movements of young children alone on the streets at night and, where necessary,

taking children home and warning parents of the dangers they are allowing their children to fall into. Children selling magazines on the streets, begging and frequenting undesirable places [are] taken under supervision.

Not much had changed, it would seem, since J.J. Kelso's campaigns fifty years earlier on behalf of street children.

In a minority of cases, perhaps one or two hundred a year, protection workers had to take action through the juvenile court to commit youngsters to the guardianship of the CAS. The largest numbers of these were babies born to unwed mothers who were unable to care for them. The society took these cases to court on behalf of the Infants' Home, which, as will be discussed later in this chapter, had assumed the full responsibility of working with the city's Protestant unmarried mothers. If guardianship was granted, the babies were placed with Infants' Home foster families, with the CAS of Toronto assuming financial responsibility.

The second-largest group consisted of young people "growing up without salutary parental control and under circumstances tending to make them idle and dissolute." Children deserted by their parents formed the third-largest group of those who were apprehended.

The society's annual reports regularly gave case examples of its child protection work. Mary, Jesse and Tim, for instance, aged six, four and three, were found living in a house in a wretched condition.

"Piles of dirty clothing and garbage on the floor, the three little children huddled in one filthy bed crying with cold and hunger. Mother staggering about just lighting fire although it was [already midday] and the temperature outside was below zero."

Case study from CAS of Toronto annual report

Piles of dirty clothing and garbage on the floor, the three little children huddled in one filthy bed crying with cold and hunger. Mother staggering about just lighting fire although it was [already midday] and the temperature outside was below zero.

The children were admitted to the agency's care while the mother, once sober and confronted with the loss of her children, began to plan with the worker for their care. Arrangements were made for them to live with an aunt in the country for a few months. Meanwhile, the worker helped the mother to deal with her drinking, move to a less dilapidated house and obtain a mothers' allowance cheque from the government. She was successful and, before long, the children were back home, attending school regularly, with "no signs of drunkenness" on the part of the mother.

Another example is that of ten-year-old Sarah, who was brought to the office by a woman asking that the agency "adopt her out." Sarah's father had disappeared, leaving her in the care of the woman.

> Illegitimate and unwanted, she had been transferred from the mother to the father and thus was living with his so-called third "wife." This woman hated the child and was very cruel to her and so the little one was passed from one place to another, the father constantly evading his obligation to support her.

The worker apprehended Sarah and placed her with foster parents, then worked to find the father. He was eventually located and started paying the society for her care. Sarah remained in the agency's care and was reported as being "well clothed and happy and to be making good progress."

The development of boarding home care at the CAS

Following the lead of Vera Moberly, with whom he worked closely, Bob Mills began to experiment with care for children in closely supervised foster homes where board was paid. Proceeding cautiously, in 1924 the society placed only two children in boarding homes. By 1927, however, there were 169 children living in this category of foster family care.

Unlike the so-called "free homes" that the agency had largely depended on until this time, boarding homes would often take sibling groups of children into their care. One example was the four immigrant Ukrainian children, featured in the 1928 annual report, who were placed with the same foster parents following the sudden death of their mother:

Unlike the so-called "free homes" that the agency had largely depended on until this time, boarding homes would often take sibling groups of children into their care.

There is no more appreciative group of children in the world than these little Russian-Canadian children. They know that all their success and happiness is due to kindly foster parents who came to their rescue when they needed assistance the most. As Olga says impatiently when she meets some of her former friends who sigh and shake their heads and say "Poor Olga," "I don't know why they should cry. We're better off now than we ever were before [in the shelter] and happier than we ever dreamed of being."

Increasingly, many youngsters with a behavioural problem, a developmental handicap or other special needs, who previously would have been considered suitable only for institutional care, began to be placed successfully in boarding homes.

Increasingly, many youngsters with a behavioural problem, a developmental handicap or other special needs, who previously would have been considered suitable only for institutional care, began to be placed successfully in boarding homes. Six-year-old Teddy was one such child. The son of a single, developmentally handicapped mother, he had been in and out of the CAS shelter. According to the 1927 annual report:

> At the age of three he was made a ward. Markedly retarded and unable to talk, he was an impossibility for adoption. Placed in a boarding home, he had made splendid progress. A mental examination two years later showed almost normal intelligence. Last January, he was admitted to special speech training classes. His improvement has been so favourable that he was selected to demonstrate to the recent teachers' convention the effectiveness of [boarding home care].

"At the age of three Teddy was made a ward. Markedly retarded and unable to talk, he was an impossibility for adoption. Placed in a boarding home, he had made splendid progress. A mental examination two years later showed almost normal intelligence. Last January, he was admitted to special speech training classes. His improvement has been so favourable that he was selected to demonstrate to the recent teachers' convention the effectiveness of [boarding home care]."
— CAS Annual Report, 1927

The introduction of boarding home care also allowed for the placement in foster homes of non-wards (children admitted to the society's temporary care while a parent was sick or family problems were being sorted out). Until this time, non-wards had always spent their time in care living in the shelter because free homes were regarded as more or less permanent placements.

Boarding homes quickly became an integral part of the agency's services, as evidenced by this comment in the 1928 annual report:

A great deal of work has gone into securing proper foster homes and we regard our boarding fathers and mothers as much a part of our staff as our field workers or supervisor. In order to foster *esprit de corps*, we had a series of conferences on various problems and started a monthly bulletin, *Co-operation*, which now has a circulation of about 350 copies.

Home supervisors — staff members who were part of the society's child-placing department — supported the foster parents and the children placed with them. The frequency of their visits to the child and foster family varied according to the type of care the child was receiving. Free homes were visited, on average, every two months. Boarding homes, on the other hand, were visited at least every three weeks. Health, psychological and dental services were provided at the agency's own medical clinic — an important benefit before the days of universal public health insurance.

In 1930, two staff took a course in group work at the University of Toronto and subsequently led regular workshops for boarding home parents on caring for foster children. Later that decade, seminars were added specifically for foster fathers. Dr. Marion Hilliard, the agency's physician, gave regular talks about child health.

Despite the demonstrated success of boarding home care, the old opinion that paying foster parents would somehow diminish the quality of care they provided took a long time to disappear. The annual report of 1925, was, however, emphatic:

> We feel that [boarding homes] are as much inspired by motives of service as [free homes]. As one foster father said, "I am beginning to feel of real use in the world now, helping to bring up these two boys to be good and honourable and useful men."

Free homes, in the meantime, remained an important resource for many children in the agency's care. Following the introduction of legal adoption in Ontario in 1921, many became adoption homes after a statutory two-year probationary period.

"A great deal of work has gone into securing proper foster homes and we regard our boarding fathers and mothers as much a part of our staff as our field workers or supervisor. In order to foster esprit de corps, we had a series of conferences on various problems and started a monthly bulletin, Co-operation, *which now has a circulation of about 350 copies."*
— CAS Annual Report, 1928

In 1930, two staff took a course in group work at the University of Toronto and subsequently led regular workshops for boarding home parents on caring for foster children.

A Legacy of Caring

At the end of 1939, the society had 1,446 children in its care. Of these, 808 were in paid care (13 in the shelter, 679 in boarding homes and 116 in outside paid institutions) with the remaining 638 in free care (555 in free foster homes and 83 in outside free institutions).

At the end of 1939, the society had 1,446 children in its care. Of these, 808 were in paid care (13 in the shelter, 679 in boarding homes and 116 in outside paid institutions) with the remaining 638 in free care (555 in free foster homes and 83 in outside free institutions).

Excerpt from the 1924 annual report, showing CAS services and funding.

Financial stability

Of all Bob Mills's reforms, he considered his greatest contribution to be the stabilization of the society's finances and the guarantee of funding for its programs.

Early in his career as managing director of the society, Mills began to work closely with the city auditor to analyze the actual cost of maintaining children in the agency's care. Soon, court orders began to be made on that basis. Funding from the city no longer came in an annual grant but was allocated based on the number of children made wards of the society by the juvenile court. In 1925, the agency received $26,000 from the city to care for its 800 or so wards. This represented almost 45 percent of its overall annual expenditure of $60,000.

The costs of protection work in the community and of caring for non-wards were funded by the Federation for Community Service. The society had joined the federation in 1922 — participating in its fifth campaign — and quickly became one of its leading members. In 1925, the CAS's grant from the federation was $13,275.

That year, Mills obtained $4,000 in financial assistance from J.J. Kelso, the province's superintendent of neglected and dependent children. As a direct result of the antipathy other children's aid societies expressed over this unusual aid, a provincial rating system was created under which societies received grants on the basis of their assessed efficiency and the amount of responsibility they accepted within their communities. The records are silent as to how the province initially rated the CAS of Toronto. However, in 1935 the agency was awarded only a B grade because, as described below, it did not accept the full responsibilities that Kelso wished to delegate to it under the Children of Unmarried Parents Act.

Direct voluntary donations, in addition to those made through the Federation for Community Service, remained important. In 1925, these direct donations amounted to $10,000. To keep the agency in the public eye and help maintain the flow of charitable dollars, communications activities were strengthened. The work of the society was regularly featured in newspaper articles. Slide show presentations were made to community groups. Information bulletins — which were updated frequently — were posted on the University Avenue side of the shelter building to catch the attention of passersby. In the mid-1930s, the society commissioned a colour movie of children in foster homes. It was often shown at service clubs and church meetings as a publicity vehicle for both the society and the Infants' Home.

By 1939, at the end of the era covered by this chapter, the society's operating budget was about $300,000. Of this, $66,000 came from the Federation for Community Service, $211,000 from the City of Toronto and other municipalities, $2,500 from the government of Ontario and $2,000 from voluntary contributions. The books were balanced by income from investments and a small bank loan.

A large part of the society's annual spending covered the day-to-day care it provided to its wards. By 1939, this amounted to more than $100,000 annually. To save money, children in care were supplied with clothes from a central clothing room, many of them handmade by volunteers. While this may have been understandable during the financial hardships of the 1930s, the custom had actually been established long before the Depression. This suggests that little thought was given to the practice's psychological effect on the children, as it further set them apart from others in the community who presumably purchased at least some of their clothing from local stores.

Staff salaries were another large expense; in 1939, they amounted to about $70,000. When Bob Mills was appointed managing director in 1923, the board granted him a salary of $4,500 a year. This was high for a social work administrator — Vera Moberly's starting salary, in contrast, had been only $1,800, plus free board and lodging — and bore no relationship to the amounts paid to the field workers, who earned about $1,300. Salaries remained at these levels until 1933, when they were cut by 10 percent as an economizing measure. (The reduction was lifted in 1938.)

Through the 1930s, considerable tension mounted between Mills and the society's board of management as the Depression threatened the agency's financial

To keep the agency in the public eye and help maintain the flow of donations, communications activities were strengthened. The work of the society was regularly featured in newspaper articles. Slide show presentations were made to community groups. Information bulletins — which were updated frequently — were posted on the University Avenue side of the shelter building to catch the attention of passersby.

By 1939, the society's operating budget was about $300,000.

Salaries for field workers stayed at about $1,300 in the decade between 1923 and 1933, in which year they were cut by 10 percent as an economizing measure.

stability and each contended with their evolving roles in policy formation, administration and service delivery. Mills, however, was highly regarded across Canada — and beyond — as a skilled and knowledgeable child welfare manager; so, in the end, his views usually prevailed.

The Infants' Home's work with unmarried mothers

The public, driven by a belief that unmarried mothers deserved punishment, was intolerant of them. Such attitudes were reflected by a Toronto police department ban on officers and their wives becoming foster parents. The department feared a scandal would result if an unwed mother were seen visiting an officer's home.

In the early years of the twentieth century, the question of what to do about unmarried parents and their children was a topic of heated debate, in which J.J. Kelso played an influential role. Public opinion, driven by a belief that such mothers deserved punishment, was intolerant. These attitudes were reflected by a Toronto police department ban on officers and their wives becoming foster parents. The department feared a scandal would result if an unwed mother were seen visiting an officer's home.

Although sympathetic toward unmarried mothers because they were all too often cut off from relatives and friends and had no access to the money needed to care for their children, Kelso's main concern was for the welfare of the child:

"The experience of ages has proved conclusively that no unmarried mother can successfully bring up her child and save it from disgrace and obloquy, whereas the child, if adopted young by respectable, childless people, will grow up creditably and without any painful reminder of its origin."

— J.J. Kelso

> The experience of ages has proved conclusively that no unmarried mother can successfully bring up her child and save it from disgrace and obloquy, whereas the child, if adopted young by respectable, childless people, will grow up creditably and without any painful reminder of its origin.

Concerns had also arisen during the First World War about the increase in the number of children born to married women as a result of relationships with men other than their soldier husbands. Twenty percent of the children in the care of the Infants Home at the end of the war fell into this category.

The demands for government action to meet the needs of children born out of wedlock prompted Queen's Park to pass the Children of Unmarried Parents Act of 1921. Under it, Kelso's office was made responsible for supervising children born to unmarried mothers, to make whatever arrangements for the child's welfare he deemed appropriate, to prove who the father was and to obtain support payments from him.

Kelso found the legislation difficult to implement, not least because the government of Premier E.C. Drury allocated no additional staff or funds for the purpose. His new responsibilities, along with those related to a recently introduced adoption act, described below, took up most of his time. This meant that he no longer had the opportunity to visit and supervise children's aid societies across the province, one of the issues that had led former CAS of Toronto president John MacDonald to dismiss Kelso's concerns about his management of the society.

It was not long, therefore, before Kelso began negotiating with local children's aid societies to undertake, on his behalf, the work with unmarried mothers. The CAS of Toronto, however, refused all cooperation with Kelso on this issue, both because the agency would receive no government funds for the purpose and because all final decision making authority on individual cases would still remain with Kelso's office.

As a result, work that the society might have undertaken with unmarried mothers and their children fell by default to the Infants' Home. Although the agency's board revisited the decision on several occasions, the CAS of Toronto did not assume responsibility for working with unwed mothers and their children until 1951, when the CAS merged with the Infants' Home.

This situation highlights the rather complex division of responsibilities between the CAS and the Infants' Home. The CAS was the protection agency, but it was also a child placement agency. The Infants' Home was a child placement agency, but it also worked in the community with unmarried mothers. The amicable working relationship between Bob Mills and Vera Moberly seemed to allow both agencies to define their roles and work together cooperatively.

The Infants' Home's work with unmarried mothers was paid for out of the agency's private funds as well as a grant from the Federation for Community Service. The salaries paid to the experienced caseworkers required for this specialized work, however, were considered high, and it was not long before Vera Moberly was complaining that "The work was increasing faster than our income and we find it very difficult to keep a proper balance between the needs of the mothers and the endurance of our workers."

Under the Children of Unmarried Parents Act of 1921, Kelso's office was made responsible for supervising children born to unmarried mothers, to make whatever arrangements for the child's welfare he deemed appropriate, to prove who the father was and to obtain support payments from him. These responsibilities eventually fell to the Infants' Home.

The CAS was the protection agency, but it was also a child placement agency. The Infants' Home was a child placement agency, but it also worked in the community with unmarried mothers.

Moberly pushed on regardless. A progressive thinker and practitioner, she encouraged workers to consider the needs of the children of unmarried mothers a family matter. "Encourage the girls," she urged them, "to tell their parents so there will be no need to banish them away." As was cited earlier in this chapter, she opened specialized foster homes, known as nursing homes, where both the mother and baby could live together. She appointed a male social worker to work with the babies' fathers and encouraged them to visit, while the mother was taught how to care effectively for her child. Thus, the parents would be better able to decide if it would be in the mother's and the child's interest for her to keep the baby.

These approaches, revolutionary at the time, made the Infants' Home an undisputed leader in the provision of services to unmarried mothers and their children. By 1939, the agency was serving almost 900 such families annually. Of these, about half were supported in their own homes. The mothers of the remaining children placed their babies in agency foster homes. About 130 mothers lived with their children in nursing foster homes.

Most of the children whose mothers could not care for them went on to adoption homes. The Infants' Home made arrangements for those not considered suitable for adoption to be made wards of the CAS of Toronto.

Alma's story, reported in the 1933 annual report, is typical of the services the Infants' Home provided to unmarried mothers. Alma was completely stunned when she gave birth to baby Bobby. The father was forty years her senior and the future looked bleak indeed:

> Feeling like one lost in a maze, Alma was admitted with her baby to a well-ordered nursing foster home. Here, the welcome of the kindly, capable foster mother soon dissolved the terrors of the previous months. During this time, Alma made the first big decision of her life. "I am going to keep Bobby, if I have to walk the street with him," she stated with almost defiant determination.

After gradually gaining self-confidence, Alma found domestic service with an understanding family. An elderly aunt was located and she took considerable inter-

Moberly appointed a male social worker to work with the babies' fathers and encouraged them to visit, while the mother was taught how to care effectively for her child. Thus, the parents would be better able to decide if it would be in the mother's and the child's interest for her to keep the baby.

est in her great nephew. Meanwhile, the Infants' Home caseworker was working with Alma to bring close the day when Bobby would be returned to the loving care of his mother.

Adoption Act, 1921

It was not until 1921 that Ontario introduced its first Adoption Act. Until that time, there had been no legal provision for adoption as a formal process, other than the non-binding indentures described in earlier chapters. Under the new legislation, the courts were authorized — if all the parties agreed, and at the end of a two-year probationary period — to issue an order granting adoptive parents all the legal rights to which they would be entitled had they been the child's birth parents. (This two-year probationary period remained the rule until 1965, when it was reduced to a maximum period of one year. In 1978, it was again reduced, in most instances, to six months.)

Like the Children of Unmarried Parents Act, passed in the same year, the Adoption Act was to be administered by J.J. Kelso's office. The CAS of Toronto, and other children's aid societies, helped by assessing the families who applied to adopt. The societies willingly entered into this joint arrangement with the province, even though they received no additional funds for doing so, because it relieved them of any long-term financial and supervisory responsibilities for children placed in such homes.

There was no shortage of adoption applicants. Initially, the majority were free-home foster parents wishing to adopt the children in their care. In time, the majority of candidates were couples that could not have children of their own. The children themselves were mainly those born to unmarried mothers, as well as some whose parents were considered permanently unfit to care for them.

By the onset of the Depression, however, adoption became a difficult financial proposition for many families. That is why, in 1935, at the nadir of the economic downturn, Premier Mitch Hepburn helped raise awareness of the continuing need for adoption homes by proclaiming an "Adopt a Child Week" and adopting a child himself.

Under Ontario's first Adoption Act of 1921, the courts were authorized — if all the parties agreed, and at the end of a two-year probationary period — to issue an order granting adoptive parents all the legal rights to which they would be entitled had they been the child's birth parents.

Toronto, Nov. 24, 1933.

Dear Mr. Mills:

Would it be possible to modify somewhat the regulation of your Society that applicants for a child should require to have six friends certify to their fitness as foster parents - this with special reference to city applicants whose home life and social position could easily be ascertained by a little personal enquiry. For instance a lady spoke to me this week about the hardship of having her friends know that she was thinking of adopting a baby - her aim being to keep this more or less a secret. Then there was recently a City family who applied to one of the baby boarding homes for a baby and was referred to your Society, no she replied,I would never go there for they would require me to be under their supervision for two years, etc. My own view is that anything that stands in the way of a helpless baby getting a free home should be removed if it can be done without sacrificing any vital principle.

Yours sincerely,

R. E. Mills, Esq.,
32 Isabella St.,
Toronto.

In 1935, in the midst of the Depression, Premier Mitch Hepburn helped raise awareness of the continuing need for adoption homes by proclaiming an "Adopt a Child Week" and adopting a child himself.

Kelso wrote articles for newspapers, church bulletins and women's magazines, offering advice to prospective adoptive parents on how to choose and parent a child. He counselled them to "See the child for yourself and instinct will tell you whether or not you can love it as your own."

He cautioned adoptive parents against letting the child, or others, know about the adoption:

> When you take the baby home, don't call in the neighbours to show them your treasure. Publicity of that kind is hurtful to the child's future … It is not necessary to tell the child he has been adopted until he asks the question himself. A child will always yield a quicker obedience and respect when he considers himself an integral part of the family.

Parents were encouraged to select children as much like themselves as possible, in the belief that only a child who looked as though he or she had been born to a couple could counteract the pain of childlessness. This, in turn, led to the rights and needs of children being treated as less of a priority than the demands of childless adoption applicants for very young infants. Public acceptance of these values hindered a more open attitude toward adoption until well into the 1980s.

These views influenced for many years the way adoption was perceived. Parents were encouraged to select children as much like themselves as possible, in the belief that only a child who looked as though he or she had been born to a couple could counteract the pain of childlessness. This, in turn, led to the rights and needs of children being treated as less of a priority than the demands of childless adoption applicants for very young infants. Public acceptance of these values hindered a more open attitude toward adoption until well into the 1980s.

Then as now, the adoption process was not an easy one for prospective adoptive parents. The "for better or worse" implications of legal adoption, fears that the placement might fail during the probationary period, and concerns about the effect of heredity put a heavy burden on CAS adoption workers, of whom there were five by 1935.

In 1935, the number of children under supervision in adoption probation homes, pending legal adoption, was almost 500.

That year, the society placed 211 children in adoption homes, of whom 47 were wards of the society and 164 non-wards. The society also arranged the adoption of 21 children where the husband or a relative of the birth mother was adopting the child. The number of children under supervision in adoption probation homes, pending legal adoption, was almost 500.

Most of the children were adopted into families where the adoptive father was a professional, a manager, a skilled tradesman, a salesman or a clerk. Relatively few were adopted by factory workers or unskilled labourers.

The CAS of Toronto developed a cooperative arrangement with the Jewish Federation of Philanthropies whereby that organization would be responsible for arranging foster care and adoption of Jewish children who had been made wards of the society by the juvenile court. The arrangement also earmarked a seat on the society's board of management for a member of the federation.

The Infants' Home, on the other hand, never became involved in adoption work, despite its responsibility for working with unmarried mothers. It referred all its children that were considered available for adoption to the Children's Aid Society.

The end of the Kelso era

In 1930, the government of Premier Howard Ferguson created a Department of Public Welfare to gather under one administrative umbrella the province's responsibilities for mothers' allowances, old age pensions, child welfare, mental health, physically and developmentally handicapped children and young offenders.

J.J. Kelso's office, responsible for supervising children's aid societies and other children's institutions, adoptions and work with unmarried parents, was integrated into this new department as its children's aid branch. Kelso managed the new branch until his retirement, at age seventy, in 1934. He was replaced by B.W. Heise, the managing director of the Hamilton CAS. Heise sought increased funding for children's aid societies, and in return demanded greater accountability and increased professional training for child welfare workers.

The end of Kelso's almost-fifty-year career brought a flood of commendations, including a silver jubilee medal from King George V for his work on behalf of neglected and abused children. Letters of congratulation flowed in from friends and colleagues, including one from Mackenzie King, then the leader of the Opposition in the House of Commons, and another from Charlotte Whitton, by then director of the Canadian Welfare Council.

Kelso's dogmatic views on moral issues defined for many years how child welfare matters would be handled.

Sadly, Kelso did not live to enjoy a long retirement. At his death in September 1935, newspapers across the country praised his contributions to the well-being of children. His old employer, *The Globe*, described him as one of Canada's greatest social reformers. His unique achievement was the creation of Ontario's child welfare system.

Against that success, however, must be weighed his shortcomings as the ongoing administrator of that system. Kelso's dogmatic views on moral issues defined for many years how child welfare matters would be handled. An example is his belief in volunteerism and his consequent failure to support children's aid societies financially during the crucial early years of their development. He also made little effort to adapt to emerging trends, particularly the development of social casework and child psychology.

His enthusiasm and self-confidence sometimes made it hard for J.J. to listen to the concerns of others, or to accept criticism of his work. These qualities hindered his ability to maintain effective provincial supervision over the work of children's aid societies. As a result, the government increasingly looked to others, principally Bob Mills, the managing director of the CAS of Toronto, for advice on child welfare policy. (Queen's Park asked Mills, for example, to devise a formula for municipal funding of CAS work, and to ensure that the societies received the dollars to which they were entitled.)

By the mid-1920s, most people involved in child welfare thought that Kelso's day had passed, as is illustrated by a confidential 1924 letter Mills wrote to Lincoln Goldie, the cabinet member responsible for child welfare, in which he expressed the opinion that "[J.J. Kelso's] standards of social work have not always been up to the level recognized by social workers and his general laissez-faire attitude has lost him the confidence of progressive people in social work."

Kelso was, in many ways, ahead of his time. He was a child welfare visionary who worked to make his visions a reality by founding the CAS of Toronto and he single-handedly established the role of government in child welfare.

Despite these criticisms, Kelso was, in many ways, ahead of his time. He was a child welfare visionary who worked to make his visions a reality by founding the CAS of Toronto. He single-handedly established the role of government in child welfare. He understood the crucial importance of placing children in family settings rather than institutions, and, to achieve this, he developed an extensive network of foster homes across the province. His greatest legacy, however, is undisputedly the work that still lives on in Canada's present-day child welfare systems.

Kelso's departure marked the beginning of more extensive provincial involvement in child welfare matters. Perhaps no single event illustrates this more clearly than the Department of Public Welfare's assumption of control over the lives of the Dionne quintuplets, who were born near North Bay in May 1934. The survival of these five identical girls, considered a medical miracle, brought worldwide attention. The children were separated from their family and put on public display, providing an opportunity for the government of Premier Mitch Hepburn to profit from what became Ontario's biggest tourist attraction. (In the late 1990s, the surviving Dionne sisters sued the Ontario government for their treatment as children and received a public apology and compensation from Premier Mike Harris.)

The well-known story of the Dionne quintuplets is now regarded as a human tragedy, but it illustrates the increasingly dominant role the province would play in child protection matters. Events in the 1940s would lead led to even greater pressure for the province to increase its responsibilities in this area.

CHAPTER 4

War and its Aftermath, 1940–1949

Canada at war

Beginning in September 1939, Canada was at war for the second time in a generation. Men from Toronto enlisted in large numbers, as did some women. Economic activity was focused on the war effort and expanded rapidly, not only reducing unemployment but creating a shortage of labour. The province responded by phasing out relief to people who could work, instead offering social assistance only to those who were considered unemployable. Many jobs in factories and offices were filled by women — including mothers with children — as well as people with disabilities and those drawing old age pensions.

With business and industry concentrating on the provision of munitions and other materiel, food and consumer goods were in short supply. Taxation and rationing brought about further austerity, which was mitigated by rent and price controls.

Women were being called upon to balance the dual roles of parenting and working in ways that were previously unheard of. In response, day nurseries — regulated under the provincial Day Nurseries Act of 1942 — began to appear, although the demand for day care spaces far exceeded the supply. The federal government raised mothers' allowances by 20 percent, although unmarried mothers remained ineligible for the program.

Child welfare agencies noted increasing numbers of abused and neglected children as many mothers, their husbands away on active service, struggled with the stress of lone parenthood.

During the war, child welfare agencies noted increasing numbers of abused and neglected children as many mothers, their husbands away on active service, struggled with the stress of lone parenthood.

After the war ended in 1945, the economy continued to grow, ushering in an era of increased employment and prosperity. Many couples who had postponed marriage during the Great Depression and the war years, and who were now united after long absences, began having children. Meanwhile, prosperous times allowed others to start families at a younger age than they might have done in the 1930s. Both trends sparked an increase in post-war marriage and fertility rates and triggered the phenomenon known as the "baby boom." This demographic shift was, in turn, to drive many of the social and political trends of subsequent decades.

The post-war years also saw a change in the structure of nuclear families, which to an increasing degree consisted only of parents and their children, with fewer grandparents and other relatives living in the same household. The divorce rate also grew rapidly, if temporarily, as many impulse-driven wartime marriages were dissolved.

The increasing affluence of the post-war years was not shared by all families, including many of those served by child welfare agencies, for whom the rapid increase in the cost of living and the lack of affordable housing represented a serious predicament. The era was marked by an increase in admissions of children to agency care.

The prosperity of the late 1940s led to a growing interest in social welfare planning. One result was the creation of Regent Park in downtown Toronto, the city's first large-scale public housing project. The increasing affluence of the era, however, was not shared by all families, including many of those served by child welfare agencies, for whom the rapid increase in the cost of living and the lack of affordable housing represented a serious predicament. The era was therefore marked by an increase in admissions of children to agency care.

The prosperity of the post-war years nevertheless created a mood of generosity toward social services, in steep contrast to the attitudes prevalent during the Depression era of the 1930s.

The child welfare field benefited, however, from a provincial policy of supporting the work with substantial new funding. In 1949, the Department of Public Welfare assumed responsibility for 25 percent of the costs that municipalities paid to children's aid societies to maintain children in agency care. The province also began paying the agencies that delivered the service a direct grant equal to 25 percent of the funds they raised from private sources. The effect was to transfer $1,160,000 in annual child welfare expenditures from the municipalities to the province. The prosperity of the post-war years clearly created a mood of generosity toward social services, in steep contrast to the attitudes prevalent during the Depression era of the 1930s.

British "war guests"

In 1940, people in Britain were preparing to be bombed or even invaded by German forces. There was widespread fear that London and other large industrial cities might be devastated. For their own safety, children of all ages were evacuated to small towns and rural villages — and, in a pilot project, more than 1,400 were sent across the Atlantic to be boarded with families in Canada. This government scheme was supplemented by private arrangements that sent children to live with relatives or family friends, as well as by an evacuation of students from British schools to collaborating Canadian schools.

Children's aid societies throughout the province were asked to help find homes for and to supervise these "war guests," as the children participating in the government scheme were called. There was no shortage of families interested in "doing their bit." In Toronto, people wrote letters, telephoned and came to the CAS offices offering to help. In addition to those volunteering their homes, 400 volunteered their time to work for the agency. These included eighteen people who acted as telephone operators, one of whom wrote:

> To appreciate [our experience as telephone operators], one must keep in mind that the coming of the children was quite uncertain and the anxiety on the part of friends was very great. Telephones rang all day, asking such questions as: "Has the boat arrived?" — "This is my nephew John here" — "Can we see the children?" — "Have you got my name down for Mary Jones?" — "What must I do to get a war guest?" etc., etc. More delays brought more telephone calls until we were dizzy trying to satisfy inquirers. It was a nerve-wracking job, entirely done by volunteers, [but I believe we were able to] calm and comfort many an anxious inquirer.

To conduct home studies of those volunteering to take in a child, the society enlisted the help of the Infants' Home, the Protestant Children's Home, the Jewish Children's Bureau, the Neighbourhood Workers' Association and the Big

Children's aid societies throughout the province were asked to help find homes for and supervise the "war guests," as the children evacuated to Canada were called. In addition to those volunteering their homes, 400 volunteered their time to work for the agency. These included eighteen people who acted as telephone operators.

Brothers' Association. As Jean Roberts, a worker at the Infants' Home, wrote in a contemporary article:

> There are many stories I could tell you of our visits ... but what impressed us most was that no matter what class of home we entered, from that of the family on the verge of relief to those with cultured, comfortable surroundings, there were few exceptions to the same offer: "We want a child in our home and we want to share all we have."

More than 2,200 homes were approved, although it transpired that the CAS of Toronto needed to place only 145 children, while its Catholic counterpart, the St. Vincent de Paul CAS, needed to place only sixteen. The "Blitz" (as the bombing raids during the Battle of Britain of 1940–41 were called), although it was destructive and caused loss of life, proved to be not as dangerous as had been predicted, and parents soon stopped sending their sons and daughters away and brought their evacuated children back home.

However, the dangers of the Atlantic crossing — more than one ship carrying evacuated children was torpedoed — prevented most of those sent to Canada from returning to Britain. Both the CAS of Toronto and the St. Vincent de Paul CAS therefore found themselves supervising these young people's placements until the end of the war. To do so, the CAS of Toronto created a war guest service department with a supervisor, a social worker and sixty-two volunteer home visitors. Many of these volunteers were former staff members or schoolteachers who gave up their evenings and weekends to help out.

Officially, the children themselves were made wards of the Department of Public Welfare under the British Child Guests Act. One of those wards supervised by the CAS of Toronto was thirteen-year-old Robert Brown, who broadcast a message across Canada and to his homeland on a radio program at Christmas 1940:

> I have been asked: "Is it very different living in Canada?" — fashions in clothes, for example. I'm afraid I don't know much

about that, but the things we eat, yes. Ice cream is Canada's staple diet. It suits us down to the ground. Sports? Well, there's baseball, skating, skiing and other jolly sports. Is school different? Well, Oakwood Collegiate in Toronto, where I go, is a great school. But there are things here that are not different. There is love — of country and Empire and freedom — so strong that it has made us strangers feel at home.

Many parents sent letters of appreciation to the agency. One wrote:

> We are not a bit worried about our little girl — she is in safe hands, in addition to which, she is in the midst of what appears to us a whole nation of would-be fathers and mothers. It is rather startling in a way but, nevertheless, a magnificent display of human kindness and good will, standing out more clearly in comparison with the conditions over here [in Europe] where the lust of power and the ruthless will to dominate has for the time being crushed all peace and good will.

By 1946, most of the war guests in the care of the agency had sailed home on the ships that had brought returning servicemen and women back across the sea to Canada. The few that remained were mostly those completing university degree courses.

"Our boys in the King's Forces"

When war broke out, many older wards of the society were eager to serve with the King's Forces, as the Canadian army, Royal Canadian Navy and Royal Canadian Air Force were collectively known. By the end of 1942, two hundred young men in the agency's care had enlisted. Four subsequently died during active service, and several became prisoners of war.

Young boys in the agency's care at play.

By the end of 1942, two hundred young men in the agency's care had enlisted. Four subsequently died during active service, and several became prisoners of war.

The agency went to great lengths to support these wards and former wards by sending them letters, care packages, newspapers and magazines and — most valued it would seem — cigarettes. Many of the young men wrote back letters trying to be cheerful, but they looked forward to the day when the war would be over and they could return home. One of them, named Jack, wrote to his worker just before he was seriously wounded in the Dieppe raid of August 2, 1942, when more than half the Canadian soldiers deployed were killed or taken prisoner:

> I'm keeping in good health and not too awful bad spirits, though a person is bound to get lonesome for home and the ones they love, especially after two years. But maybe Christmas will be spent in different surroundings, who knows? I shall not forget what the folks have done for me when the war is over. It makes it so much easier to do your duties when you know the people back home are pulling for you. So thanking you once again and hoping to see you again to thank you in person.

"I'm keeping in good health and not too awful bad spirits, though a person is bound to get lonesome for home and the ones they love, especially after two years. But maybe Christmas will be spent in different surroundings, who knows? I shall not forget what the folks have done for me when the war is over. It makes it so much easier to do your duties when you know the people back home are pulling for you. So thanking you once again and hoping to see you again to thank you in person."

— Jack, a former ward and Canadian soldier writing in 1942

Services to soldiers' families

For the duration of the Second World War, children's aid societies administered living allowances and helped families to set budgets.

During the First World War, a Soldiers' Aid Commission had been established to support families where fathers were absent on military duty. Such was not the case during the Second World War, when this task fell to the children's aid societies.

In some cases, the societies were already supervising homes before the father enlisted because of child neglect or potential neglect, and they continued to do so after he joined up because the protection concerns persisted. In other instances, the father's absence was itself considered to be the cause of the neglect. Despite their husbands' duties overseas for years at a time, and the fear these wives felt that they would never see them again should they be killed while on active service, CAS of Toronto records speak of workers' concerns about mothers who neglected their family responsibilities because "[a] freedom from the restraining influence of the partner in the home [can lead] the mothers, whose marriage tie has never been very strong, to open infidelity and consequent moral neglect of the children."

The CAS workers who wrote such reports, all women themselves, seemed unaware of, or perhaps, given the values of the time, felt unable to act on an understanding that it would be only natural for wives to seek the companionship and support of another partner at such a difficult time.

A second large category of services provided by children's aid societies to the families of servicemen and women was the administration of living allowances. As Williams writes:

> [Children's aid societies] determined the eligibility for living allowances of wives, children, parents and other relatives of the thousands of men and women in uniform. [They] also assumed responsibility for counselling and adjusting family problems [and] investigated and recommended upon supplementary grants to the regular allowances and advised the military whether "compassionate leave" should be granted to service personnel where family problems were acute. As the war went on and members of the armed forces were discharged, many for reasons of ill health or injury, there were applications for pensions and veterans' allowances to be investigated and evaluated.

At the CAS of Toronto, this work took a great toll on an already overburdened staff. It required the establishment of careful bookkeeping and reporting, the analysis of liabilities and needs, and the setting of an individual budget for each family. These cases were particularly difficult for workers because, in most situations, the family resented the society's interference in their right to plan their own spending.

Along with dealing with these challenges, CAS workers continued throughout the war years to fulfil their primary tasks of protecting children and, where necessary, providing them with substitute care. The agency's resources were tightly stretched, with foster homes in unusually short supply in a community preoccupied by war and survival. Workers, some of whom were seconded to other civilian and military duties, were busy with a continuously increasing caseload in protection, child-placing and adoption services.

All this put tremendous pressure on society staff, foster parents, volunteers and board members, which prompted managing director Bob Mills to write: "In the face of continually increasing workloads, the spirit of our staff has been magnificent and their response unfailing. My personal pride in them is unbounded and I [wish] to express my own appreciation and that of the society."

In addition, the press and the public at large both recognized the commitment and leadership in the welfare of children undertaken by the CAS of Toronto during the years of wartime crisis.

Post-war staffing challenges

Immediately after the war's end in August 1945, both the CAS of Toronto and the Infants' Home struggled to maintain a full complement of qualified and experienced staff, despite the return of workers from war-related jobs. Many married women resigned their jobs at the agencies to resume homemaking responsibilities. There were also concerns that the heavy workload and low salaries paid to social workers compared with those in other professions would hinder the agencies' ability to recruit new staff.

At the end of the war, the annual salary for social workers at the society was only $1,400, just a hundred dollars more than the rate established in 1923. This issue prompted the formation of a staff association in 1942 (there was also one at the Infants' Home) and led its members to vote four years later on a resolution that it reconstitute itself as a trade union. When the results of this poll were counted, however, only a few had voted in favour of a unionized workplace. This came as a relief to the board of management, which, predictably, had argued strongly against such a development.

The society's board, in response to its own and its workers' concerns, undertook a number of initiatives to make CAS work more rewarding and competitive. Annual salaries for workers were raised to a maximum of $2,260 if they were professionally qualified and $1,950 for those who were untrained. These salary levels

Annual salaries for workers were raised to a maximum of $2,260 if they were professionally qualified and $1,950 for those who were untrained. A contributory pension scheme was introduced, the number of annual vacation days was increased, and staff were given every other Saturday off.

were regularly improved over the succeeding years so that, by the end of the decade, the top of the front-line worker scale reached $2,900, while supervisors were paid $3,300. Administrative and clerical staff received comparable increases. A contributory pension scheme was introduced, the number of annual vacation days was increased, and staff were given every other Saturday off. The agency was frequently reorganized to make the best use of all available resources.

Similar changes were made at the Infants' Home, which had, in 1942, belatedly obtained a new charter to reflect that it was now solely a child placement agency. At that time, the agency also changed its name from the Infants' Home and Infirmary to the Infants' Homes of Toronto.

At both agencies, in-service training programs were expanded to strengthen supervisory supports and increase worker skills. At the Infants' Homes, where most front-line workers were nurses, staff were taught casework theory and were trained to apply knowledge of human behaviour to their everyday practice. Caseloads were gradually reduced through the hiring of additional staff. At the CAS, this again raised the need for additional office space as the accommodation at 32 Isabella Street became very crowded, so the society began to either purchase or rent the neighbouring properties at 22, 24, 26, 28 and 34 Isabella Street.

"Child in Swaddling Clothes" was created by Florence Wyle, R.C.A, O.S.A. This artwork marked for many years the entrance to the Infants' Homes on Huntley Street.

Foster home shortage and a new Receiving Centre

The foster home shortage, first experienced during the war years, remained, partly due to the increase in the cost of living and partly because foster parents were becoming more choosy about which children they would accept — they were particularly shy to provide homes for adolescent boys, as well as the increasing number of emotionally disturbed children being admitted to agency care.

Both the CAS and the Infants' Homes tried to find ways to address these issues and give foster parents greater satisfaction so that they would serve the agencies over longer periods. Their initiatives included a raise in board rates — with a special supplement going to those homes taking children considered hard to serve — improved training and support programs and better publicity about the need for foster families.

Kid-size facilities.

More kid-size facilities.

The President and Members of the Board of the
Infants' Homes of Toronto

request the honour of your presence at the opening of the

Receiving Centre

by

Her Excellency-Viscountess Alexander of Tunis

on Thursday afternoon, May the first

nineteen hundred and forty-seven

at three o'clock

15 Huntley Street
Toronto

The foster parent shortage meant there were more children living in outside institutions and at the CAS shelter at 33 Charles Street East — and they were staying there longer. To alleviate the pressure for beds, the society rented a building across the street at number 38 to use as an annex to the shelter.

In the meantime, the Infants' Homes had purchased, in 1941, a semi-detached house at 40 Huntley Street. It would serve as a reception home to give temporary care to infants from emergency situations, to aid children in the transfer from foster families to adoptive ones and to assess children whose behaviour had become too difficult for their foster parents. This building quickly proved not to be big enough to meet the demand, so the agency acquired the other half of the house, at number 38, with the intention of converting both houses into one unit. However, seeing that the reception home concept had quickly proved its value, the agency decided instead to erect a modern, purpose-built centre.

A fundraising campaign secured $20,000, which, combined with a grant from the city and the proceeds from the sale of 38–40 Huntley Street, enabled the agency to purchase land at 15 Huntley. On this site, the agency built the Infants' Homes Receiving Centre, which opened its doors on February 28, 1947. It accommodated twenty-five children and seven live-in staff on two floors. An additional ten staff lived off the premises. The building would be used as a receiving home until 1974.

Retirements of Vera Moberly and Bob Mills

In October 1945, Vera Moberly handed in her resignation as executive secretary of the Infants' Homes, but agreed to stay on until the end of the year while the agency searched for a successor. Two years later, in December 1947, Bob Mills resigned as managing director of the CAS of Toronto.

These two extraordinary leaders, whose careers ran in tandem, were similar in a number of ways. Both possessed a marked ability to adapt to changing times as they steered their agencies for the better part of three decades. Both stimulated growth in those organizations, turning them from well-meaning but often ineptly run operations into modern, professional social service agencies. Both were skilled managers and successful fundraisers. Both held and exercised a quiet power that was well regarded by their boards, staff, foster parents and volunteers, as well as other professionals and the child welfare community at large. Both negotiated with governments and other funders from a position of strength, technical knowledge and practical experience, to the lasting benefit of their respective agencies. Governments and funders, in return, often sought their advice on child welfare and other social service matters.

Moberly and Mills met together regularly throughout their careers. In latter years, they held weekly conferences, in which the city's welfare department also participated, to provide a team approach to managing issues of common concern as well as to determine how specific client situations might best be handled. Although they both could see how an amalgamation of their two agencies would likely create a more stable and dynamic organization to protect and care for Toronto's needy children, the times were not yet propitious for such a move.

Moberly died in November 1945 while still at her post as executive secretary of the Infants' Homes. Since 1919, she had led the agency through the gradual change from a nursery and infirmary caring for largely sick infants to an organization that became a network of central office, clinics, foster parents, field staff and volunteers caring for youngsters who were usually physically healthy and living in substitute family settings. Before her death, she saw her ambition of a receiving centre for the observation and assessment of children at least partially achieved. In 1956, a group living program for children was opened at 136 Isabella Street, on the receiving centre campus, and named in her honour.

Upon leaving the society, Mills was invited by B.W. Heise, J.J. Kelso's successor at the province, to work as a child welfare consultant in the Department of Public Welfare. He stayed there for about two years. Although he eventually developed Parkinson's disease, Mills enjoyed ten years of retirement before his death in March 1959.

Writing his obituary for *The Globe and Mail*, Charlotte Whitton commemorated Mills as one of the first people in North America to have tried to assess the cost of services provided by the not-for-profit sector, to devise standards to measure efficiency, and to require that financial support be justified based on results

Foster parents were particularly shy to provide homes for adolescent boys as well as the increasing number of emotionally disturbed children being admitted to agency care.

Mills and Moberly, whose careers ran in tandem, were similar in a number of ways. Both stimulated growth in their organizations, turning them from well-meaning but often ineptly run operations into modern, professional social service agencies.

achieved. His enlightened policies and uniting efforts did much to shape the present-day CAS of Toronto

Both Mills and Moberly were child welfare pioneers whose compassion, integrity and insight contributed to making Toronto a better place for children.

Belle Carver and Stewart Sutton

In 1945, Belle Carver, a former protection worker at the CAS of Toronto, replaced Vera Moberly as executive secretary of the Infants' Homes. The following year, Stewart Sutton succeeded Bob Mills as the new managing director of the CAS.

Sutton was the first professional social worker to hold a senior administrative position at the Children's Aid Society of Toronto. Previous to joining the society, he had worked for the Protestant Children's Home, at York County CAS and in Kingston at Frontenac County CAS. During the Second World War, he was a lieutenant-colonel in the Canadian armed forces and set up the army's first social service corps. Sutton later ran the forces' directorate of social science and, before resigning his commission, spent some time organizing social services for the federal Department of Veterans' Affairs.

Both Sutton and Carver were to work together cooperatively to achieve the next milestone in Toronto's child welfare history — the amalgamation of the Infants' Homes and the Children's Aid Society.

CHAPTER 5

Amalgamation and Growth, 1950–1964

Toronto at mid-century

During the 1950s and '60s, Greater Toronto's population nearly doubled, from just over one million to nearly two million. There were a number of reasons for this unprecedented growth. Besides the baby boom, municipal reorganization had extended the city's boundaries, while increased industrialization attracted rural families and a new influx of immigrants to the city.

At first, these immigrants came mainly from the British Isles, the traditional source of newcomers to Canada. They were followed by migrants from western and central Europe, including Germany, the Netherlands, Poland and Yugoslavia. The onset of the cold war, however, restricted immigration from countries under the influence of the Soviet Union, and migrants from southern European countries, particularly Greece, Italy and Portugal, replaced them in large numbers.

These immigrants headed for the cities, particularly Toronto, where they worked in the expanding manufacturing and construction industries or aspired to jobs in the professions. Although still primarily Christian, these new Canadians began the process of changing Toronto's demographic character from predominantly Protestant Anglo-Celtic to a multi-racial, multi-ethnic community of many faiths.

The characteristics of family life also changed gradually during the post-war decades. Families got smaller. More and more married women began to work outside the home, slowly moving beyond their traditional roles as wives, mothers and care providers. A major problem they experienced, however, was the ongoing lack

Although still primarily Christian, new Canadians began the process of changing Toronto's demographic character from predominantly Protestant Anglo-Celtic to a multi-racial, multi-ethnic community of many faiths.

A major problem working married women experienced was the ongoing lack of appropriate child care and home help services. A growing number of children was being cared for inadequately, increasing the incidence of "latchkey kids" left unsupervised after school.

of appropriate child care and home help services. A growing number of children was being cared for inadequately, increasing the incidence of "latchkey kids" left unsupervised after school.

There were, nevertheless, still very strong conventions about the sorts of family relationships that were socially acceptable. The divorce rate was low and, until the late 1960s, common law relationships were disparaged and legally disadvantaged, while same-sex relationships were against the law. The stigma against unmarried parenthood remained, and church-run maternity homes in Toronto were very busy as young women from around the province — and further afield — sought a place to give birth to their babies in secrecy and anonymity. Almost all of these mothers relinquished their children for adoption, which was why adoption services were a major focus of the work of children's aid societies during this era.

During the 1950s and 1960s, the adolescent years between childhood and adulthood gradually came to be identified as distinct, and the teenage population began to develop its own culture, with identifiable traits, mores and behaviour. Young people stayed in school longer and attained greater autonomy than ever before. Gaps between the generations were frequently disruptive to family life. This trend was reflected by the development of specialized services for youth, such as those described in Chapter 6.

Meanwhile, the face of the Toronto region was changing extensively as a byproduct of the rapid urbanization of former agricultural lands in the townships beyond the city limits. To administer this growing community, a federated urban government, the first of its kind in North America, was formed in 1953, when thirteen adjoining but separate jurisdictions were united into the Municipality of Metropolitan Toronto. (In 1967, further reorganization reduced the thirteen communities to six.) It was not long before Torontonians were referring to this new municipality, and the geographical area it administered, simply as "Metro."

Increased affluence made this a time of greater government spending in support of low-income families. One outcome was the development and management by the Ontario Housing Corporation — a provincial government agency — of thousands of public housing units, both in the city and the burgeoning suburban communities.

This was also an era of consolidation and growing professionalism in the social services. The Master of Social Work (MSW) degree enjoyed a high level of credibility, and children's aid societies hired increasing numbers of workers with such a background. This led to a better understanding among CAS workers of the unique and complex needs of children, insight that was enhanced by the work of John Bowlby and Henry Kempe.

Bowlby, a British child psychiatrist and psychoanalyst, published research in 1951 in a report called *Maternal Care and Mental Health*. (A popular, abridged version of this work appeared in 1965 under the title *Child Care and the Growth of Love*.) In it, he demonstrated how important it was for a child to have a loving relationship with a mother figure, and how children who lacked such a relationship developed problems becoming emotionally attached. His work had a significant influence over the decisions CAS workers made about the admission and placement of children in care and for adoption.

British child psychiatrist and psychoanalyst John Bowlby's research showed how important it was for a child to have a loving relationship with a mother figure, and how children who lacked such a relationship developed problems becoming emotionally attached.

Kempe, a Colorado pediatrician, invented the term "battered child syndrome" to describe physical violence against children. (He deliberately coined the phrase to bring home to the public the reality of the physical abuse of children that, until that time, was referred to by the catch-all expression "cruelty to children." The term "abuse" did not gain currency until the 1970s.) In his research, he found that this violence was more common than most people realized, and that many of the children who were abused were under three years of age. His paper, published in 1962 in the *Journal of the American Medical Association*, made a considerable impression on the way CAS workers investigated and intervened in these situations.

Colorado pediatrician Henry Kempe invented the term "battered child syndrome" to describe physical violence against children. His research made a considerable impression on the way CAS workers investigated and intervened in these situations.

Improving social conditions and the widespread use of antibiotics contributed to a dramatic reduction in the infant death rate — from sixty-one to twenty-seven deaths for every 1,000 live births over the twenty years from 1941 to 1961. Conversely, in the late 1950s, more than 50 percent of the deaths of children between one and twelve months old, and about a third of the deaths of children between one and five years of age, were due to infectious diseases. While some of these diseases were associated with families of low socioeconomic status, others, like poliomyelitis, which swept the city in the early 1950s, did not respect any income group.

The introduction of government-funded hospital insurance in 1957 and of universal public medical insurance in 1966, reduced the vast disparities of access to medical resources between the insured and the 50 percent of the population that had been uninsured in the early 1950s.

Although these advances, and a buoyant economy, contributed to the health and well-being of both the city and the province, the children and families served by children's aid societies generally remained poor. The population explosion, the increasing complexities of urban life and the other changes referenced above produced more families in need of professional help. The apparently simple needs of the pre-war years were long gone.

Amalgamation of the CAS and Infants' Homes

In 1935, the Federation for Community Service had asked the Children's Aid Society of Toronto, the Infant's Home and the Protestant Children's Home to consider amalgamating. All three agencies prepared position papers on the advantages and disadvantages of such a merger, and although discussions went on for a couple of years — and Vera Moberly of the Infants' Home and Bob Mills of the CAS were generally in favour — no action was taken, largely because the boards of the Infants' Home and the Protestant Children's Home did not wish to lose their separate identities or the expertise they believed they had developed as specialized child placement agencies.

Greater collaboration between the Infants' Homes and the CAS of Toronto would improve services to children, eliminate situations where the two agencies duplicated each other's work and reduce competition for scarce resources.

After the war, the issue of amalgamation was once more placed on the table. While the Protestant Children's Home continued to believe that a merger "would compromise service to children and families in need," the Infants' Homes took the opposite view. Under the leadership of Belle Carver, they thought that greater collaboration between the Infants' Homes and the CAS of Toronto would improve services, eliminate situations where the two agencies duplicated each other's work and reduce competition for scarce resources.

Carver and Stewart Sutton of the CAS began discussions in earnest in 1949. Their arguments in favour of a merger persuaded the boards, staff and foster parents of both organizations. The rationale was summed up in the minutes of a joint meeting of both boards:

> There is no reason to believe that the amalgamation will bring about any reduction in staff or expenditures, but it should mean substantial economy in that better services should be provided for children and other clients at a cost represented by the combined budgets of the two agencies.

As the desire was for a friendly merger, many hours were spent discussing how the many difficulties and problems common to amalgamations — particularly those between organizations with valued and settled traditions — would be resolved. With goodwill on both sides, it was thought that these issues would not be insurmountable.

Thus, on May 31, 1951, the two agencies amalgamated under the name Children's Aid and Infants' Homes of Toronto, becoming one of the largest child welfare organizations in North America. It was a merger of equals, not a takeover of the Infants' Homes by the CAS, which is why the historical connections to both predecessor agencies were maintained in the name of the new organization.

Sutton, who had run the CAS of Toronto since 1947, was appointed executive director of the amalgamated agency. Lloyd Richardson, director of the CAS of Lincoln County in St. Catharines, was recruited as deputy director. March Dickens of the Infants' Homes rounded out the senior management team, as casework consultant.

The new agency had a full-time staff of 219 — social workers, child and youth workers, nurses, physicians, psychologists, accountants, clerical workers and caretakers. They gave protection to neglected children in their own homes, counselled unmarried mothers and fathers, found the best possible foster homes for children and placed hundreds in adoption homes. They worked out of the CAS offices at 32 Isabella Street and adjacent buildings, at the Charles Street shelter, the Huntley Street Receiving Centre and the Infants' Homes' former offices at 34 Grosvenor Street.

The agency's budget for its first year of operation was a little over $1.25 million, the largest portion of which came in the form of grants from the City of Toronto and the Community Chest of Greater Toronto, which had taken over the respon-

On May 31, 1951, the two agencies amalgamated under the name Children's Aid and Infants' Homes of Toronto, becoming one of the largest child welfare organizations in North America.

The new agency had a full-time staff of 219 — social workers, child and youth workers, nurses, physicians, psychologists, accountants, clerical workers and caretakers.

The agency's combined budget for its first year of operation was a little over $1.25 million.

sibilities of the Federation for Community Service when the latter organization sus-
pended operations at the end of the war. Most of the budget went to staff salaries,
boarding payments to foster parents and to pay the costs incurred in running the
shelter and the Receiving Centre.

That year, the new agency cared for 2,687 children who were born to unmarried mothers or whose parents could not provide a home for them. Most were
placed with agency foster parents or in adoption probation homes, with adoption
plans being made for 1,045 youngsters. The agency helped another 3,179 children
and their parents in their own homes.

The challenges posed by amalgamation

Although much work had been done prior to amalgamation, the senior management team had to ensure that the new agency had a sound organizational structure
and strong administrative and casework staff. They needed to develop policies to
govern such issues as the way that foster homes were to be supported and supervised, the rationalization of the two agencies' caseloads, and the development of
new working relationships with other agencies in the community.

Most importantly, they had to make sure that the combined staffs of the two
agencies were able to work together cooperatively. This was of particular concern
because the staff of the Infants' Homes were primarily nurses, while those who had
worked at the CAS were mainly social workers. The agency also inherited a large
number of employees who did not have a professional qualification, some of whom
felt threatened by a new emphasis on professional training. Long-time staff member Jessie Watters remembers a difficult meeting when one such employee commented, "It seems you have to believe in Freud to get a raise around here."

The agency also had to cope with the fact that newly minted holders of the
MSW degree graduated with only a cursory education in child welfare work.
Rarely did their training equip them with the knowledge required to work in a children's aid society. Writing in 1962, Watters, who had succeeded March Dickens as
the agency's casework consultant, estimated that it took a further three to five years

In its first year, the new agency cared for 2,687 children who were born to unmarried mothers or whose parents could not provide a home for them.

"It seems you have to believe in Freud to get a raise around here."

— CAS employee, referring to the society's new emphasis on professional training

of supervised work experience for new graduates to translate theory into skilled practice. Although there have been some improvements over the years, the society confronts the same issue today.

The agency responded by investing heavily in in-service training programs to keep staff up to date with developments in child welfare. Supervisors were also helped to build the skills they would need to teach new workers the specifics of child welfare practice. A system of bursaries was instituted to enable promising unqualified staff to return to school and secure their professional training.

In the years following the merger, employing enough qualified and skilled staff to manage an increasingly complex and difficult caseload was an ongoing concern. There were many reasons why. For instance, CAS work was not considered prestigious. Caseloads were high — it was not unusual for a protection worker to be responsible for fifty families. And there was intense competition among social service agencies for MSW graduates — and the agency often found itself priced out of the market because its salary scales were not always competitive with those of other employers.

CAS work was not considered prestigious. Caseloads were high — it was not unusual for a protection worker to be responsible for fifty families. And there was intense competition among social service agencies for MSW graduates.

An additional challenge was that social work was still a profession taken up mainly by women. Although values were gradually changing, most women still considered marriage and a career mutually incompatible. Many employees remained on staff only until they got married and started families.

A *new Child Welfare Centre*

Even before amalgamation, the Children's Aid Society of Toronto had long outgrown its offices in the row of houses between 22 and 34 Isabella Street. By the mid-1940s, pressures for space had reached the breaking point. A solution to this long-felt need seemed to be near in 1946, when 2,500 of the agency's friends — with support from the City of Toronto — donated $389,000 for the construction of a modern building to house staff, clinics, private interviewing rooms and waiting rooms and to meet other administrative needs.

Supply scarcities, and the subsequent plan to amalgamate with the Infants' Homes, postponed the building program until a plan could be developed to provide

The CAS of Toronto had long outgrown its offices in the row of houses between 22 and 34 Isabella Street. By the mid-1940s, pressures for space had reached the breaking point.

facilities that would be adequate for the enlarged organization. This was doubtless a wise decision but, in the meantime, it meant that staff were still squeezed into every nook and cranny of the existing buildings, where they interviewed about 270 children and families every day. These working conditions were described in a contemporary fundraising brochure:

> Walk through the worn corridors, the drab offices and the bare, lonely waiting room. You will see desperate, unmarried, deserted mothers who are searching for understanding and help, sitting out in the open, under the scrutiny of those present — a mother and a father discussing their most intimate problems before their own children and within earshot of people all around. Walk upstairs and watch some of the hampered caseworkers, 12 in one room, 17 in another, trying to talk on telephones about the delicate problems of those in their care. See the social worker dictating in what was once a linen closet in this old house.

"Walk upstairs and watch some of the hampered caseworkers, 12 in one room, 17 in another, trying to talk on telephones about the delicate problems of those in their care. See the social worker dictating in what was once a linen closet in this old house."

— CAS fundraising brochure

Seventeen workers in one room

In 1952, a new building program, with a budget of nearly $750,000, was launched. It called for the demolition of the old CAS shelter at 33 Charles Street East, which would be replaced by a new, purpose-built children's residence and a state-of-the-art Child Welfare Centre with 2,700 square metres of office and clinic space spread over three floors.

In 1952, a new building program, with a budget of nearly $750,000, was launched. It called for the demolition of the old CAS shelter at 33 Charles Street East, which would be replaced by a new, purpose-built children's residence and a state-of-the-art Child Welfare Centre. The structure would contain 2,700 square metres of office and clinic space spread over three floors. A building campaign, to which each staff member contributed a day's salary, raised $300,000. This money was added to proceeds from the sale of the Infants' Homes offices at 34 Grosvenor Street and the $389,000 that had been raised during the 1946 campaign.

A year later, the new Child Welfare Centre, for which Mayor Allan Lamport had laid the cornerstone, opened its doors. It housed all of the agency's professional and administrative staff as well as its medical and dental clinics.

A special effort was made to make the centre open and accessible to the public. Jessie Watters remembers why:

Stewart Sutton knew that the children in the shelter found it hard to go to classes at Jesse Ketchum Public School because the other students referred to them as the "home children." They did not want to play with them, they said, "because you don't have a mother or father." So when plans were made for the new building, Stewart insisted that the grounds should be arranged for the general public to use and that they be made welcome so that CAS children would not feel so isolated. That is the origin of the sunken garden in front of the Charles Street offices. When the new building was opened, Stewart quoted a twelve-year-old boy who said, "Today, I'm proud to belong to the Aid."

On the same occasion, board president A.E. Eastmure declared:

Following many years of careful planning and thanks to the generosity of the citizens of this community, [we have completed and are ready to occupy] our new Child Welfare Centre. Of equal, if not greater, importance, this move into our new quarters has symbolized and cemented the amalgamation of the two former agencies who came together to create the Children's Aid and Infants' Homes.

The children's residence called for in the plans was never built, to a large extent because the agency was about to inherit York Cottage, a residential facility in Willowdale, as the result of yet another merger — this time with part of York County CAS. In the meantime, children who would formerly have been placed in the CAS shelter were now being cared for at the former Infants' Homes Receiving Centre at 15 Huntley Street.

"Stewart Sutton knew that the children in the shelter found it hard to go to classes at Jesse Ketchum public school because the other students referred to them as the "home children." They did not want to play with them, they said, "because you don't have a mother or father." So when plans were made for the new building, Stewart insisted that the grounds should be arranged for the general public to use and that they be made welcome so that CAS children would not feel so isolated. That is the origin of the sunken garden in front of the Charles Street offices. When the new building was opened, Stewart quoted a twelve-year-old boy who said, "Today, I'm proud to belong to the Aid."

— Jessie Watters

Tree house in front of the then North Branch and York Cottage

To reflect its expanded responsibilities, the Children's Aid and Infants' Homes adopted a new name: the Children's Aid Society of Metropolitan Toronto, a mouthful that most people shortened to CASMT, or Metro CAS. It is a sign of the success of the earlier amalgamation with the Infants' Homes that no objections were raised about the loss of the title "Infants' Homes," which it had been so important to retain only six years before.

The decentralized branch system was intended to bring workers in the protection and unmarried parents departments, as well as those who worked with foster and adoptive families, closer to the communities they served.

Expansion to the suburbs

This second amalgamation would extend the jurisdiction of the Children's Aid and Infants' Homes of Toronto beyond the city limits and into the suburbs that now formed an integral part of the new municipality of Metropolitan Toronto. Until 1953, the territory that made up Metro had been part of York County, and for the first four years of the new district's existence, York County CAS continued to take responsibility for child welfare services in the parts of Metro outside the City of Toronto. That changed as of January 1, 1957, in accordance with the recommendations of a report commissioned by Metro Council.

To reflect these expanded responsibilities, the Children's Aid and Infants' Homes adopted a new name: the Children's Aid Society of Metropolitan Toronto, a mouthful that most people shortened to CASMT, or Metro CAS. It is a sign of the success of the earlier amalgamation with the Infants' Homes that no objections were raised about the loss of the title "Infants' Homes," which it had been so important to retain only six years before.

A gradual shifting of cases from York CAS to Metro CAS began in the fall of 1956, while at the same time some members of the York board joined the board of the Toronto agency. Metro CAS took over York Cottage, the 150-year-old farmhouse at 5412 Yonge Street that had operated as the York CAS shelter (Metro CAS converted it into a group living program for children who were unsuited to foster care), as well as that agency's offices at 112 St. Clair Avenue West in Toronto. All York CAS staff who transferred to Metro CAS were guaranteed their existing salaries, although they were told that their job descriptions might change.

The merger was followed by a restructuring of the agency which resulted in the development of a decentralized branch system, intended to bring workers in the protection and unmarried parents departments, as well as those who worked with foster and adoptive families, closer to the communities they served.

Two purpose-built Child Welfare Centres were opened in the fall of 1958: North Branch, on the grounds of York Cottage at 5414 Yonge Street, serving the northern townships; and East Branch, at 843 Kennedy Road, serving Scarborough Township and the eastern part of North York Township. Each cost about $100,000 to build, plus the cost of the land at the East Branch location. Financing was obtained through the sale of the St. Clair Avenue offices inherited from York CAS, as well as grants from the province and Metro and from the agency's depreciation fund.

In 1962–63, the agency's operations within the city of Toronto were also decentralized, as units of protection workers were deployed in five districts.

Stewart Sutton resigns

In 1954, after seven years at the agency's helm, executive director Stewart Sutton resigned to take up a senior position with UNICEF, the United Nations Children's Fund. He would have a distinguished career on the world stage. He worked first in UNICEF's operations in southern and eastern Africa, then became the agency's regional director for the Middle East. In 1963, he left UNICEF and moved to Geneva to become director of International Social Service, an agency that facilitates cooperation between social welfare agencies around the world. He moved back to Canada in 1966 to become the first secretary-general of the newly formed Vanier Institute of the Family. After stepping down from that position in 1971, he continued for several years to work as a consultant. He died in 1988.

Staff and board alike took pride in Sutton's international work, but they also lauded him for what he had achieved at Metro CAS, notably his outstanding success in merging the society with both the Infants' Homes and York County CAS.

According to those who knew him best, including Jessie Watters, whom he brought into the agency in 1947 and who became a lifelong friend, Sutton's most important contribution was his work to update the agency's attitudes toward children.

> Stewart felt there had been too much emphasis on rules and regulations, on what children could and couldn't do, and not enough on children's needs. He felt that policies should be guidelines for staff but that children's needs should come first. He hated that "I know what's best for the child" attitude. He also made the CAS an

North Branch, 5414 Yonge Street

East Branch, 843 Kennedy Road

Former executive director Stewart Sutton.

exciting place to work. You could try out new ideas, new ways of helping people.

Lloyd Richardson

John Yaremko, Ontario's minister of community and social services (left), Lloyd Richardson (right) and a young friend cut the ribbon at the new residence.

In 1954, the board of Metro CAS appointed Sutton's deputy, Lloyd Richardson, as the agency's new executive director. Richardson had extensive experience working with children and adolescents, including some time in the 1930s as a caseworker at the Protestant Children's Home. Sutton said that he asked Richardson in 1947 to give up his position as executive director of Lincoln County CAS to come to Toronto as his deputy because:

> I liked him, trusted him, and had complete confidence in him. We were enough alike that there could be no real friction between us and yet we were different. I trusted him as a friend and colleague to do his utmost to keep me on track when he and our colleagues felt that I was straying. To my great delight, relief and surprise, Lloyd accepted my offer. We worked happily together and maintained harmonious relationships with the board of directors, the staff and the community at large without any of us having such a thing as a job description.

Largely because of his warmth and interpersonal skills, agency staff held Richardson in the same high esteem as they had Sutton. Mona Robinson, who transferred to Metro CAS from York CAS at the time of the 1957 amalgamation to assume the job of intake supervisor, recalls:

"Among Richardson's strengths was his ability to inspire loyalty and respect. This was demonstrated by what became known as his Friday afternoon "walkabouts," when he greeted each staff member by name and asked about their week's work."
— Mona Robinson

> I had the greatest admiration for Lloyd Richardson. He had a facility for delegating responsibility and giving staff scope to use their potential. Among his strengths was his ability to inspire loyalty and respect. This was demonstrated by what became known as his Friday after-

noon "walkabouts," when he greeted each staff member by name and asked about their week's work.

This personal, hands-on approach extended to clients, as is evidenced by his involvement with a teenage couple seeking his permission as CAS wards to marry.

Richardson worried about negotiating the agency's budget with the board of directors, the Department of Public Welfare and the Municipality of Metropolitan Toronto. Jessie Watters, however, remembers his competence:

> He had the most remarkable combination of shrewd judgment, common sense and a wide vision. He saw CAS as something you had to look after and you had to back up the workers, especially front-line staff.

Child Welfare Act, 1954

Immediately upon assuming the executive directorship, Richardson had to grapple with the implications of new child welfare legislation that had come into effect a month earlier.

The post-war baby boom was in full swing and the child population was soaring. Although the agency's caseload was not growing at as high a rate, the young people it was serving were older than in the past and, as a result of the changes in family life that were outlined at the beginning of this chapter, their needs were more complex.

Premier Leslie Frost's government reacted by passing the Child Welfare Act, 1954, which consolidated the Children's Protection Act of 1893 with two pieces of 1921 legislation, the Children of Unmarried Parents Act and the Adoption Act.

The new law reflected the continuing but gradual movement, begun in the 1940s, away from funding child welfare through philanthropic and municipal means and in the direction of entrenching children's services within the auspices of the expanding welfare state, with its increasing regulatory powers. The act was intended to provide a more stable foundation upon which to finance

The new Child Welfare Act reflected the continuing but gradual movement, begun in the 1940s, away from funding child welfare through philanthropic and municipal means and in the direction of entrenching children's services within the auspices of the expanding welfare state, with its increasing regulatory powers.

protection and adoption services. It also, to some extent, clarified the different responsibilities of the provincial Department of Public Welfare, the municipalities and the societies.

The act continued the 25 percent provincial contribution — extended to 40 percent in 1957 — to maintain children in CAS care. Societies also received a provincial grant to cover 25 percent of their capital costs. This was accompanied by increased government monitoring and supervision of the societies in the form of periodic visits by Department of Public Welfare staff. (The title of these government visitors has varied over the years, from child welfare supervisor, field supervisor and field consultant to the present-day term: program supervisor).

There were, however, not yet any provincial standards by which CAS services could be judged. Nor were there any mechanisms that protected the rights of children in foster homes and group homes. The assumption was that those who provided these services did so with altruistic motives, and therefore standards were not necessary.

The visitors held discussions with society staff, visited agency programs and reviewed files. There were, however, not yet any provincial standards by which CAS services could be judged. Nor were there any mechanisms that protected the rights of children in foster homes and group homes. The assumption was that those who provided these services did so with altruistic motives, and therefore standards were not necessary.

The Child Welfare Act stressed that the selection of adoption and foster homes should be suited to each child's individual needs, a best-practice approach long undertaken by both the CAS of Toronto and the Infants' Homes. Another outcome was the establishment of a central adoption registry, known as the Adoption Clearing Service, to match children and adoptive parents across the province. Yet another was that children were not to remain in temporary care for longer than twenty-four months; after that time, but hopefully sooner, they were either to return to their parents or be made permanent wards of the society and, if possible, adopted. In a report to the board, Richardson said he thought that:

A central adoption registry, known as the Adoption Clearing Service, was established to match children and adoptive parents across the province.

> This [new Child Welfare Act] does seem to be progressive, but it has increased the number of court actions, since one must always be conscious of the two-year limit set forth in the act for temporary wardship. With the help of [Metro], three workers have been detailed to the supervision of temporary wards and their families to concentrate on returning them quickly to their own homes. The court situation,

"This [new Child Welfare Act] does seem to be progressive, but it has increased the number of court actions, since one must always be conscious of the two-year limit set forth in the act for temporary wardship. The court situation, though, is at its saturation point because of the increase in court actions and the high frequency of short-term adjournments."
— Lloyd Richardson, speaking about the new Child Welfare Act

though, is at its saturation point because of the increase in court actions and the high frequency of short-term adjournments.

The act also reduced the maximum age that a child could remain in care to eighteen years from twenty-one. At the time the legislation came into effect, the agency had about 300 young people between those ages in its care. Most had been admitted during the war years, when protection services were minimal and permanent guardianship was the favoured means of meeting the needs of children requiring protection.

"Changing the course of human life"

The agency was growing rapidly. By 1958, it had about 350 staff, 200 of whom were professionals — social workers, child and youth workers, nurses, physicians, dentists and psychologists. They were assisted by almost 1,200 foster homes and many individual volunteers and community groups. Between them that year, they supported almost 8,000 families and more than 15,000 children, 3,000 of whom were in care at any given moment. Adoptions were legally completed for almost 430 children.

These services were paid for partly through tax dollars and partly through donations. Metro Council and other municipalities spent almost $1.5 million a year for the direct maintenance of children in care. The United Community Chest contributed about $350,000 toward protection services, work with unmarried parents and adoption services. The province granted more than $1 million a year toward the society's work, while the federal government passed on almost $200,000 in family allowance benefits (as part of a program established in 1945). The agency relied on voluntary contributions to pay for such "extras" as birthday gifts, bicycles, and Boy Scout and Girl Guide uniforms for the children in its care.

In 1950, Stewart Sutton summed up the work of the society: "What we do, and what we leave undone, may change the course of a human life."

The society's fundamental purpose was described at that time as the protection of children from cruelty and neglect on the part of parents, guardians or others. Based on contemporary research into behavioural psychology, not least the work of

By 1958, the society had about 350 staff, 200 of whom were professionals — social workers, child and youth workers, nurses, physicians, dentists and psychologists. They were assisted by almost 1,200 foster homes and many individual volunteers and community groups. Between them that year, they supported almost 8,000 families and more than 15,000 children.

"What we do, and what we leave undone, may change the course of a human life."
— *Stewart Sutton*

Workers believed that the best place for a child was in his or her own home. They made every effort to put that belief into practice by counselling families, helping unmarried parents plan for their child's future and assisting in custody and access matters in divorce proceedings.

Each child in the society's care had a social worker — or, if they were very young, a nurse — from the Child Care department who was responsible for their welfare, health and schooling. These staff made a major effort to maintain the child's ties to his or her family, when appropriate, and to the community at large. Plans for the children were reviewed consistently to see if it were possible to return them to their own homes or to place them for adoption.

Bowlby and others on the damaging effects of maternal deprivation, workers believed that the best place for a child was in his or her own home.

They made every effort to put that belief into practice by counselling families, helping unmarried parents plan for their child's future and assisting in custody and access matters in divorce proceedings. When it was not possible for children to remain safely at home, they admitted them to the agency's care or arranged for their adoption. They devoted much energy to recruiting and supporting foster parents and potential adoptive parents.

Many children were voluntarily admitted to care at the request of unmarried mothers or parents for whom a short-term placement would help them through a difficult period. Others were admitted through legal action under the Child Welfare Act, the society being entrusted with their guardianship.

Each child in the society's care had a social worker — or, if they were very young, a nurse — from the Child Care department who was responsible for their welfare, health and schooling. These staff made a major effort to maintain the child's ties to his or her family, when appropriate, and to the community at large. Plans for the children were reviewed consistently to see if it were possible to return them to their own homes or to place them for adoption.

Those who were not placed for adoption were, for the most part, cared for by foster families or in group homes. About 12 percent of the children lived either in one of four agency-run institutions (described below and in Chapter 6) or in numerous "outside institutions" operated by other organizations.

The society was also required by law to make recommendations in the case of adoptions made privately — for example, through a family doctor — and on behalf of families who were adopting a child related to them. In 1958, it was involved in 900 such adoptions.

Protection work

By now, there were almost fifty workers whose job it was to investigate and intervene in situations where children were being neglected. Many of these staff were located at the new decentralized branch offices in Scarborough and Willowdale, but most still worked in the central areas of Metro, where social problems were still more prevalent than in the suburban communities.

The Metro area's growth created shortages of both affordable housing and employment, and for many parents the resultant pressure was too much to bear. Alcoholism, desertion, physical abuse and incest (as intra-familial sexual abuse was usually called before the 1980s) were the unfortunate outcomes. The society and other social agencies found it hard to meet the ever-increasing demands.

Requests for service generally came by way of a complaint or referral from the police, hospitals or other social service agencies. Because the crisis was often immediate, workers frequently had to respond quickly. Their ability to do so was enhanced by the introduction of an agency "radio car" that kept field workers in touch with the office via two-way radio — an early example of information technology.

Sheila McDermott, who emigrated from England in 1955 to join the agency's protection department, describes one of her earliest experiences:

> In those days, we had to work Tuesday evenings. That's why I was sitting at my desk after the supper hour, when I received a phone call from one of my clients — let's call her Janet — asking me to come to her house right away because she was worried about her two boys.
>
> When I arrived, I found that Janet and her partner — I'll call him Peter — had been drinking heavily. Obviously the worse for wear, Peter had passed out on the living room floor. The two boys were in bed but Janet was insisting she had to go to work — she had an overnight job as a nursing aide in a private home.
>
> Her sister-in-law and I eventually persuaded her that this would not be a good idea and that it would be best for her to sleep it off now. As we were helping her to bed, I discovered two unopened bottles of liquor under the pillow. As the two boys were fast asleep by this time, it seemed safe to leave them, so I "apprehended" the bottles instead.

The Metro area's growth created shortages of both affordable housing and employment, and for many parents the resultant pressure was too much to bear. The society and other social agencies found it hard to meet the ever-increasing demands.

The agency "radio car" that kept field workers in touch with the office via two-way radio

"Early the next morning, I went back to the house to see what was going on and found Peter was already up and away to the bootlegger. I helped Janet clean up the place and remember pouring half-filled glasses of liquor down the sink. At this point, Peter returned home joyfully clutching a bottle of rye. He graciously offered me a drink!"

— Sheila McDermott, about one of her earliest protection department experiences

The society's workers tried to broaden their role to include working with families to prevent family crises and the resulting upsets for children. More often than not, though, they found themselves being called in to families when it was too late to do anything other than admit children to care. Usually, they had to settle for such limited goals, so busy were they in moving from one crisis to another, while often feeling drowned in work.

Early the next morning, I went back to the house to see what was going on and found Peter was already up and away to the boot legger. I helped Janet clean up the place and remember pouring half-filled glasses of liquor down the sink. At this point, Peter returned home joyfully clutching a bottle of rye. He graciously offered me a drink!

I sold the two bottles of liquor to my colleagues and put the money in the Protection department's "slush fund." However, when [executive director] Lloyd Richardson heard about this he told me in his dry, humorous way that if the Liquor Control Board [LCBO] ever got to know about it, I would be in deep trouble as (unbeknownst to me as a new immigrant) only the LCBO was permitted to sell liquor in Ontario!

The society's workers tried to broaden their role to include working with families to prevent family crises and the resulting upsets for children. More often than not, though, they found themselves being called in to families when it was too late to do anything other than admit children to care. Usually, they had to settle for such limited goals, so busy were they in moving from one crisis to another, while often feeling drowned in work.

Work with unmarried parents

Although the war years had loosened the community's negative attitude toward unmarried parents, giving birth to a so-called "illegitimate" baby would still be considered a shameful act well into the 1960s. While some unwed mothers were willing to face the social stigma of being a single parent, few could afford to raise a child alone despite the extension of provincial mothers' allowance payments to unwed parents in 1951. And those who signed a declaration of paternity, in an attempt to put legal pressure on the father to provide financially for their child, usually found that he had no resources with which to do so.

Because of the prevailing attitude, these pregnant young women, who were often teenagers, continued to feel the need to give birth in anonymous circumstances — and Toronto was still their preferred destination. This created a massive workload for the agency; in 1959, for example, the unmarried parent department admitted to care more than 700 children of unwed parents. Workers in the department worked hard, usually in close cooperation with their colleagues in the Adoption department, to find permanent homes for these children.

Ruth Mankie, who joined in the unmarried parent department as a young worker in the late 1950s, remembers one of her of her mentors:

> We called Gladys Bastedo "The Angel of Moss Park" [after the inner-city housing project where she worked]. She was a tiny woman, quick as anything, and even though she seemed to us very old, [she] would run circles around us younger workers. She was a very committed and professional woman who nevertheless referred to her clients as "her little girls." She seemed to be made of iron but she had a huge heart. She was very resourceful and incredibly independent.

Adoption

In 1949, the society had updated its adoption policy to state that "the prime responsibility of the society regarding adoption is to consider the possibility of adoption for all children in the care of the society and to find the best possible home for each child entrusted to our care." This policy statement represented an important shift of emphasis in Metro CAS's adoption practice. As described in Chapter 3, for years the society had tended to respond to requests from white, economically secure but often infertile couples for perfect newborn babies who would appear in almost every respect to be their birth children. Gradually, however, the CAS of Toronto, the Infants' Homes and other agencies had begun to gain public support for shifting the primary focus away from the needs of the potential adoptive parents and toward those of the children requiring adoption.

Pregnant young women, who were often teenagers, continued to feel the need to give birth in anonymous circumstances — and Toronto was still their preferred destination. This created a massive workload for the agency.

The Angel of Moss Park
"We called Gladys Bastedo "The Angel of Moss Park" [after the inner-city housing project where she worked]. She was a tiny woman, quick as anything, and even though she seemed to us very old, [she] would run circles around us younger workers. She was a very committed and professional woman who nevertheless referred to her clients as "her little girls." She seemed to be made of iron but she had a huge heart. She was very resourceful and incredibly independent."
— Ruth Mankie

For many years, potential adoptive parents would continue to demand newborn Caucasian babies of impeccable background.

It remained a challenge, however, for the society to put its new policy into practice. For many years, potential adoptive parents would continue to demand newborn Caucasian babies of impeccable background. While many of the children available for adoption met this criterion, many others did not.

Nor were they all children of unmarried parents. Many were already wards of the society for whom permanent plans had to be made. These children tended to have special needs or were older, often having already spent a considerable amount of time in a foster home. In 1954, Lloyd Richardson described the challenge some of these children presented:

> Peter is an attractive child with a gentle, loving nature but has developed at a slower pace than the average child. Among applicants, we find that adopting a child of limited ability such as Peter is one of the hardest things for them to consider. Children with temper tantrums or with medical problems such as epilepsy in their background are as a rule more readily appreciated than the retarded child.
>
> Mary was born with a severe harelip and cleft palate. The repair to the lip was so skilfully done that it is barely noticeable. The repair to Mary's palate seems miraculous, for she talks well in spite of the fact that there is a gap at one side of her upper jaw. Nevertheless, while we have been successful in finding adoption homes for children with allergies, heart defects and other internal deficiencies, a facial deformity has proven to be most difficult for couples to accept. "Mary's Story" is to appear in the December issue of *Chatelaine*. Through it, we hope at last to find adopting parents for her.
>
> Mae is an attractive, pert little half-Chinese girl of four. Although we have visited Chinese doctors and ministers armed with her photograph, we have still not found parents for her. Her appearance has been too Anglo-Saxon for some oriental couples and too Chinese for occidental couples.

"Mary was born with a severe harelip and cleft palate. The repair to the lip was so skilfully done that it is barely noticeable. The repair to Mary's palate seems miraculous, for she talks well in spite of the fact that there is a gap at one side of her upper jaw. Nevertheless, while we have been successful in finding adoption homes for children with allergies, heart defects and other internal deficiencies, a facial deformity has proven to be most difficult for couples to accept. "Mary's Story" is to appear in the December issue of Chatelaine. *Through it, we hope at last to find adopting parents for her."*

— Lloyd Richardson

Adoption workers tried hard to find homes for the children who needed them, including young people like Peter, Mary and Mae, and to prepare the children and applicants for adoption. Nevertheless, according to Jessie Watters, "Workers often found it was hard to convey to adoption applicants the needs of those children who presented a higher risk while facing the perception of the public at large that they were trying to control destiny in seeking to find exactly the right parents for each child."

Fortunately, through hard work and a strong commitment to the needs of children, workers managed to place the majority of young people needing adoption with people who had demonstrated they were willing and able to meet their varying needs.

Workers conducted home studies of couples — adoption in this era being limited to applicants who were married. Some of these couples could best respond to an outgoing, boisterous child, while others may have had more understanding of one who was shy and sensitive. There were those who could readily undertake the care of a child with a medical problem but who would be uncomfortable with a child whose ethnicity was other than their own. There were those who could accept as their own the child who came to them as a toddler or older, whereas others could be parents to an adopted child only if he or she came to them in early infancy.

One of the reasons agency staff were successful in finding so many suitable homes for children whose needs were not always straightforward was that there were more families seeking children than there were children needing homes. (A situation that left many applicants disappointed.) Another reason was the province's establishment of the Adoption Clearing Service, which brought the needs of children who were hard to place to the attention of potential adopters.

Although the society rarely had contact with adoptive families once their probationary period was over, most placements were regarded as successful because each year fewer than a dozen of the hundreds of children it placed for adoption were "returned" to the agency.

Agency staff were successful in finding so many suitable homes for children because there were more families seeking children than there were children needing homes, and because the Adoption Clearing Service brought the needs of hard-to-place children to the attention of potential adopters.

Foster family and group home care

As described in earlier chapters, both the Infants' Homes and the CAS of Toronto were pioneers in the use of foster families to look after children in care. When the two agencies merged, this tradition continued. However, times were changing and workers had become more aware of the children's needs. One outcome was that children were not admitted to care as readily as before, and those who were admitted were often more troubled. This frequently resulted in foster parents being asked to provide a level of care that, in many cases, was beyond their capabilities.

Although the society approved 181 new foster homes in 1953, up from 156 the year before, the number was far from adequate, as Lloyd Richardson told board members:

> The foster home situation for younger children has improved somewhat and the staff are now finding that the more adequate boarding home rate is beginning to attract more and better homes, but the situation in this regard is not yet by any means solved.
>
> The major difficulty is our inability to find homes suited to the peculiar needs of individual children and more particularly we are still a long way from finding foster homes that will accept or handle the problems common to teenage and adolescent children. I am still inclined to doubt that we will ever find adequate foster homes for this older group of children.

As Richardson's comments clearly illustrate, for many children foster care was beginning to be seen as insufficient. This is why, by the 1960s, the therapeutic group home was viewed as one answer. Such homes might provide remedial care especially to children with emotional and behavioural disorders — a fast-growing percentage of the agency's caseload.

As early as 1952, Stewart Sutton had expressed the opinion that:

"The major difficulty is our inability to find homes suited to the peculiar needs of individual children and more particularly we are still a long way from finding foster homes that will accept or handle the problems common to teenage and adolescent children. I am still inclined to doubt that we will ever find adequate foster homes for this older group of children."
— Lloyd Richardson

For many children foster care was beginning to be seen as insufficient. This is why, by the 1960s, the therapeutic group home was viewed as one answer. Such homes might provide remedial care especially to children with emotional and behavioural disorders — a fast-growing percentage of the agency's caseload.

Some years ago, we entered an era when it was felt that all institutions were bad and that the foster home provided the only way to care for a child. We now recognize that the pendulum has swung too far, and I feel safe in predicting that within the next decade it will be recognized that many children will have to be cared for in small, adequate institutions. Many of these children can live happily and develop usefully only in the more impersonal atmosphere of a warm, human institution, where they can keep their distance from people whom they are not prepared to accept as replacements for their own mother and father.

Marnie Bruce, who supervised the society's new group care program, expanded on Sutton's theme:

A group home provides care for a small group of up to six children in a family type setting where the emphasis is on meeting the needs of the children. It is a warm, family setting geared to understanding children who cannot take the close parental relationship of a foster home but who do not require institutional care. They are especially good for adolescents and disturbed youngsters.

Group parents are very carefully selected and are hopefully of high quality. The group mother is paid for her services, the close relationship with the agency social worker is that of colleague and group parents are expected to accept more responsibility than are foster parents or child care attendants in institutions.

On the other side of the coin, the agency's active responsibility is greater and the agency determines the basic mode of living, which is geared to meeting the children's needs more than in a foster home.

Despite the development of group homes, foster families still looked after the majority of children in the agency's care, and most did an excellent job. Barb was one of those children. Born in 1953, she recalls a childhood filled with "unpredictability, mistrust and great sorrow." Family conditions deteriorated to the extent that she was admitted to care and placed with foster parents. Reflecting back, she recalls: "I can truthfully say I had a positive experience as a 'system kid.' But it had a lot more to do with my foster parents than the system itself. They were genuinely interested in giving me — someone else's child — a chance to become a successful adult."

Many staff and foster parents regarded the nerve centre of the agency's foster care system to have been Margarita Deary, fondly known to all simply as Deary. She worked at the society for four decades, starting in the 1930s, as the placement worker who matched children with foster families. Although faced with what often seemed an impossible task, she would somehow come up with a bed, even if it meant that she had to cajole foster families into changing their plans for the evening. Ron Poole remembers her from his time as a young social worker in the 1960s:

> Deary had her own system of remembering all of the foster parents and knew their strengths and weaknesses. She sat in her office surrounded by stacks of cards in rubber bands with her illegible (to us) scrawl on each of the cards. We often said that if Deary was ever hit by a truck and hospitalized, the whole foster care system would be doomed.

"Margarita Deary, fondly known to all simply as Deary, had her own system of remembering all of the foster parents and knew their strengths and weaknesses. She sat in her office surrounded by stacks of cards in rubber bands with her illegible (to us) scrawl on each of the cards. We often said that if Deary was ever hit by a truck and hospitalized, the whole foster care system would be doomed."

— Ron Poole, social worker

Institutional care

Despite the successes of foster care (the numbers of children in foster homes peaked in the 1960s) and group homes, Metro CAS, along with other children's aid societies, also began to place children who needed specialized care because of emotional disturbance or "maladjusted behaviour" in treatment institutions. Williams writes that:

> New institutions appeared, some of a charitable, some of a profit making nature, each advocating the efficacy of its own regime, yet differing markedly in everything from the psychiatric and child

nurturing theories of its professional staff, the moral and social values to be inculcated through training regimes, conduct and discipline to the varied techniques of treatment. There were advocates of "permissiveness" and "free expression" and those who promised firm discipline to produce a "proper and well-behaved personality." In the field of treatment of disturbed children, there was, in fact, no one proven and generally accepted theory of practice with ascertainable and predictable results.

Although these institutions were originally regulated under the Charitable Institutions Act of 1931, according to Williams they were vulnerable to charlatans, eccentrics and mere incompetents. Fortunately, the good judgment of agencies such as Metro CAS kept these to a minimum. The passage of the Children's Institutions Act of 1963 strengthened the province's ability to regulate them by setting appropriate standards and monitoring compliance. As a result of this legislation, 500 beds in children's institutions across Ontario were closed because of a failure to meet the standards.

Another piece of child welfare legislation, the Children's Boarding Home Act of 1957, was a response to newly discovered dangers that unregulated care posed to children. Williams recounts how the legislation came about:

> Bertha "Mom" Whyte and her husband lived on a thirty-acre [12 hectare] property near Bowmanville. From serving as foster parents for the local children's aid society, the couple began to expand their operation, which they called Whytehaven, by taking in children from various sources. Eventually, they had up to 140 children on the property, with usually no more than five or six adults present to attempt the twenty-four-hour tasks of physical care and parenting.
>
> Mom Whyte found that she had a talent for publicity and received a warm response from the public and the media [who] assumed she was carrying out a noble, self-sacrificing service. The Department of Public Welfare and the children's aid society saw

the matter quite otherwise. They considered her operation wrong in principle and hazardous in practice. The very identities of the children had become obscure, their names changed, their history forgotten [as] they merged with the heterogeneous crowd that was Mom Whyte's "family."

Jessie Watters recalls that the Department of Public Welfare eventually stepped in and closed Whytehaven after a hepatitis epidemic broke out among the children:

> Staff were called in from Metro CAS and other children's aid societies, and we all had to go down and get the kids that weekend and sort out who they were, which ones had parents and which ones needed to be admitted to CAS care.

This situation at Whytehaven gave rise to a report on children's institutions in Ontario and was one of the factors that, in 1962, prompted the government of Premier John Robarts to establish the Advisory Committee on Child Welfare mentioned in Chapter 6.

The Receiving Centre

In the 1950s, the society operated four institutions of its own: the Receiving Centre, at 15 Huntley Street; Moberly House, at 136 Isabella Street; York Cottage, in Willowdale; and the Christie Street Boys' Residence, described in Chapter 6.

This was an era when most children in the society's care were infants and toddlers, who were usually placed with foster parents directly after being admitted. Children four years of age and older were, more often than not, placed initially at the Receiving Centre, which a contemporary report described as a shelter for "[c]hildren who have recently, and in many cases suddenly, separated from their homes and families or who have been rejected and deserted. They are, therefore, usually confused, angry, frightened and unhappy. Frequently they

"Staff were called in from Metro CAS and other children's aid societies and we all had to go down and get the kids that weekend and sort out who they were and which ones had parents and which ones needed to be admitted to CAS care."
— Jessie Watters on Whytehaven, an unregulated children's institution

The 1950s were an era when most children in the society's care were infants and toddlers, who were usually placed with foster parents directly after being admitted. Children four years of age and older were, more often than not, placed initially at the Receiving Centre.

have come from unstable and chaotic family situations where [unreasonable] demands were placed on them."

The society's Receiving Centre, which grew out of the program first developed by the Infants' Home in the 1940s, provided a short-term program for up to twenty-four children, designed to assess their needs while helping them cope with the trauma of separation. Residents were offered a balance of routines that included daily living, schooling, church programs, recreational activities, individual and group counselling and, where appropriate, family visits.

Full-time child and youth workers, known as houseparents, provided physical and emotional warmth and day-to-day care, while caseworkers provided counselling, handled relationships with the child's family, and planned and prepared his or her ongoing living arrangements. This might mean the child would return home to an improved family situation or be placed in a foster home or a specialized treatment residence.

In 1963, two hundred and forty children were admitted to the Receiving Centre. About two-thirds were placed in more permanent settings within three months of their admission. The remaining third, who stayed for up to seven months — and in some cases more than a year — were considered hard to place. Staff usually saw these latter children as having many difficulties and behaviours that presented special challenges.

Tony Diniz, who was employed in several positions at the agency from the 1960s to the 1980s, remembers working at the Receiving Centre:

> In the 1960s, as a summer student, I worked at the Receiving Centre — then run by Shirley Pearse and Dick Phillips. As kids came directly there on admission to care, many of them were very upset. I worked in B Unit with Bill "Morgey" Morgan and many other fine folk.
>
> The summer nights were very hot and the kids couldn't sleep. Sometimes, the place almost fell apart at bedtime. To cool the kids off, we took them swimming at Christie Pits or the John McInnes Community Centre. To this day, when I walk into 15 Huntley

Full-time child and youth workers, known as houseparents, provided physical and emotional warmth and day-to-day care, while caseworkers provided counselling, handled relationships with the child's family, and planned and prepared his or her ongoing living arrangements.

"To this day, when I walk into 15 Huntley Street, I can still see the faces of the kids — Jamie, Glen, Billie — and hear their voices and remember the hard times and the good times as if it were yesterday."

— Tony Diniz

Street, I can still see the faces of the kids — Jamie, Glen, Billie — and hear their voices and remember the hard times and the good times as if it were yesterday.

Melvine Petroff, who also worked at the Receiving Centre at that time, recalls that:

> The teenage girls lived on the top floor. They were carefully monitored so that they would not come into unsupervised contact with the teenage boys resident downstairs. Even male staff had to seek permission from their female colleagues before venturing upstairs, so that they could make sure that the girls were decently covered. Thus, it was a major breakthrough when, in the early 1970s, the agency hired Jack Scanlon as the Receiving Centre's first male child and youth worker assigned to work with female adolescents.

Moberly House

As was illustrated above, many of the children in the Receiving Centre needed specialized care and were considered inappropriate for placement with foster families. While the agency often arranged for such children to be cared for in outside institutions, the desire to meet their specialized needs was the impetus behind the society's decision to open its own "institution for disturbed children."

With grants from Metro and the province, and with the surplus from the Charles Street Child Welfare Centre building campaign of 1952, Moberly House was opened in June 1956. It was designed as a home for twelve boys between the ages of six and fourteen.

The program was named for Vera Moberly, who, although she had pioneered the move away from institutional care in favour of foster care during her long term as executive secretary of the Infants' Homes, nevertheless foresaw the need for a residential program of this nature. Its goal was to eventually return the children to their own families or to enable them to be placed successfully with foster parents.

Richard Phillips, who is the agency's longest-serving staff member, joined the staff of Moberly House in 1957 as a live-in houseparent. He recalls working seven-hour shifts during the day, as well as five night shifts a week, "at the grand starting salary of $1,800 per year, less board, which was deducted at source." He recalls two incidents among many that are firmly engraved on his mind:

> The first is of a thirteen-year-old boy who was in trouble with the staff. He played hooky one fine spring day. When he returned late for supper, he went straight to his room carrying a box. He stood on guard over his clothes cupboard door while the other boys whispered and laughed. An air of mischievous excitement filled the residence.
>
> I asked Billy to open the door to his clothes cupboard. Naturally, he refused, so I decided to open the door without his permission. Out leaped the fox, which Billy had caught that afternoon in the Rosedale ravine. Bedlam erupted in the residence, as Billy ran up and down stairs trying to catch the petrified animal. I, in turn, called the Humane Society.
>
> The fox finally escaped out of an open door, but not before several of the boys and myself had had contact with it. Of course, it happened to be one of the years that there was a serious outbreak of rabies in the province. That resulted in a steady parade of reluctant boys and staff attending the medical clinic for a series of very unpleasant injections, which, at that time, were given in the belly.
>
> The other story is of an eleven-year-old boy who was a sleep-walker. Working nights, I was expected to sleep in the staff bedroom with an open door. On this particular night, I awoke to a feeling of water splashing down my body. When I came to, I saw the eleven-year-old boy standing over my bed urinating. As the bathroom was adjacent to the staff bedroom, I can only assume that he had travelled one door too many.

Richard Phillips, who is the agency's longest-serving staff member, joined the staff of Moberly House in 1957 as a live-in houseparent. He recalls working seven-hour shifts during the day, as well as five night shifts a week, "at the grand starting salary of $1,800 per year, less board, which was deducted at source."

"The fox finally escaped out of an open door but not before several of the boys and myself had had contact with it. Of course, it happened to be one of the years that there was a serious outbreak of rabies in the province. That resulted in a steady parade of reluctant boys and staff attending the medical clinic for a series of very unpleasant injections, which, at that time, were given in the belly."
— Richard Phillips

After about four years of operation, Moberly House was redesignated as a residence for teenage girls who had difficulty adjusting to foster homes. The neighbourhood, however, was in transition, and by the early 1960s many staff were concerned about "the deterioration of the [area] which is making it morally unsafe for the girls." The agency made the decision, therefore, to transfer most of the residents to the society's new group home program.

Another reason for this development was a steady increase in number of admissions to the Receiving Centre. It was operating well over capacity, despite the creation of three admission group homes to manage the overflow. If it were no longer a residence for adolescent girls, Moberly House could be incorporated into the Receiving Centre program to relieve the stress it was experiencing. Conveniently, both programs shared the same site at the corner of Huntley and Isabella Streets.

Thus, in 1963, Moberly House became one of the four living units into which the Receiving Centre program was organized, increasing the number of beds at the Centre from twenty-four to thirty-six. This growth was to presage the exponential expansion of the society's programs for children and their families that began in the late 1960s and continued throughout the 1970s.

The society's busiest year

Nineteen sixty-four was the busiest year to date in the society's long history. Protection workers were involved with almost 4,000 active cases involving more than 10,000 children. Unmarried parent workers worked with 2,040 unwed mothers and 956 unwed fathers. Almost 2,000 children were admitted to care, while 863 were placed in adoption homes. The provision of these services cost the agency almost $4,400,000, of which Metro contributed 45 percent, the Department of Public Welfare 35 percent and the United Community Fund 8 percent. The balance came from the federal government, other municipalities and sundry fees.

Most of the money was designated for the maintenance and provision of services to children in care. Expenditures on protection and other services to children in their own homes amounted to only $634,000, which was clearly an inadequate amount to fund the agency's growing work in this area. As Edmund Meredith, the society's president that year, noted:

> By arriving early, we can often straighten out a troubled family. The human savings are great. The financial savings are substantial and demonstrable. The cost of maintaining a family intact is only a fraction of the cost of financing children apart from their families. You may ask why, if the road to success is clear, progress is slow. The strange answer is that the community will provide money for the child once neglected but little to prevent neglect.

There were, however, encouraging signs of change in the community's conscience, particularly in the press. Revisions to the Child Welfare Act in 1965 would reflect this change by providing for better protection services for children.

"By arriving early, we can often straighten out a troubled family. The human savings are great. The financial savings are substantial and demonstrable. The cost of maintaining a family intact is only a fraction of the cost of financing children apart from their families. You may ask why, if the road to success is clear, progress is slow. The strange answer is that the community will provide money for the child once neglected but little to prevent neglect."
— Edmund Meredith

CHAPTER 6

The Golden Years, 1965–1977

Toronto in the 1960s and 1970s

Throughout the 1960s and 1970s, the Anglo-Celtic, Protestant nature of Toronto increasingly gave way to vibrant communities of many races, faiths and cultures. Most immigrants were now of non-European ancestry, arriving mainly from countries in the Caribbean, South Asia and East Asia.

Meanwhile, the children of the families who immigrated after the Second World War had become middle class and politically active, developing a vibrant press and diverse cultures. Their demands for an end to discriminatory laws and behaviours in accommodation, education, employment and immigration resulted in federal and provincial human rights legislation and an emphasis on multiculturalism — the recognition of all Canadians as full and equal partners in society. These changes in attitudes were also mirrored by a greater tolerance toward First Nations peoples and a growing sensitivity toward, and appreciation of, aboriginal culture.

The Metro population now exceeded two million people and its growth was accompanied by rapid suburban development. For those who could not readily find affordable accommodation, the Ontario Housing Corporation and other public agencies, along with some private developers, built significant numbers of units of high-density, lower-cost housing, much of it in the suburbs. Increasingly, however, concerns were raised over the concentration of low-income families in these large-scale projects, as well as the fact that their construction often required the destruction of existing neighbourhoods. In

There were extraordinary changes in family life in this era. Young people gained much greater freedom to do as they chose.

As a consequence of the popularity of the birth control pill and the liberalization of abortion laws, families continued to get smaller, although the number of children born to unwed mothers increased.

response, nonprofit and cooperative approaches to social housing — emphasizing respect for neighbourhoods, low-rise architecture and a variety of income groups as tenants — developed.

There were extraordinary changes in family life in this era. Young people gained much greater freedom to do as they chose. Instead of living with their families, many left home to live alone or with peers. Premarital sex and common law relationships were increasingly accepted, leading to a sharp drop in the rates of marriage. In 1969, same-sex relationships were decriminalized, and the years that followed would see organized gay liberation campaigns that helped to increase tolerance toward lesbian and gay people.

As a consequence of the popularity of the birth control pill and the liberalization of abortion laws, families continued to get smaller, although the number of children born to unwed mothers increased. Most unmarried women, however, continued to relinquish their babies for adoption until the late 1960s. The rate of divorce climbed spectacularly after 1968, when marriage breakdown was added to the legal grounds on which divorces could be granted.

The lives of women, in particular, were changed irrevocably by these developments. They often postponed marriage and entered the full-time work force in increasing numbers, as did women with children. Feminist organizations pressed for changes to laws that discriminated against women and they were influential in lobbying for social change.

Throughout the 1960s, major reforms in human services affected the population's material well-being, among them the introduction of universal medicare and the Canada Assistance Plan, a federal-provincial cost-sharing plan for social assistance and other social services.

The decade was also one in which governments came to be preoccupied with modernization. These developments led the Department of Public Welfare to change its name in 1967 to the Department of Social and Family Services, reflecting the wider range of programs it was now supporting and funding. In 1972, to reflect the government's increasing support of community endeavours in the provision of social services, the department's name was changed yet again, to the Ministry of Community and Social Services (MCSS).

In this era, social agencies mushroomed and training programs in the human services greatly expanded. (And organizations such as Metro CAS were the ultimate beneficiaries.) For this reason, these years have been described as "the golden years" for child welfare. They lasted until a downturn in the economy ushered in a period of retrenchment in the mid- to late 1970s.

Despite increased funding, a major problem facing children's aid societies, and the families with whom they worked, was the constant lack of resources for children with disabilities and those with mental health needs. During this time, the government embarked on a course of closing institutions without providing alternate community supports, a program that gathered steam over the succeeding two decades. This process was motivated partly by concerns about the inadequacies of institutional care, but it was also due to the introduction of psychotropic drugs to treat mental illness.

The role of children's aid societies

Immigration and the baby boom had combined to cause a significant increase in Ontario's child population. By the early 1960s, three million of the province's seven million people were younger than nineteen years of age. How these young people were to be cared for and educated became a topic of intense public debate that included discussions about the role of children's aid societies and how they should be governed.

According to Williams, one of the concerns was a belief that "[c]hildren's aid societies were too addicted to removing children from parental care and too reluctant to return their wards to the family or to offer them for adoption. The consequence was a large use of foster homes, which [many thought] was itself proving injurious to the children."

As James Band, the deputy minister of the Department of Public Welfare, observed in his annual report for 1961:

> It is frightful to consider that when a child is taken into permanent
> care by a [children's aid] society he may face, if not placed on adop-

tion, the deteriorating experience of being moved time and again from one set of foster parents to another ... Perhaps we should be giving recognition to the development of group care facilities on a smaller scale than in the [large orphanages of the past] for certain children who find it difficult to adjust to a normal family life.

These were sentiments with which child welfare leaders such as Metro CAS executive director Lloyd Richardson did not disagree, and they were to have a potent effect over the coming years, as children's aid societies and other providers established expensive group care and other residential programs for "hard-to-serve" children.

Meanwhile, controversy over the societies' autonomy was intense, due in part to revelations about inadequate resources and questions about the quality of the services provided by children's aid societies. Many commentators, including *The Globe and Mail*, thought that the province should take over the societies' operation.

> A charitable society is ultimately successful when it has done itself to death, and when it has yielded its duties to a department of government which comes under the control of elected representatives of the people.

Others, however (notably the Roman Catholic Church), were vehemently opposed to the government having control over the lives of children.

These debates came together in an Advisory Committee on Child Welfare, which the province established to address "issues relating to the organization, structure, financing and administrative policies and practices of the children's aid societies." During its deliberations, the committee expressed an interest in developing standards by which child welfare services could be judged. Its report, published in 1964, concluded that "The provincial government is ultimately responsible for laying down basic standards, founded in the public interest and sound professional principles, as well as stating the requirements to meet these standards."

Despite the committee's belief in the importance of client rights, and its recommendations to that effect, the government developed no specific mechanisms to

Controversy over the societies' autonomy was intense, due in part to revelations about inadequate resources and questions about the quality of the services provided by children's aid societies. Many commentators, including The Globe and Mail, *thought that the province should take over the societies' operation.*

address them. One might only conclude that the ministry continued to have faith in the professional judgment of those operating the system.

Child Welfare Act, 1965

In response to the advisory committee's report, the Robarts government passed the Child Welfare Act, 1965, in which the legislature, avoiding political conflict, backed away from any reorganization of child welfare services that would result in direct administration by either the province or the municipalities. The act did, however, give the province greater control over many of the operations of children's aid societies, removing any pretence that they were organizations with the freedom to act independently of government.

Qualifications for CAS staff and rules for the composition of boards of directors were established. Municipalities, which had traditionally provided most of the funding for child welfare services, were mandated to have four representatives on a nine-member executive committee of CAS boards of directors, a move with the potential to give them a powerful voice in the societies' governance.

The societies' authority over children in care was reduced, with the guardianship of young people in permanent care — now to be known as Crown wards — exercised by the Department of Public Welfare. A limit of two years was placed on children in the temporary care of a children's aid society, who from now on were to be known as "society wards." For educational and humanitarian reasons, children's aid societies were allowed to extend their "care and maintenance" of wards until age twenty-one.

Under the new act, those who suspected that a child was being abused were, for the first time, required by law to report that suspicion to a children's aid society. Perhaps the most important aspect of the legislation, however, was the new direction it gave to children's aid societies to intervene early to prevent the development of circumstances that might lead to a child being abused, rather than getting involved only when that child was in imminent danger. This new provision gave societies the responsibility to "provide guidance, counselling and

The new Child Welfare Act gave the province greater control over many of the operations of children's aid societies, removing any pretence that they were organizations with the freedom to act independently of government.

Under the new act, those who suspected that a child was being abused were, for the first time, required by law to report that suspicion to a children's aid society. Perhaps the most important aspect of the legislation, however, was the new direction it gave to children's aid societies to intervene early to prevent the development of circumstances that might lead to a child being abused, rather than getting involved only when that child was in imminent danger. This new provision gave societies the responsibility to "provide guidance, counselling and other services to families for protecting children or for the prevention of circumstances requiring the protection of children."

other services to families for protecting children or for the prevention of circumstances requiring the protection of children."

This preventive approach was supported by a new funding mechanism that paid societies for comprehensive services to children and families. The existing system of grants for various aspects of CAS work was abandoned. Governments now accepted full responsibility for funding approved child welfare services, with the province contributing 60 percent (raised in 1975 to 80 percent) and the municipalities the balance.

Despite the legislative changes, the new act did not always result in the hoped-for harmony and trust between Metro CAS and the provincial government. This was in part because Queen's Park vacillated over the extent of its role and focused on only a limited range of child welfare services, including a declaration that the prevention component of CAS work was to be permissive rather than mandatory. The overall result was that there was little new money for the society.

Executive director Lloyd Richardson was nonetheless optimistic. He thought the agency was coping well with the rapid changes in society and was able to meet the challenges of implementing the legislation. This optimism, combined with the promise of stable and full government funding for child welfare services, allowed the agency to withdraw from a four-decade-long membership in the Community Chest and its predecessor, the Federation for Community Service.

The agency reorganizes

The emphasis of the agency reorganization of the late 1960s was on increased integration with the community, so that workers got to understand what was going on in their neighbourhoods and became better known to local residents as sources of both advice and practical help.

In 1965, the new Child Welfare Act spurred the society to flatten and decentralize its organizational structure. The new arrangements, which were to remain the agency's organizing principle for almost three decades, were designed to bring Metro CAS services closer to the people who needed them. The emphasis was also on increased integration with the community, so that workers got to understand what was going on in their neighbourhoods and became better known to local residents as sources of both advice and practical help.

This approach to service delivery led to the long-delayed establishment of a West Branch to serve Etobicoke and other western municipalities. It opened in 1965 in a house the society had purchased at 5162 Dundas Street West. The Central Branch on Charles Street expanded into four large district offices and, in 1975, was itself subdivided into two branches, Toronto East and Toronto West. The North and East branches (respectively renamed North York and Scarborough) developed sub-offices, while several of Metro's largest housing projects had service units employing CAS and other community workers.

Within the branches, family services and children's services departments provided community-based programs and services. Family Services workers included those who worked in prevention and protection services as well as those who worked with unmarried parents. Children's services workers supported children — and their care providers — in foster homes and provided adoption services.

For the first time in the society's history, most of the agency's social work staff were professionally qualified. By 1975, their average annual salary was $13,000, a rate that was competitive in the marketplace. By contrast, ten years earlier the workers' annual salaries had averaged only $6,000.

Services that needed to be quickly available to all were located in Centralized and Specialized Services. These included homefinding and placement, institutions, group homes, homemakers, medical clinics and the emergency after-hours service. Finance and Administration Services included accounting, purchasing, statistical and service information, property and agency planning. Staff Resources included personnel administration, staff development, operational research and public relations.

The joint annual meeting of CAS of Metropolitan Toronto and the Catholic Children's Aid Society of Toronto was held at the Royal York Hotel in 1968.

For the first time in the society's history, most of the agency's social work staff were professionally qualified. By 1975, their average annual salary was $13,000, a rate that was competitive in the marketplace. By contrast, ten years earlier the workers' annual salaries had averaged only $6,000.

Prevention and early intervention

Many discussions had taken place at Metro CAS about the need to examine the role of protection workers and to team up with other agencies in the community to prevent abuse, neglect and admissions to care. Writing in the early 1960s, Mona Robinson, supervisor of the Protection department, expressed the goal:

"We believe that we must demonstrate to the community and to ourselves that a group of CAS workers with skill, imagination and desire can do a "preventive" job [by providing a helpful service] before a family actually breaks down."

— Mona Robinson

We believe that we must demonstrate to the community and to ourselves that a group of CAS workers with skill, imagination and desire can do a "preventive" job [by providing a helpful service] before a family actually breaks down.

We would like to plan a project here in Protection, where we would use one supervisor and three or four workers who will work in a certain district, serving all requests from that district and providing the most appropriate assistance we can identify and diagnose for a particular family.

It may be this team will have one or two skilled, experienced caseworkers to give intensive service to certain cases. It may be that some cases will receive service aimed at modifying or sustaining a family, not really solving basic problems, but helping the family to function.

We hope that we will work very closely with schools, churches, police, nurses, etc., and that communication between these groups and ourselves will be clear, honest and mutually helpful.

This vision formed the basis of the society's recommendations to the province's Advisory Committee on Child Welfare that children's aid societies be mandated by the government to do prevention work. The agency's lobbying efforts were reflected in the 1965 legislation that authorized, and led to the development of, the range of prevention programs described below.

Family services

The concept of protection workers was dropped in favour of family service workers, since, with the addition of prevention responsibilities, workers were placing emphasis on working with whole families and with the community pressures that affected them.

Protection services quickly came to cover a wide and ever-changing spectrum of child welfare. Indeed, with the agency reorganization described above, the concept of protection workers was dropped in favour of family service workers, since, with the addition of prevention responsibilities, workers were placing emphasis on working with whole families and with the community pressures that affected them.

Workers who provided services to children and families in the community began to focus more and more on helping children remain safely in their own homes and in assisting parents to care for them more effectively. They counselled families, talked with school principals, consulted with the police and made referrals to appropriate community services. What was a typical day for these front-line staff and how did they go about it? A 1972 article in *Our Children*, a Metro CAS journal that had been founded in 1964, provides the answer:

There's no such thing [as a typical day] according to Angie Beckstead, who's located at [Central Branch's] District 4 offices at 951 Queen Street East. "You come in organized with your day's work planned and then the phone starts to ring." It may be a call from the police station where they're holding a juvenile runaway … or a call from a mother who's packing to leave home and kids.

These are the urgent calls. Others are not as critical, but are time consuming and can be frustrating. There's the single parent who moves from place to place without notifying the agency. There's the youngster with both physical and emotional problems who's gone through all the available placements.

For Angie, who speaks Greek, there are also cases where she's needed as an interpreter … and there are always the routine chores like correspondence with other agencies and endless paperwork. But it all gets done. The interruptions and emergencies are superimposed on the regular day's work and if the result is overtime … well, that's Family Service.

Former district supervisor Connie Ross remembers ruefully the ever-present CAS worker's dilemma, one that remains as potent today as it was then:

Half our life was spent explaining to the community that we're not baby snatchers and the other half explaining why we can't snatch babies when the neighbours think we should.

"There's no such thing [as a typical day] according to Angie Beckstead. You come in organized with your day's work planned and then the phone starts to ring. It may be a call from the police station where they're holding a juvenile runaway … or a call from a mother who's packing to leave home and kids.

These are the urgent calls. Others are not as critical, but are time consuming and can be frustrating. There's the single parent who moves from place to place without notifying the agency. There's the youngster with both physical and emotional problems who's gone through all the available placements.

For Angie, who speaks Greek, there are also cases where she's needed as an interpreter … and there are always the routine chores like correspondence with other agencies and endless paperwork. But it all gets done. The interruptions and emergencies are superimposed on the regular day's work and if the result is overtime … well, that's Family Service."

— 1972 article from Our Children

"Half our life was spent explaining to the community that we're not baby snatchers and the other half explaining why we can't snatch babies when the neighbours think we should."

— Connie Ross

Despite these criticisms, workers focused on rehabilitating families, which they did through counselling as well as referrals for outside help, for medical care and day care, and for a friendly visit from a volunteer. With the assistance of night duty staff, they offered protection services twenty-four hours a day. It may have taken perseverance, but when there were positive results, it was one of the greatest satisfactions of the job.

Community development

The society believed that, to achieve lasting results, individual family service work needed to be supported by the development of skills and resources in the local community that would benefit all members of the community.

The society believed that, to achieve lasting results, individual family service work needed to be supported by the development of skills and resources in the local community that would benefit all members of the community. The philosophy was quite simple. Children needed help, but so did their parents, and the agency had to work as closely as possible with those who were the most common sources of child welfare referrals: the police, public health departments, schools and local community organizations.

Out of this belief rose the Community Protection Program. Each branch designated a number of staff as community protection workers who spent two days a week on work that was not related to cases. *Our Children* described how these workers put the theory into practice.

> Jim Ziliotto works in the Ontario Housing project at McCowan Road and Eglinton Avenue. With colleagues from the Family Service Association and public health, he meets regularly with Ontario Housing representatives to address the many problems that centre around housing. One project is a play school for which the CAS has provided volunteer group leaders. This provides preparation for pre-kindergarten programs for the kids while giving their mothers a break. It is cooperative with mothers contributing 50 cents a week for juice and playthings if they are able and also helping to make toys and assist in the cleaning up.

Barbara Ander works in the Alexandra Park area, a neighbourhood of increasingly immigrant populations speaking Ukrainian, Portuguese, Italian and Chinese. She has focused much of her activity around the HELP unit, designed to handle emergencies over the weekend when most agencies are closed. From Friday through Monday afternoon, one local volunteer and one agency person is on duty.

The Community Protection Program tied in with the work begun by the agency and its community partners to develop interagency and interdisciplinary units located in public housing projects at Warden Woods, Lawrence Heights and Regent Park.

The unit in Regent Park, the large downtown housing project that arose from the slum clearances described in Chapter 5, illustrates the effectiveness of this approach to prevention work. It was established in 1968 as the result of a tenants' meeting organized by Doug Barr of Metro CAS. Traditional programs and individual casework were not having much effect, and residents had complained of duplication of services, having to travel to get assistance, and the "agency runaround." The caseworkers who worked with them were frustrated by the continued cycle of poverty and hopelessness.

Doug Barr was on the site every day, along with staff from several other agencies, social assistance workers, lawyers and doctors. Sheila Holmes, a resident, was coordinator of the unit, while many other residents volunteered their services to answer phones and serve as receptionists, stenographers and clerks. They took children to special classes, visited newcomers and baby-sat. Provision was made for teenage drop-ins, sewing groups and English as a Second Language classes for new immigrants.

The unit was able to practice prevention by identifying neighbourhood needs and coping with them on the spot. Close contact with Ontario Housing staff enabled workers to prevent evictions by addressing the causes that led to families being asked to vacate their apartments. Juvenile offences were reduced and the number of children coming into the CAS's care declined dramatically.

Doug Barr was on the site [of the Community Protection Program in Regent Park] every day, along with staff from several other agencies, social assistance workers, lawyers and doctors. Sheila Holmes, a resident, was coordinator of the unit, while many other residents volunteered their services to answer phones and serve as receptionists, stenographers and clerks. They took children to special classes, visited newcomers and baby-sat. Provision was made for teenage drop-ins, sewing groups and English as a Second Language classes for new immigrants.

The unit was able to practice prevention by identifying neighbourhood needs and coping with them on the spot. Close contact with Ontario Housing staff enabled workers to prevent evictions by addressing the causes that led to families being asked to vacate their apartments. Juvenile offences were reduced and the number of children coming into the CAS's care declined dramatically.

The unit workers were strongly encouraged by the results of their work. Still, there were some society staff and board members who did not fully support the community development concept and who, because of an inability to appreciate more abstract community development issues, were constantly asking the workers to justify what they did on the basis of numbers of individuals helped. At the same time, there were questions about the suitability of the program, which arose from beliefs held by some that community workers engaged too heavily in partisan political activity. In part to deflect these criticisms, the society continued until 1979 to divide community workers' time between protection and prevention activities.

Homemaker service

In many situations, however, families needed to be given immediate, practical support to prevent children being admitted to care. In the 1960s and 1970s, agency homemakers provided an innovative program that did just this. *Our Children* described their work as emergency parents.

A mother suffering a mixture of poverty, too many children and limited intelligence, attempts suicide. Fortunately, her efforts failed to find a way out of deep depression and, because her children are suffering neglect, the Children's Aid is called by the police.

Rather than bring the large family of children into care, one of the CAS's ten staff homemakers is dispatched with her rollaway bed in a taxi to the family — tiding the children over a rough patch in their lives, teaching the mother as much as possible about budgeting, meal planning — all the homemaking and mothering skills the distraught mother may never have learned. She may have been a neglected child herself.

The homemaker reports to the worker the strengths and weaknesses she finds in the family — at the same time sharing her skills with all its members. She hugs and comforts the children (some

"Rather than bring the large family of children into care, one of the CAS's ten staff homemakers is dispatched with her rollaway bed in a taxi to the family — tiding the children over a rough patch in their lives, teaching the mother as much as possible about budgeting, meal planning — all the homemaking and mothering skills the distraught mother may never have learned. She may have been a neglected child herself."

*— Our Children describes the
role of agency homemakers*

mothers have not learned their most basic needs), teaches them to clean their cuts with disinfectant, lets the harassed husband pour out his heart and shows the whole family that doing things together need not cost money and can be fun.

She acts as an emergency parent and her role is a teaching one rather than a housekeeping one. She is not a char, although many a time homemakers have rolled up their sleeves and scrubbed a filthy floor.

If the situation obviously requires longer than two weeks to get the family functioning again, Visiting Homemakers or another agency is called in. Our homemaker only handles emergencies — and the next day there will be another crisis in another family.

Alternate care

Alternate care was another preventive program, developed by the agency in the mid-1970s, intended to respond to the increasing number of older children — those over twelve years of age — who were being admitted to the society's care. The outcome of out-of-home placements of teenagers was often seen as unsatisfactory, while budget restraints rendered problematic the expensive residential programs frequently required by these young people.

Community-based alternative care programs were designed to provide support for youth to enable them to remain in their own homes while providing them with the counselling and resources they needed. The first one got under way in 1976 and involved phasing out Moberly House as a residence and using it as a base for alternate care. Another was the Family Centre, a warehouse space in Parkdale, which agency staff and the families they served worked together to decorate colourfully. Program supervisor Hanna McDonough reminisces:

> We tried to address the problem of the escalating numbers of teens coming into CAS care. We wondered if we could help parents to

Community-based alternative care programs were designed to provide support for youth to enable them to remain in their own homes while providing them with the counselling and resources they needed.

keep their kids at home by teaching parents child management and teaching kids self-management.

So several of us created the Family Centre. It had a homey kitchen, a well-stocked craft area, a big gym with a bright yellow floor and group rooms with pillows and comfortable sofas. The "Know Thyself Room," soothingly equipped with wraparound pillows and a shag rug, was reserved for therapy with the kids. The kids came after school, had snacks, played basketball or did crafts. They talked to their worker and their parents came to group therapy once a week.

Self-help and peer support were the hallmarks of the program. Parents in the group supported each other by offering practical help. One week, for example, two parents, fed up with their children, in the group decided to exchange kids for the weekend. This exchange had a good payoff for all involved. Each parent had a break from their own problems and became much more insightful about each other's difficulties managing their children.

Over time we created a positive peer culture where the kids with whom we had worked became mentors of the more recent arrivals. The parents and kids were very proud of their program.

> *"Self help and peer support were the hallmarks of the program. Parents in the group supported each other by offering practical help. One week, for example, two parents, fed up with their children, in the group decided to exchange kids for the weekend. This exchange had a good payoff for all involved. Each parent had a break from their own problems and became much more insightful about each other's difficulties managing their children."*
> — *Hanna McDonough describes the Family Centre*

Services to youth

In the 1960s, Canadians were obsessed with young people who were challenging the norms and values of an older generation. An article in *Our Children* summarized these concerns.

By now everyone has seen them. Like others of their generation, they drift around the streets in weird garb, hair long and stringy — a desperate earnestness in their pale faces. The hippies.

Children's aid societies have dealt with rebellious youth for decades but this phenomenon is a new thing. Running away is as

> *"By now everyone has seen them. Like others of their generation, they drift around the streets in weird garb, hair long and stringy — a desperate earnestness in their pale faces. The hippies. Children's aid societies have dealt with rebellious youth for decades but this phenomenon is a new thing. Running away is as old as time, but children opting out, living off the streets in hordes, begging and turning to drugs is new."*
> — *Excerpt from an article in Our Children about '60s youth*

old as time, but children opting out, living off the streets in hordes, begging and turning to drugs is new.

Talking to the kids themselves a picture emerges of deep discontent with school, unhappiness at home, feelings of futility, a desperate urgent need to feel wanted for themselves and their attitudes and a certain peace in having each other.

There is also sickness — physical and mental. And there are drugs with blatant publicists such as The Beatles and Bob Dylan, brilliant musicians who sing of drug taking.

The agency was in a quandary over how to handle the problem. Workers had to be concerned about the safety of youngsters wandering around at will. But to the children, the CAS represented the very society and adult authority from which they were trying to break loose.

Among them were many out-of-town "transient" youth running away from indifferent or hostile parents. For years, many of them had appeared in juvenile court, charged with vagrancy, until other approaches were developed. One was a program called The Trailer, in which Metro CAS and several other agencies collaborated. The program — it literally was a trailer — operated in the middle of the Yorkville "hippie" community and was a place these young people could get medical help, financial assistance and counselling. Many were returned to their home communities through the society's Transient Program — in 1972 alone, it worked with 229 youth — while others were taken into care.

The Trailer program — it literally was a trailer — operated in the middle of the Yorkville "hippie" community and was a place these young people could get medical help, financial assistance and counselling. Many were returned to their home communities through the society's Transient Program — in 1972 alone, it worked with 229 youth — while others were taken into care.

Another agency initiative was the purchase of a three-story house at 28 Simpson Avenue to be used by teenage girls who were alienated from their families. Unlike other group homes, it had a minimum of rules. The atmosphere was designed to be conducive to helping the residents sort out their issues so that they could return to their own homes after a short time.

The reasons why these youth were running away from home were barely understood at the time; most adults and child welfare workers simply believed that they were looking "for fun and adventure." It took the tragic sexual assault and murder in 1977 of twelve-year-old Emanuel Jaques, described by the media as a "shoeshine boy," to raise awareness among social service workers and the community at large about the needs of street-involved youth and to understand that most were escaping unhappy or abusive homes in the only way they knew how.

Although the hippie movement eventually faded away, the Jaques murder led, among other initiatives, to the establishment of Inner City Youth, a forerunner of the programs provided in later years, by the society and others, to meet the needs of homeless and runaway youth.

Child abuse and neglect

In 1973, the society established a central abuse committee to validate and monitor all new referrals of alleged abuse of children less than five years of age. It developed resources needed to provide service effectively, tried to increase the level of knowledge and practice skills in the area of high-risk protective service, and measured the effectiveness of various methods of treatment.

Although Metro CAS's work expanded to include prevention services, efforts to protect abused and neglected children remained the society's priority. In 1973, a central abuse committee was established to validate and monitor all new referrals of alleged abuse of children less than five years of age. It developed resources needed to provide service effectively, tried to increase the level of knowledge and practice skills in the area of high-risk protective service, and measured the effectiveness of various methods of treatment. Local branch committees provided an opportunity for workers to consult with colleagues and specialists on difficult case situations.

The committee structure was supplemented by a training program for nurse practitioners who would not only conduct medical examinations and consultations but would also support the abuse committees. Each nurse practitioner served as a member of the branch abuse committee. She accompanied family service workers when an abuse situation needed medical assessment and, if necessary, gave evidence in court. She made follow-up visits in high-risk situations and assisted with community education.

Marilyn Pearson, who became the nurse practitioner for Toronto East and Toronto West branches, recalls:

"Establishing a trusting relationship was the key to success with abusive parents. Trust grew from the very first contact when the presence of a nurse trained to assess damages may have avoided the threatening experience of taking the child to hospital. Even giving evidence in court was not necessarily damaging to a good relationship. On one occasion, I remember testifying that a mother was giving only adequate care and noticed that she was listening intently and nodding her head in agreement!"

— Marilyn Pearson on the agency's nurse practitioners

Establishing a trusting relationship was the key to success with abusive parents. Trust grew from the very first contact when the presence of a nurse trained to assess damages may have avoided the threatening experience of taking the child to hospital. Even giving evidence in court was not necessarily damaging to a good relationship. On one occasion, I remember testifying that a mother was giving only adequate care and noticed that she was listening intently and nodding her head in agreement!

Services to children in care

Society staff who worked with children in foster care, group homes and residences, along with those in adoption, were serving a changing population. This was the result of shifting social conditions, such as those described at the beginning of this chapter, and legislation that helped shift the focus of child welfare work to maintaining children safely in their own homes.

As a result, many of the children now being admitted to Metro CAS care were older than in the past and were increasingly living with physical or developmental disabilities. The society had to direct its efforts toward new and more skilled uses of foster family care. A home care program, a specialized foster home program, foster family group homes and admission-assessment foster homes were all examples of the continuing development of the foster family as the best placement for children who must live away from home. Meanwhile, the higher percentage of teenage children needing care prompted the development of an array of youth residences.

These changes dramatically altered the agency's adoption program, as will be described later in this chapter. It had to adjust to older children, as well as those who were handicapped and slow learners, while placing increased emphasis on early permanent adoption placements for those children.

Homefinding

The challenge for the society, therefore, was to recruit suitable foster and adoptive families to care for these young people. In 1972, the agency supported 1,485 foster

Marilyn Pearson, nurse practitioner for Toronto East and Toronto West branches and the originator of the High Risk Infant Nurse Program

A home care program, a specialized foster home program, foster family group homes and admission-assessment foster homes were all examples of the continuing development of the foster family as the best placement for children who must live away from home.

homes. As part of the approval process, each was studied and assessed by the society's homefinding staff.

After an initial telephone conversation and an office visit, and after securing permission to obtain pertinent medical information, the homefinder made between three and six visits to the family home to acquaint the parents with the hazards and pitfalls involved in caring for someone else's child, especially one who had come from a deprived home situation and might present unexpected problems.

The society was innovative in its use of the media to inform a broad segment of the population about its need for homes. Every Monday morning in the early 1970s, for example, while mothers were getting their children ready for school, Jim Paulson of radio station CKEY wound up his morning show by talking about one of the agency's children. The segment was called "Our Foster Child of the Week," and each was a thumbnail sketch of a hard-to-place youngster in Metro CAS care. The idea was later taken up by CFTO Television, which created a weekly program called *Family Finder*. Baby Jessica was one of the children featured:

The society was innovative in its use of the media to inform a broad segment of the population about its need for homes.

> Baby Jessica has never known what it is to like have a mother of her own and a home. She has spent the three months of her life in hospital under the watchful eyes of nurses and doctors. Jessica has a heart condition and suspected epilepsy. She may need an operation eventually. She is well enough to leave the tiny iron crib and learn what it is to be cuddled by people. She is on digitalis every day and her foster mother must be able to take her to hospital frequently for observations.

"Baby Jessica has never known what it is to like have a mother of her own and a home. She has spent the three months of her life in hospital under the watchful eyes of nurses and doctors. Jessica has a heart condition and suspected epilepsy. She may need an operation eventually. She is well enough to leave the tiny iron crib and learn what it is to be cuddled by people. She is on digitalis every day and her foster mother must be able to take her to hospital frequently for observations."
— Family Finder, CFTO Television

Danny was another child whose story was told on the radio:

> Danny has stirred up a peck of trouble in his eight and a half years. But he hasn't had much from the world but trouble, either. His mother is a prostitute and an alcoholic and he has known no father. He has been expelled from school for fighting and truancy. So he has home tuition until he learns how to get along with other

children. Danny has brown eyes and brown hair and is small and wiry. He smashes toys at a rapid rate and has learned no table manners. As you can see, this boy is a real challenge. He must have the kind of foster parents who can see him through psychiatric treatment. He may be unlovable just now — but oh, how this lad needs a loving foster home.

A popular syndicated newspaper column, "Today's Child," was another way in which the agency, along with other children's aid societies, alerted the public to the need for good homes for children in care, this time for adoption homes. It began in 1964 when Helen Allen, a reporter for the Toronto *Telegram*, had the idea of using photographs of children available for adoption. Hardly a world-shaking idea in itself, perhaps, but the use of photographs of CAS wards — advertising them in the paper, no less — was so controversial that at first only the Metro, Hamilton and Kenora societies went along with the idea.

It took a remarkable number of phone calls to acquire photos of the first twenty-three children — and get permission to use them. Luckily, the twenty-three published pictures and stories resulted in eighteen adoptions. Before the program was three weeks old, many of the reluctant societies had changed their thinking and were asking if they, too, could take part. What began as a six-week pilot project continued for many years to tell readers about the variety of children needing homes and turning up families for them. Mikey, Cindy and Frankie were among them:

> Mikey is a good-looking blue-eyed boy whose early development was slow. For a while, we thought he had mild cerebral palsy and we were worried about muscular dystrophy. This last was unfortunately confirmed about a month ago. We must provide for his needs with a family who are prepared to care for a boy with this handicap.
>
> Cindy is a very attractive part-Indian lass who was born with a heart defect which will require surgery sometime during her childhood. She is legally free for adoption. Will she have to wait in a fos-

A popular syndicated newspaper column, "Today's Child," was one way in which the agency, along with other children's aid societies, alerted the public to the need for good homes for children in care, this time for adoption homes. It began in 1964 when Helen Allen, a reporter for the Toronto Telegram, had the idea of using photographs of children available for adoption. Hardly a world-shaking idea in itself, perhaps, but the use of photographs of CAS wards — advertising them in the paper, no less — was so controversial that at first only the Metro, Hamilton and Kenora societies went along with the idea.

ter home until after the surgery before we can find her a family? Will it be too late then to move her?

Frankie, aged 10, is hoping to find an adoptive home where parents will appreciate a super-active but thoroughly lovable kid! He loves fishing, camping and animals and would, in fact, prefer to live outdoors if he could! He's also mad about hockey and likes to read a lot. Need we say that he has bright red hair to go with those freckles!

Foster family care

As described in earlier chapters, foster families had been the cornerstone of support for children in the care of the CAS of Toronto since its earliest beginnings. Boarding home care, a specialized service that eventually became the norm, had begun at the Infants' Home at the end of the First World War, when, because of severe epidemics, it was medically dangerous to leave large numbers of small children together in institutions where infection spread rapidly. Successful efforts were made to place these children in families, and the mortality rate declined rapidly.

Almost as an additional bonus, both the CAS of Toronto and the Infants' Home later discovered that children raised in foster families were able to make a better adjustment to adult life than those who grew up in the then-prevalent large institutions or orphanages.

Almost as an additional bonus, both the CAS of Toronto and the Infants' Home later discovered that children raised in foster families were able to make a better adjustment to adult life than those who grew up in the then-prevalent large institutions or orphanages. Out of this grew the conviction that child welfare agencies should place all the children in its care, except for the most seriously disturbed or handicapped ones, in foster homes. The continuation of this long tradition was reflected in a 1977 article in *Our Children* that told the story of foster parents Joy and Harry Chong:

Joy and Harry Chong have been foster parents for nine years and during that time have fostered a total of 158 children! The shortest stay in that period was four hours and the longest seven and a half years!

One of those children was Georgie, who came to them "for three months" when he was three years old. Georgie's young mother had had no idea of parenting and his natural father had taken no interest in the boy at all. Little Georgie consequently spent most of his first two years in a crib in a semi-dark room.

When CAS discovered him he was covered in sores from the infrequent changing, his eyes had been affected by the lack of light and his lower jaw and teeth were deformed. He couldn't walk, could sit only for a short period and he was not used to taking solid food, only a bottle.

For a long period of time, Joy had to take him to Sick Kids [hospital] weekly for his physical problems but gradually they responded to loving care. His emotional trauma was more deep seated. Accustomed to the safety of his crib, Georgie was fearful of larger spaces and only felt secure when he was in his playpen. Attempts to help him stand only frightened him. It took a long time and much patience to help him gain confidence.

One sheltered spot in the kitchen seemed less frightening than others and there he was willing to make an attempt to stand. Harry, who works for the Post Office, encouraged him patiently whenever he was at home and the whole family clapped and cheered whenever Georgie made an effort. He loved the attention and the applause. "One good thing," says Joy Chong, "Georgie was able to learn to trust."

Stimulation and encouragement from all the family were the remedies that brought Georgie out of himself and helped him develop into an interesting, warm and loving youngster. Meanwhile, Georgie and the Chongs became more and more attached to each other.

Eventually, however, Georgie was made a ward of the Crown and became free for adoption. Although the separation was traumatic for all concerned, Joy said that the adoption workers couldn't have

"When CAS discovered him he was covered in sores from the infrequent changing, his eyes had been affected by the lack of light and his lower jaw and teeth were deformed. He couldn't walk, could sit only for a short period and he was not used to taking solid food, only a bottle."
— *Excerpt from* Our Children
about society ward Georgie

been better. "They were really sensitive and helpful and Georgie's adopting family is super." At last report, Georgie and his new family appeared to be living happily ever after.

In the mid-1960s, the society had started a specialized foster home program, supervised by Maureen Duffy, to care for children whose needs were too extensive for most foster parents. These specialized foster homes were recruited from applicants who had child care or some other related training as well as the exceptional qualities required to care for these young people.

A Home Care program was set up to provide extra support and guidance for the care providers of developmentally handicapped children in the agency's care. Run by Lillian Keys, it taught foster parents how to understand and meet the needs of the child they were caring for and to encourage whatever potential that child may have had.

A 1970 survey reported that the society was caring for 700 children of below-average intelligence (19 percent of those in its care), of whom more than 400 were being cared for in foster homes. To support them, a Home Care program was set up to provide extra support and guidance for their care providers. Run by Lillian Keys, it taught foster parents how to understand and meet the needs of the child they were caring for and to encourage whatever potential that child may have had.

Foster Parent Association

The Metro CAS Foster Parent Association established in 1967 was set up to improve communication between foster parents and the agency, to support foster parents in providing quality care to children, and to improve the community's perception of foster parenting.

An important development in terms of support to foster families was the establishment in 1967 of the Metro CAS Foster Parent Association (FPA). It was set up at the request of executive director Lloyd Richardson to improve communication between foster parents and the agency, to support foster parents in providing quality care to children, and to improve the community's perception of foster parenting.

Training courses for foster parents were established — one year there were 120 foster care providers attending courses at George Brown College.

Groups of foster parents, led by Sue Barclay and Lois Wicks, began to meet regularly to exchange ideas, set goals and plan activities. Training courses were established — one year there were 120 foster parents attending courses at George Brown College. Foster parents, through the FPA, now had a voice in decisions that concerned them. They were involved in discussions regarding boarding rates and policies and procedures. They assisted in recruitment, sat on branch advisory groups and board committees and met regularly with staff.

Speaking to the FPA on the occasion of its tenth anniversary in 1977, Ed Watson, the executive director of the day, shared these thoughts about the new responsibilities undertaken by foster parents:

Fostering is in the process of change. We as agency staff fully realize that the expectations placed on you are increasing year by year. The children you get are usually seriously emotionally or physically deprived. We are often unsure how long they will be with you. You are asked to help them with the upset of visiting natural families, sometimes in your own homes. Many are in treatment and you must be a part of the process. As more older children are being adopted you must be involved in adoption placement. Many of you maintain contact with children who have returned to their natural families. Some of you are asked to testify in court.

Where you were asked in the past to accept a child into your home and treat him as you would your own, you are now expected to provide treatment for a few months or a couple of years so that the child may return home to his own family. In many cases, you cannot treat him like your own because he is different from your own children. Often you and your family have become very attached to him and you must sometimes help him to leave before you think he or his family are ready. You are in the business of treating children rather than just loving them.

What this means to you as foster parents and to us as staff is that we must work closely together to provide the best possible experience for that child while he is in care. You must share with us the knowledge and assessment of the child and we must listen to what you have to say. You must be involved with us in planning for the child and in deciding what kind of child you work with best.

A big job? You know it. That is why we would like to salute the FPA on their ten years of giving active support to foster parents, one of the agency's most valuable and valued resources.

"Where you were asked in the past to accept a child into your home and treat him as you would your own, you are now expected to provide treatment for a few months or a couple of years so that the child may return home to his own family. In many cases, you cannot treat him like your own because he is different from your own children. Often you and your family have become very attached to him and you must sometimes help him to leave before you think he or his family are ready. You are in the business of treating children rather than just loving them."

— Ed Watson addressing the FPA in 1977

Reading clockwise
from bottom left:
York Cottage,
Richardson Residence,
Moberly House,
the Receiving Centre,
Horsham House
and the Boys' Residence.

Residences

The society's philosophy had long been to keep children in the community if it could be done safely and, if not, to place them in foster family care or in group home programs such as those described in Chapter 5. However, institutional care was still required for some children, including those who were seriously mentally ill, developmentally delayed or physically disabled, as well as youngsters — such as those who violently attacked others — whose behaviour was considered too aggressive for most families.

As the percentage of youth and children with special needs being admitted to care increased during the 1960s and 1970s, the numbers in residential care began to rise. In 1972, for example, as many as 105 children were living in various kinds of residences owned and run by the society, while even more — 449 — were placed by the agency in outside institutions. Besides the Receiving Centre and Moberly House, the society's residential programs in the early 1970s consisted of York Cottage and Horsham House in Willowdale, the Boys' Residence at 305 Dawes Road in Toronto's east end and the purpose-built Lloyd S. Richardson Residence in Scarborough.

The Boys' Residence was described in a 1972 article:

> The Boys' Residence is a Tudor-style country mansion that doesn't look at all like an "institution." Set in nine acres [3.6 hectares] of rolling woodsy grounds it has a secluded country feeling in spite of high rises on the horizon and the thirteen boys ages 12 to 18 who live there obviously enjoy their surroundings to the full.
>
> Though the house and its grounds seem rather too grand for an agency institution, they were acquired on a lease basis when [the borough of] East York appropriated the nine acres as parkland over a year ago. The house and an acre [0.4 hectares] of land are leased to Metro CAS and the rest of the acreage remains a public park.
>
> Presiding over this impressive domain are Mr. and Mrs. Corrigan who moved here with the boys in December 1971 after 14 years of supervising the Christie Street Residence (it opened in

August 1957). The Corrigans have had great success with their charges and can count more than 100 "graduates." They plan a program that is both pleasant and structured, with much emphasis placed on schooling. When a boy is ready to leave, the Corrigans help him to find a job and offer support to him and his employer. Many come back for visits after they have become self-supporting, some bringing a wife and children.

Built on the grounds of the society's East Branch at a cost of $600,000 and named for the agency's executive director, the Lloyd S. Richardson Residence — or LSR, as it became known — opened its doors on May 21, 1969. It consisted of four self-contained "houses," each holding six children. A contemporary report described its work:

> The program's aim is to be a temporary home for moderately disturbed children. The staff work toward rehabilitating the children to their own homes or if this is impossible they may move on to an adoption or foster home or whatever is the best alternative. Parents are very much involved in the program through individual and family counselling and a plan of sending children home on weekends has been working well. This keeps the parents in touch and lessens risks involved when the child must return home for good.
>
> The children are cared for and helped individually and in groups. When a child enters the residence his behaviour is evaluated and a second evaluation is carried out when he returns home. The average length of stay is between three months and 14 months. A follow up service is provided as long as three to six months as required after the child goes home.

The cost of this kind of residential treatment was high — estimated in 1967 at about $12,000 per child per year. The society was uncomfortable with the fact that children in need of institutional placement were not regarded as being just as sick

"Presiding over [the Boys' Residence] are Mr. and Mrs. Corrigan who moved [to 305 Dawes Road] with the boys in December 1971 after 14 years of supervising the Christie Street Residence (it opened in August 1957). The Corrigans have had great success with their charges and can count more than 100 "graduates." They plan a program that is both pleasant and structured, with much emphasis placed on schooling. When a boy is ready to leave, the Corrigans help him to find a job and offer support to him and his employer. Many come back for visits after they have become self-supporting, some bringing a wife and children."
— Excerpt from a 1972 article
in Our Children

"The [LSR] program's aim is to be a temporary home for moderately disturbed children. The staff work towards rehabilitating the children to their own homes or if this is impossible they may move on to an adoption or foster home or whatever is the best alternative. Parents are very much involved in the program through individual and family counselling and a plan of sending children home on weekends has been working well. This keeps the parents in touch and lessens risks involved when the child must return home for good."
— A report on the opening of the Lloyd S. Richardson Residence in 1969

as a child rushed to hospital for a physical ailment. Lloyd Richardson expressed the general sentiment of staff when he wrote: "Treatment [for children in residential care] should be financed in the same way — by hospital insurance. Eighty-five percent of these children are wards of the Crown. Children's aid societies should not be left with the unbearable burden of deciding which children are expendable."

By the mid-1970s there was once again a move away from large institutions toward placing children in smaller, staff-operated homes in the community.

By the mid-1970s, however, there was once again a move away from large institutions toward placing children in smaller, staff-operated homes in the community. Three operated as "admission-assessment" homes (where the needs of older children and youth were assessed) and seven as "hostels" (temporary homes for teenagers who could not live at home because of family conflict). At this time, the Receiving Centre and Moberly House were both closed and the buildings converted to non-residential use.

Meanwhile, the society recognized that a substantial number of adolescents who had spent a number of years in care needed help in preparing to live on their own in the community. It purchased or rented a number of houses and apartments as transitional "LIFE" homes, each for four to six youths, sixteen years of age or older, together with a volunteer adult mentor.

Meanwhile, the society recognized that a substantial number of adolescents who had spent a number of years in care needed help in preparing to live on their own in the community. It purchased or rented a number of houses and apartments as transitional homes, each for four to six youths, sixteen years of age or older, together with a volunteer adult mentor. These so-called LIFE houses — the acronym stands for Living Independently For Experience — were an immediate success and remain to this day an integral part of the agency's efforts to help youth prepare to leave agency care.

Adoption

In the 1960s, the agency began to experience a decline in the number of infants needing adoption homes but an increase in the number of older children and those with special needs.

The changes that took place in society during the 1960s were reflected directly — and dramatically — in the agency's adoption service. As a result of the availability of the new birth control pill, liberalized abortion and the trend toward unmarried mothers keeping their babies, the agency began to experience a decline in the number of infants needing adoption homes. At the same time, the number of older children and those with special needs was on the rise.

For example, in 1969 — the peak year for infant adoptions — the agency placed 1,239 children for adoption. Of these, 961 were under a year old and only 66 were over four years old. Four years later, in 1973, completed adoptions numbered just 436; of these, only 281 were babies under a year old, while 98 were older children. Sandra Scarth, who worked in the society's adoption department, remembers:

> Traditionally, school-aged children had been considered not only hard to place but generally unadoptable. Those with developmental delays, moderate to severe medical or physical problems, or with mental illness in their backgrounds, were likely to remain in foster or institutional care.
>
> We, on the other hand, felt passionately that no child was unadoptable, but the prevailing attitude to adoption was that it was a service for childless couples wanting babies. Then the Today's Child column appeared and began to break down that barrier as the public began to see photographs and hear about older children who needed families.
>
> The response was overwhelming at times. The agency began to hear from couples that were interested in adopting older and handicapped youngsters. One of the first placements through the column was a child with Down's Syndrome. When workers heard how well that placement was proceeding, they referred several more children with Down's Syndrome. We quickly realized that there were strong adoptive families out there who could provide the long-term commitment and sense of belonging that our children needed.

The society was also an innovator in the field of recruitment by collaborating with the province to set up parent meetings at the adoption exchange conferences. These meetings allowed potential adoptive parents from throughout Ontario to see slides of waiting children and talk to their workers. Prospective parents were also able to take part in adoption parties at which they could meet, in an informal setting, children available for adoption while playing games and enjoying refreshments with them.

Scarth and her colleagues in the adoption department also began to recognize that the traditional casework method of assessing and approving adoptive families

"We felt passionately that no child was unadoptable, but the prevailing attitude to adoption was that it was a service for childless couples wanting babies. Then the Today's Child *column appeared and began to break down that barrier as the public began to see photographs and hear about older children who needed families."*
— Sandra Scarth

Beginning in 1971, the adoption department offered support groups for adoptive families during the post-placement period, as well as a post-adoption course, in conjunction with Humber College and the YWCA.

Joan Davis, then a social worker, now director of the Central Intake Branch, in the Scarborough clinic

"There were a lot more infants in care in those days and they had to be seen regularly. At first, we used residents at the Hospital for Sick Children until the hospital clamped down, saying their residents were not supposed to be moonlighting. That was too bad because some of them were really good."
— Maggie Hunter

was not providing the kind of special preparation and support they needed. Starting in 1971, therefore, they offered support groups for adoptive families during the post-placement period, as well as a post-adoption course, in conjunction with Humber College and the YWCA.

Medical services

At both the CAS of Toronto and the Infants' Home, there had been a long history of medical clinics, where children in the agency's care received specialized medical attention. Now, with one at the Charles Street offices and in each suburban branch, these were under the supervision of nurse practitioners. The clinics relied on the work of sessional physicians and the many volunteers who drove the children in for their appointments and transferred newborn babies who were to be adopted from the maternity ward to their new homes. Maggie Hunter, who became the society's medical director in 1967, recalls:

> There were a lot more infants in care in those days and they had to be seen regularly. At first, we used residents at the Hospital for Sick Children until the hospital clamped down, saying their residents were not supposed to be moonlighting. That was too bad because some of them were really good. So we obtained the services of neighbourhood doctors to come in and do the clinics. They would talk to the foster moms about their sick babies. Mostly they were pretty good, but occasionally the clinic nurses would report back to me that "Dr. So-and-So doesn't wash his hands from one patient to another" or "This doctor doesn't think he needs to look into a child's ears because he says he could certainly tell if they were infected without doing that"! So I had to deal with that as well as make the rounds at Sick Kids [hospital] and see any of our children in there and any of the other kids who might need the protection of the CAS.

Over time, as a consequence of changes in the child population the agency cared for, more and more teenagers were seen in the medical clinics. For many, it became their anchor. Hunter remembers that:

> They were more sexually active than previous generations of adolescents and this created all sorts of problems. We had to treat a lot of sexually transmitted diseases and make arrangements for many abortions. It was also common for us to see teens with addictions to marijuana and LSD [lysergic acid diethylamide, a hallucinogen].

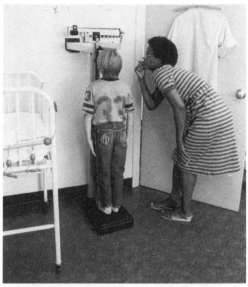

Sheila Reid and a young friend weigh in.

Volunteers

During the 1960s, the number of volunteers working for the society increased by 2,000 percent. One impetus behind this change was the development of preventive services that led the agency to use the contributions of volunteers more creatively. Another was the increasing support and supervision of volunteers by professional staff.

There were now more volunteers than paid staff. By 1975, for example, the agency employed a staff of 700, complemented by about 1,000 volunteers. These volunteers ranged from talented ten-year-olds to retired business people, and they donated approximately 4,000 hours of service a week. Writing in 1974, Lil Laforet, volunteer supervisor for Scarborough Branch, described some of their activities:

> A family service team volunteer could be phoned day or night if a client is feeling depressed or alone. The volunteer may arrange to take the mother of two active little boys to the park for a picnic lunch or to go with another to visit a teacher, sometimes a frightening experience for a parent with little formal education. Another gives individual help to a handicapped child, lessening his frustrations and relieving the mother.
>
> A volunteer might be attached to a children's service team working with foster parents in an admission-assessment home or

Volunteers outnumbered paid staff. By 1975, for example, the agency employed a staff of 700, complemented by about 1,000 volunteers. These volunteers ranged from talented ten-year-olds to retired business people, and they donated approximately 4,000 hours of service a week.

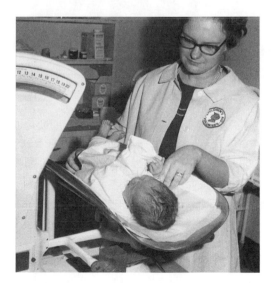

making appointments for eye, orthodontist or annual medical appointments, coordinating these and sharing the driving.

Children who are supervised in their own homes rather than in care may receive a visit from a volunteer to help make arrangements for a homemaker or babysitter. Working independently and yet with staff, these volunteers are able to keep children in their own homes.

Lloyd Richardson retires and is succeeded by Ed Watson

By the end of 1973, Lloyd Richardson was ready to give up the helm of the agency he had guided through massive expansion into an era of increasingly diverse and complex demands.

At that time, he reflected on the transformation of the agency's administrative structure, which had paved the way for better program management, decision making and communication — between management and staff and among the organization's thirty-eight separate locations. These changes in turn enabled the society to respond to its own growth as well as to the complexities created by a more permissive age and by rapidly changing client needs. He wrote:

> No longer do we regard child welfare as "the blessed work of rescuing … children found in surroundings of vice and sin," as one of the society's early annual reports put it.
>
> Today, there is a distinct trend away from "rescuing" children and punishing parents toward reinforcing the family unit to help it function as a whole again. The single mother is no longer condemned and the child with personality and behaviour problems is not regarded as wilfully "bad" and therefore to be locked up.
>
> As the public attitude toward individual rights alters, so gradually does the law of the land. The Legal Aid Act, amendments to the Child Welfare Act and the new emphasis on civil rights and

"Today, there is a distinct trend away from "rescuing" children and punishing parents towards reinforcing the family unit to help it function as a whole again. The single mother is no longer condemned and the child with personality and behaviour problems is not regarded as wilfully "bad" and therefore to be locked up."

— Lloyd Richardson

liberties contribute to the challenge and change of longstanding laws and customs.

But while we believe in the rights of parents, we feel strongly that the rights of the child must also be maintained and that legislation and practice must guarantee these rights.

"But while we believe in the rights of parents, we feel strongly that the rights of the child must also be maintained and that legislation and practice must guarantee these rights."

— Lloyd Richardson

Richardson's retirement was widely lamented; many staff felt that his departure marked the end of an era. Richardson did not strive for a high personal profile, preferring instead to work very effectively, often behind the scenes, as a child welfare advocate. He always found the time to be alert to trends and developments in the field and collaborated skilfully with those in government, other children's aid societies, community services and education. In particular, he formed a close and fruitful working relationship with Ward Markle, his counterpart at the Catholic Children's Aid Society.

Richardson was the prime mover in developing the plans for the new Child Welfare Centre at 33 Charles Street East and meticulously followed every detail with the architects and builders. He was the first senior executive at the agency to give serious attention to the development of personnel policies, salary scales and working conditions. He promoted an effective and creative working relationship with foster parents. He also developed and maintained an effective rapport with social work students, encouraging them to come to work for the society.

Lloyd Richardson enjoyed seventeen years of retirement, much of it spent at his villa on the Spanish coast, until his death in 1990.

Pressures for accountability, productivity and efficiency

As Richardson's successor, the board of directors recruited Ed Watson, executive director of the Family Service Association — a capacity in which he had worked with the society to run several community-based programs. Like Stewart Sutton and Lloyd Richardson before him, Watson was a professional social worker. He had worked initially in direct practice and as an administrator with the British Columbia

Public Welfare Department before moving to the Canadian Welfare Council in Ottawa, where he helped develop funding for social work education and training.

By the time of Watson's appointment in 1974, the society was dealing with a political and economic environment that had changed dramatically from that of the previous decade.

On the economic front, a period of rapid inflation, caused by cuts in the supply of imported petroleum products, prompted the provincial government to acquire a keen interest in assessing the costs, efficiency and effectiveness of the bodies it funded, among them Metro CAS. The era was marked by a number of inquiries and structural alterations within the provincial government, and its relations with children's aid societies grew increasingly turbulent as it demanded greater accountability while at the same time the societies grew ever more anxious to preserve their independence.

By the 1970s, three studies had suggested that CASs be taken over by different levels of government.

Two inquiries, in particular, merit mention, both reported in the mid-1970s. The first was the MCSS Task Force on Selected Issues and Relationships, known as the Hanson Task Force after its chair, Hugh Hanson. Although designed primarily to examine the ministry's own activities, the task force also studied the need for more rigorous standards to direct the work of children's aid societies and even considered — although it did not recommend — that the ministry abolish CAS's and deliver child welfare services directly. (An earlier Study of the Managerial Effectiveness of Children's Aid Societies, begun in 1969 by the management consultants Urwick, Currie and Partners, reached similar conclusions, although nothing became of them.)

The second was the Royal Commission on Metropolitan Toronto, known as the Robarts Commission after its chair, the former premier John Robarts. It was established to examine and make recommendations on the structure, organization and financing of local government in the Metropolitan Toronto area. The commission criticized Metro's children's aid societies as being unaccountable to government at any level and repeated earlier recommendations that Metropolitan Toronto take them over. The municipal government, however, declined to do so.

At this time, Metro CAS was serving 19,000 children and more than 7,000 families with 750 full-time staff, 500 foster homes and more than 1,000 volunteers.

Those numbers, reflecting the size and complexity of the organization, were sufficiently daunting to prevent both the municipal and provincial governments from entertaining any thoughts about abolishing the agency or the other children's aid societies across the province.

However, during all this ferment, the press took sides. While the *Toronto Star* supported the societies, calling for adequate funding to let them do their work, *The Globe and Mail* continued its campaign in favour of transferring the societies to direct government management.

While the Toronto Star *supported the societies, calling for adequate funding to let them do their work,* The Globe and Mail *continued its campaign in favour of transferring the societies to direct government management.*

> If the autonomy of local societies has a lack of accountability (and we believe it has) and if that lack of accountability has permitted sloppy procedure to go unchecked (and the record speaks for itself), then perhaps that autonomy should be revoked. Perhaps the children's aid societies should be placed directly under provincial control.

This view was never shared by the government of Premier Bill Davis. Still, *The Globe and Mail* maintained its position on children's aid society governance until 1982, when, at a meeting with the newspaper's editor, Metro CAS persuaded the influential paper to change its editorial viewpoint.

The society's response to provincial expectations

This clamour, however, did make for increased complexity and uncertainty as the society struggled to meet the province's expectations for accountability, productivity and efficiency at a time when Queen's Park was preoccupied with fiscal matters rather than questions related to organization or programs.

It became increasingly difficult for the agency to secure — and manage — adequate financial resources. In 1965, when, for the first time, virtually all of the society's expenses were covered by the provincial and municipal governments, the agency's budget had totalled a little short of $5 million. By 1973, when Ed Watson became the executive director, it had increased almost threefold to $14 million.

In this context, the province began to demand substantial evidence of sound management, fiscal prudence and high performance before it would approve the society's annual budget estimates. In the mid-1970s, this review process deteriorated steadily, with a whole year often passing before the province made decisions on the agency's estimates. Watson described the relationship between the parties as "taut."

As funding restraints escalated, they held serious consequences for every facet of the society's operations. Watson's response was to institute important changes in the way the agency was managed, changes that he believed were necessary to meet the province's expectations. It wouldn't be easy: he had inherited the responsibility of running an organization that had developed a culture patterned in part on the personality and style of Lloyd Richardson. He recalls:

> When I took over the job of executive director, I felt that the agency was somewhat of an ingrown ship. The senior staff had been in their positions for many years and had been schooled to be responsive to Lloyd's file. I found there was some resistance to looking openly at better ways of doing things because they felt they knew what they were doing.

Watson created a service management group that involved branch directors to a greater degree in setting the agency's priorities and establishing the budget for its operations. At the same time, Paul Michaelis was appointed to a newly created position, director of field services, to oversee the work of the branches. This allowed Watson to devote more time to running what had become a very complex organization.

Harry Zwerver was hired into a new position of director of planning and development and was charged with instituting a "program planning budgeting system" that would try to set goals for, and measure the performance of, programs in a way that would strengthen the society's budget submissions to MCSS. Under the direction of Bill Hedderwick, the agency began to use more structured methods, as well as computer-assisted technology, to measure management performance, the placement of children and the deployment of staff consistent with the funding the government made available.

Under Bill Hedderwick's direction, the agency began to use more structured methods, as well as computer-assisted technology, to measure management performance, the placement of children and the deployment of staff consistent with the funding the government made available.

Serious attempts were made to save money by ensuring that children came into care only as a last resort. Youth over thirteen years of age were not admitted unless it was essential, and children were to be moved, whenever possible, from more expensive outside paid institutions into lower-cost agency programs. This was a notable change from the era of deputy minister James Band, who, as recounted at the beginning of this chapter, advocated in 1961 the benefits of limited institutional care for children.

Many staff embraced Watson's reforms enthusiastically, although there were endless discussions about how to structure the organization to respond to the issues of the day. Tony Diniz remembers how humour was often used to ease the tension:

> [Debate over how] to deliver services in the best way possible raged through Scarborough branch when I was there in the early 1970s. It had the added complication that this branch somehow always considered itself a pioneer. After what seemed like endless conversations, we determined that the best way to proceed was to bring together the very separate family service and children's service departments and to create multi-service teams which would be organized around children, families and local communities. We always needed hilarity and symbolism to mark change. Accordingly, we staged a mock shotgun wedding where the two department heads of the time vowed eternal mutual bliss. The two, Marilyn Holland and Cary Wolgelerenter, dressed up as bride and groom and you can imagine who wore which costume!

In a similar vein, long-time intake worker Ann Coulter recalls:

> When intake got particularly awful, we would bring our pet gerbil out to run about in the office. One Friday afternoon, three of us were trying to catch him on the floor at a time when we were all complaining about ministry cuts. Someone commented, "Imagine if a ministry inspector walked in now — three social workers crawl-

ing round the floor trying to catch a gerbil instead of rescuing children in need of protection!"

Humour did not help everyone, however. Despite Watson's attempts to proceed cautiously at a pace that most people could accept, several long-term employees chose to resign rather than agree to changes in which they did not believe. Still, staff and foster parents in large part managed valiantly and creatively to maintain service excellence during this turbulent period.

Union certification

Another success was a decision that made it acceptable for women staff members to wear pants instead of skirts while on agency business.

As workload demands and the effects of government funding restraints intensified, staff began to press increasingly for union certification. This development was also a reflection of the tenor of the times, as staff grew more aware of their rights as employees.

As described in Chapter 4, both the CAS of Toronto and the Infants' Homes had long had staff associations. In the 1950s, their negotiations with management had yielded a five-day work week and longer vacations. In the 1960s, further negotiations brought about better salaries and personnel practices, the establishment of a staff canteen, parking spaces and an improved heating system at the Charles Street offices. Another success was a decision that made it acceptable for women staff members to wear pants instead of skirts while on agency business.

By 1973, the staff's concerns over deteriorating morale, funding cutbacks, attrition and a sense of not being involved in decision making led to a campaign to convert the association into a certified union. The timing seemed right because the president of the board that year, Bert Edwards, was an executive of the United Steelworkers of America. Many board members and senior staff, however, thought a union was unnecessary and that good management practices should be able to provide sound leadership and protection for workers, especially for professional staff.

The staff association conducted a series of referenda in 1976 to ascertain the wishes of its members with respect to unionization and the degree to which management should be excluded from membership. A majority of front-line staff voted for unionization, but front-line supervisors did not.

The front-line workers, therefore, signed their first contract with the society in 1977. Initially the new union was not affiliated with any national organization, but in 1979 it joined the Canadian Union of Public Employees (CUPE) as its Local 2316.

Mary Lewis, who was prominent in the unionization drive, recalls some of the tactics staff used to bring their concerns to the board's attention:

> We were in the process of going for certification and we decided we'd do a silent vigil. We lined up on both sides of the stairs before a board meeting so that board members would have to walk up through the line. My memory of it is that it was quite a radicalizing experience for the staff members on the stairs because the board members were clearly of a different social class from many of the workers. I think it was awkward for the board too, because we were just silent and didn't say anything.

A *birthday celebration*

In 1975, the agency celebrated the 100th anniversary of the founding of the Infants' Home. Public forums were held, alumni meetings were organized and, at the opening of the Canadian National Exhibition (CNE) in August, there was a grand birthday party. Premier Davis attended, there was music on the bandstand, entertainment for the children and great quantities of cake to go round.

Uncle Bobby, a television personality much loved by children, celebrated at the CNE, too, on Kids Day, along with a troupe of clowns — foster parents in everyday life. They performed magic tricks and were joined by fire eaters, limbo dancers and other exciting acts for the audience to watch.

To celebrate this anniversary, the society unveiled its first trademark or, to use the term then coming into common use, logo. Brian Greggains, a board member who was chair of the public relations committee, contacted Jim Donoahue, one of

Bill Davis, then the premier of Ontario, and Uncle Bobby, the host of a local children's television show, celebrate CAS of Toronto's 100th anniversary.

Former executive director Ed Watson

"There was seldom enough time for front-line staff to invest significant hours in working with a situation. They had to run from one crisis to another, often without being able to provide sufficient support to make a difference. The balance between protection and family service, to me, has never been adequately resolved and it gets somewhat artificially divided, either to organize the work or to partialize it into a manageable piece."
— *director Ed Watson*

Canada's leading graphic artists, to ask if he would design a logo to commemorate the anniversary. Donoahue agreed and set to work right away.

His submission, a small child ensconced in the final zero of the figure 100, was so well received that that the agency regretted having to put it aside when the anniversary year ended. Because of this, Donoahue agreed to revise the logo to make it appropriate for all occasions. The product was the logo the society uses to this day — a child nestled and protected inside the letter C — which Donaohue generously donated to the agency as a public service. It captures the essence of the society's mission — the protection of children — and creates a strong visual identity for the organization.

Ed Watson resigns

Ed Watson's tenure as leader of the society was a relatively short one; in 1978, he was invited to become executive director of the Child Welfare League of America. This was a tribute not only to him personally but also to the agency's leadership of child welfare in North America. On his return to Canada, Watson was appointed the clinical director of the Addiction Research Foundation. Later, he went into health planning with the Toronto District Health Council.

In a 1999 interview, during which he looked back on his five years at Metro CAS, Watson mentioned the unresolved tension between child protection and prevention work. He described what remained a persistent concern at the agency:

> There was seldom enough time for front-line staff to invest significant hours in working with a situation. They had to run from one crisis to another, often without being able to provide sufficient support to make a difference. The balance between protection and family service, to me, has never been adequately resolved and it gets somewhat artificially divided, either to organize the work or to partialize it into a manageable piece.

It would fall to Watson's successor to try to resolve this dilemma.

CHAPTER 7

Improving the System, 1978–1988

Toronto in the 1980s

In the early 1980s, Toronto witnessed its most severe recession since the Great Depression fifty years earlier. Inflation was rampant, unemployment was high and job creation strategies failed to stem the layoffs. Demand for affordable housing outstripped supply, exacerbating homelessness, which grew to an estimated 10,000 people in Metro Toronto, many of them young people in need of protection.

During these years, scant attention was paid to enhancing social services as a way to support struggling families. Indeed, restraints and cutbacks in health and social services put added stress both on those who staffed those services and those who depended on them. Better day care and more rigorous rent controls were talked about, but there was little action.

Governments did institute some low-cost strategies, among them the study and reform of laws affecting children and developmentally handicapped adults and the provision of aid to single mothers to eliminate their need for social assistance. Another positive development was a change in the policies of the Criminal Injuries Compensation Board to allow abused children to receive criminal damages as compensation for injuries sustained at the hands of abusive parents.

The recession ebbed in the second part of the decade, although the gap between rich and poor widened. Concerns about poverty were deflected for a while by the publication in 1988 of *Transitions*, a report by a provincially appointed Social Assistance Review Committee chaired by Judge George Thompson. Calling

Restraints and cutbacks in health and social services in the 1980s put added stress both on those who staffed those services and those who depended on them.

A positive development was a change in the policies of the Criminal Injuries Compensation Board to allow abused children to receive criminal damages as compensation for injuries sustained at the hands of abusive parents.

attention to the inadequacy of social assistance benefits, *Transitions* contended that such aid should be seen as an investment in people rather than simply the alleviation of poverty. Concerned citizens and organizations such as Metro CAS campaigned aggressively in the media on the report's behalf, but little concrete action was taken to implement its recommendations.

By 1989, the number of Canadian children living in poverty led to a resolution in the House of Commons to eradicate child poverty by the year 2000. Although it received the support of all parties, politicians and influential opinion makers tended to be more concerned about the high levels of government debt and deficit financing than they were about the incidence of child poverty. Their views were to gain increasing credence over the subsequent decade.

The circumstances described above contributed to increasing illicit drug use, particularly of the cocaine derivative known as crack. This created such related problems as child neglect, particularly of "crack babies" (who were born addicted or with drug withdrawal symptoms and who were often neglected or abandoned as a result of parental drug addiction), family and adolescent violence, and an increase in the number of young people living on the streets. Exceptionally sad was the number of babies born infected with the HIV virus that leads to AIDS, usually as a result of unsafe sexual practices or hazardous drug use by their mothers.

Single parenthood and the raising of children by common law partners had now become accepted as never before, a change brought about by less restrictive social mores, easy access to divorce and legal separations, and a decline in the social pressure to marry. Many children grew up in reconstituted families or lived in flexible family arrangements — for example, by spending part of each week with different birth parents.

The 1980s were also a time of increased recognition of human rights. A new federal Charter of Rights and Freedoms became part of Canada's constitution in 1982, while the Ontario Human Rights Code was amended in 1982 and again in 1986 to broaden the categories of those whom it protected. There was a new awareness and acceptance of the equality rights of aboriginal Canadians and of the needs of First Nations children. They received greater government attention, including the funding of specialized aboriginal child welfare programs.

Illicit drug use created such problems as child neglect, particularly of "crack babies" (who were born addicted or with drug withdrawal symptoms and who were often neglected or abandoned as a result of parental drug addiction). Exceptionally sad was the number of babies born infected with the HIV virus that leads to AIDS.

Immigrant populations within Metro Toronto, particularly from Asia, the Caribbean and Central and South America, continued to grow throughout the decade, bringing with them diverse family traditions such as a greater reliance on extended family members for social, emotional and financial support. Many of the newcomers to Metro were refugees rather than migrants seeking to better their economic circumstances, a development whose roots lay in the late 1970s, when, as one of the aftereffects of the end of the American war with Vietnam, a wave of asylum seekers arrived in Toronto. Among them were unaccompanied children who needed protection. Later, a change of regime in Iran and a war with neighbouring Iraq brought another group of unaccompanied refugee youth to the city.

These developments directly influenced the program development, service delivery and hiring practices of social agencies. More slowly, similar changes affected industry and other private employers. The population of Metro itself remained relatively stable at just over two million, as the focus of growth in the Toronto area shifted to the neighbouring communities in, among others, Durham, York, Halton and Peel regions. These rapidly developing suburban communities were now beginning to face similar challenges to those that had confronted Metro since its formation three decades earlier.

The quality of children's services came under heavy scrutiny during this era. In the mid-1970s, the deaths of two children receiving child protection services shook the public's confidence in the effectiveness of Ontario's child welfare system. These tragedies would lead to many changes over the subsequent decade, changes that would profoundly affect the work of Metro CAS and of other children's aid societies across the province.

The death of Vicky Ellis

The first of these deaths was that of nineteen-month-old Kim Anne Popen, who died at her home in Sarnia in 1976 while receiving services from the local CAS. She sustained a fatal blow to her head. This was the final assault among more than seventy other injuries, including severe sexual abuse, that a postmortem examina-

Many of the newcomers to Metro were refugees rather than migrants seeking to better their economic circumstances. Among them were unaccompanied children who needed protection.

tion revealed. Kim's death led to a prolonged and acrimonious judicial inquiry headed by Judge Ward Allen, during which the Sarnia CAS's supervision of the family and MCSS's oversight of the society's operations were criticized.

The second death was that of one-month-old Vicky Ellis, who died of neglect in Toronto's west end in March 1977. According to the pathologist, the probable cause of her death was swelling of the brain brought on by improper feeding. In addition, she was suffering from gastroenteritis and high body fluid loss.

Vicky's mother, Debbie Ellis, was a long-term CAS client, first of the Catholic CAS and subsequently of Metro CAS. Vicky was her fifth child. Her first, Charlene, had been apprehended after Debbie was charged with "failing to provide [the child] with the necessities of life." The baby was returned home after six months in foster care. When her second child, Darlene, died of neglect just four months later, Charlene was apprehended once again and eventually made a Crown ward.

Three years after Darlene's death, Debbie's third child, Parrish, drowned in his bathtub — having been left unattended — when he was seventeen months old. One month before Parrish died, Debbie had given birth to her fourth child, Brooks. Metro CAS apprehended him when he was only seven weeks old because the worker found him grossly undernourished and lying in a diaper caked in excrement.

According to an anonymous social worker quoted by journalist Peter Silverman,

> Over the next eighteen months, Debbie attempted via the Family Court to get Brooks back. But the legal battle over who was to have custody demonstrated the weaknesses of the Child Welfare Act. The parents have rights and can retain legal counsel and the CAS has a legal mandate and legal counsel. The two sides brawl in court using all the rules pertaining to the adversary system. The whole thing drags on. For a critical year and a half of Brooks' life, no one could properly make arrangements for his future until the courts had decided who got the child.

Brooks was eventually made a Crown ward. In the meantime, Debbie became pregnant with Vicky. As Alan Wolfish, Metro CAS counsel, told Silverman:

We decided to apprehend at birth. We debated it at length, not just the caseworker but senior staff. We rejected a plan to supervise Mrs. Ellis twenty-four hours a day, seven days a week. It would have been impossible in terms of both execution and personnel.

During the subsequent court hearing to determine whether Vicky should remain in the agency's care or be returned to her parents, Metro CAS argued strenuously against the Family Court Clinic's recommendation that the baby be returned home. Tragically, however, the rules of evidence prevented the introduction of vital facts regarding Debbie's history as a mother, so the judge returned Vicky to her. Three weeks later, the baby was dead. (A year after Vicky's death, Metro CAS apprehended Debbie's sixth child at birth.)

The media made much of this tragedy during the inquest that followed, and seldom did Metro CAS appear in a good light. Even though Vicky was ordered home over the agency's protests, again and again the papers and broadcast news stated the opposite: that it had been the CAS workers who wanted the child sent home.

Other voices, however, tried to make themselves heard in letters to the newspapers. One child protection worker wrote: "Journalists are free to constantly attack the rare tragedies that occur in child protection work. I say rare because, while there are a number of tragedies every year, no child protection agency is ever free to publish the great number of lives saved every year."

Another letter read: "Like your editorialist, I am upset when a child dies of neglect or deprivation … but unlike your editor, I do not attribute these tragedies to the incompetence of the CAS but to the legislators who have severely limited CAS budgets … and to the existing legislation that does not give the experts sufficient muscle with which to protect children."

A team of workers in the agency's Scarborough branch — Shirley McCulloch, Charlotte Genova, Dan Freedman and Bruce Rivers — did not hesitate to make the same point:

On a daily basis, we touch the lives of family members who are subject to many sources of stress. Government cutbacks and lack

The media made much of the Vicky Ellis tragedy during the inquest that followed her death, and seldom did Metro CAS appear in a good light. Even though Vicky was ordered home over the agency's protests, again and again the papers and broadcast news stated the opposite: that it had been the CAS workers who wanted the child sent home.

"No child protection agency is ever free to publish the great number of lives saved every year."
— Excerpt from a letter to a newspaper editor written by a child protection worker

of support for human services have significant impact on many of these individuals. Lack of adequate day care and special education, insufficient financial support and poor housing are a few of the results that serve to frustrate already high-risk family situations. It is not surprising that a child welfare worker's success in helping such families is becoming extremely difficult to realize. Society and its government is demanding more for less and becoming intolerant of any failure on the part of the child welfare system.

The difficulties of protecting children

A few years later, Ron Smith, the manager of Toronto West Branch's District 2 offices, and his staff faced similar challenges after the death of another infant due to malnutrition. His recollections illustrate how difficult it is to be a child protection worker:

> The case was open to CAS because we were trying to help the child's mother. This was our client. Did we fail to meet our responsibilities? If you read *The Globe and Mail* accounts uncritically, you might well have concluded that we did.
>
> The paper's detailed daily accounts of the mother's criminal trial led even my best friends to ask, "What did you guys do there?" The two police officers investigating the case seemed to disbelieve not only what actually happened but also just about everything we reported. One medical expert disputed our evidence that the child appeared healthy two weeks prior to his death by stating that it would be impossible to draw this conclusion. Another expert disagreed with the first expert.
>
> The social worker visited the home three days prior to the death to deliver winter clothing for an older child in the home. She did not suspect the infant was at risk. Was this understandable,

was this consistent with child welfare norms and standards, was this believable, even? These and many more questions were explored repeatedly in the media and elsewhere.

For the better part of a year, those directly involved lived under a cloud of suspicion as the matter wound its way through internal agency reviews, the criminal trial of the mother, the coroner's inquest and media scrutiny.

The experience was both a follow-up to the experience of those involved in the Ellis inquest and a forerunner of the mid-nineties, which was marked by lengthier coroner's inquests and even more intense media scrutiny.

Nancy Dale, who joined the agency as a child protection worker at this time, offers an additional perspective of protection work in this era:

> We had very high caseloads, 27 to 30 families. There was an unofficial mentoring system on the team and we would pair up to do investigations for support and to get a different perspective. I remember that you'd excuse yourself for a minute and go out into the hall and discuss with your colleague what to do. The supervisor was linked into that but not in the way they are now. You'd consult with your supervisor before you went out but there was a level of trust that once you were out there you wouldn't necessarily have to call in to the office at each step along the way. You and your colleague would be able to make the decision.
>
> We worked very hard. All of us were relatively young, none of us had children, and our colleagues were our support system. I have strong memories of enjoying my clients; we had a real desire to help them.

Protection work undertaken at night could be particularly complex and dangerous because it was — and still is — done in isolation at a time of day when the

"For the better part of a year, those directly involved in working with a child who subsequently died of malnutrition lived under a cloud of suspicion as the matter wound its way through internal agency reviews, the criminal trial of the mother, the coroner's inquest and media scrutiny. The experience was both a follow up to the experience of those involved in the Ellis inquest and a forerunner of the mid-nineties, which was marked by lengthier coroner's inquests and even more intense media scrutiny."
— Ron Smith

only resources available are the police and the hospitals. Sybil Smith, for many years the supervisor of the agency's Emergency After Hours Service, remembers:

> When I began to supervise night duty work in the early 1980s, it had grown from a very small service staffed, for the most part, by contracted law students to a more professional operation where the staff was fairly large and professionally trained, albeit still working on a fee-for-service contract. They are the unsung heroes of the agency, working from five at night until nine the next morning and 24 hours a day on weekends.
>
> The adrenaline pumps at 2 a.m. when such matters as medical emergencies occur and complicated action involving numerous people must take place immediately with little information readily available. The lighter side was epitomized by one night duty worker who remarked, "Never have so many decisions been made by so many naked people sitting on the edge of the bed [at home, taking a night duty phone referral]."
>
> Night duty workers love to regale their audiences with "war stories." Who can forget the rather small worker who had to move a very large, angry adolescent [and] who meekly asked the boy, "Are you going to come quietly or are you going to hurt me?" Or the irate farmer who called from out of town to complain about his horse having become sick after being bitten by a CAS ward, and what were we going to do about it!

"The adrenaline pumps at 2 a.m. when such matters as medical emergencies occur and complicated action involving numerous people must take place immediately with little information readily available. The lighter side was epitomized by one night duty worker who remarked, "Never have so many decisions been made by so many naked people sitting on the edge of the bed [at home, taking a night duty phone referral]."

— Sybil Smith, writing about the Emergency After Hours Service

Making it easier to protect children

The deaths of Vicky Ellis and Kim Anne Popen led directly to alterations to the system designed to protect children. At the provincial level, these included legislative change, the overdue development of standards for children and families receiving services from children's aid societies, and more consistent monitoring of the work of the societies by MCSS. An operational review process was developed to assess the strengths and weaknesses of individual societies; agencies began to report such serious occurrences as the deaths of children receiving service to MCSS; CAS services to Crown wards were subjected to mandatory reviews; and guidelines for the provision of residential services were created.

At Metro CAS, services for abused children and their families had been a top priority for several years. Specialist abuse committees were well established, and each branch had its own trained abuse coordinator. Family services departments, while working on behalf of abused and neglected children, put an increasing emphasis on programs to prevent child abuse, several of them funded by the agency's new charitable foundation.

The Ellis and Popen cases also were a factor in the establishment of an MCSS Task Force on Child Abuse chaired by Ralph Garber, the dean of the University of Toronto School of Social Work. As a result of the Garber Report, training of front-line workers became more systematic, government-mandated standards and guidelines regulating CAS intervention in abuse cases were introduced and a statutory child abuse register was established.

Child Welfare Act, 1978

The changes to child protection legislation embodied in the Child Welfare Act, 1978, were a direct outcome of the Ellis and Popen cases.

Among them were provisions that ensured that children involved in child protection matters, such as Vicky Ellis and her brother Brooks, would have their opinions about what should happen to them heard through separate legal representation from that of their parents. The act also required the consent of children aged twelve and over whenever a children's aid society assumed the voluntary care of that child outside of a court hearing.

(Until 1978, all children in CAS care had been considered wards, although the idea of voluntary temporary care had first emerged between the two world wars. Through the provisions in the 1978 act, parents who needed temporary

Legislative change, the overdue development of standards for children and families receiving services from children's aid societies and more consistent monitoring of the work of the societies by the provincial government all resulted from the deaths of Vicky Ellis and Kim Anne Popen.

care and parents of children with special needs could negotiate agreements for care with CASs.)

Other sections of the act codified how judges in protection hearings were to define the best interests of a child; allowed conditions to be attached to orders requiring children's aid societies to supervise children in their own homes; and provided for professionals who failed to report child abuse to be fined. (The concept of the "best interests" of a child had been developed early on in the history of child welfare in Ontario, but was not codified until the introduction of the 1978 act.)

The act also created the more formal, statutory Child Abuse Register recommended in the Garber Report. Its purpose was to ensure that previous allegations of abuse in one jurisdiction were brought to the attention of all children's aid societies across the province. With this register, however, the suspected abuser's rights also began to be codified, just as the act codified the rights of children. Thus, the suspected abuser had to be notified when he or she was registered, and was allowed to view the entry and had the right to appeal. (Prior to this time, children's aid societies reported cases to a central abuse registry that had been established in 1966. By the late 1970s, however, the registry had become mainly administrative and was used primarily for research purposes.)

Until 1978, Metro CAS had few, if any, lawyers on staff, having relied instead on social workers with court experience — and perhaps paralegal training — to represent it in protection hearings. With the passage of the new act, the agency began to hire legal counsel to manage the added court services workload that the legislation created.

Until this time, Metro CAS had few, if any, lawyers on staff, having relied instead on social workers with court experience — and perhaps paralegal training — to represent it in protection hearings. With the passage of the new act, the agency began to hire legal counsel to manage the added court services workload that the legislation created.

Doug Barr

In 1978, the year the new Child Welfare Act was implemented, Doug Barr succeeded Ed Watson as executive director of Metro CAS. Barr was a popular man whose vision, vitality and success in working with people — as well as his knowledge of the agency — made him an appealing leader, even though, at the time of his appointment, he did not have senior management experience.

Barr had been a community worker with the society in Regent Park as well as a member of the agency's board of directors, a social planner and a school trustee. He had also spent time at the National Council of Welfare. Based on these qualifications, the staff had high expectations of him. As he recounted in a 1980 article for the agency journal *Our Children*, he had written a letter on behalf of the staff association to the president of the agency's board of directors seven years earlier outlining the qualifications for the position of executive director:

Former executive director Doug Barr

> Someone in the middle of his/her professional career with some but not necessarily all of his/her experience in the child welfare field. Someone who would consult with staff, who would speak out publicly concerning the political and institutional roadblocks to client well-being, who could deal positively with the media and who was committed to operationalizing prevention.

He achieved all these objectives and more in his almost seven years at the helm of the agency. The challenges during those years were certainly many: public expectations of children's aid societies were higher, the law was more specific about what was required of workers, the provincial government was more involved in setting service standards and guidelines, and a severe recession made financial restraint in the provision of social services the norm. Barr, however, viewed these as opportunities rather than dangers. He characterized the society's activities during his years as executive director as "reform under fiscal restraint."

Public expectations of children's aid societies were higher, the law was more specific about what was required of workers, the provincial government was more involved in setting service standards and guidelines and a severe recession made financial restraint in the provision of social services the norm.

Child and Family Services Act, 1984

The Child Welfare Act of 1978 was considered a short-term measure pending the introduction of omnibus children's services legislation. This took place in 1984, when, after extensive consultation, the Child and Family Services Act was passed.

This new act repealed not only the Child Welfare Act but also a number of other pieces of legislation that affected children, including the Children's Institutions Act,

The intent of the Child and Family Services Act was to consolidate the separate streams of programs designed to benefit children — child welfare, young offenders and services to those who were developmentally handicapped and those who needed treatment.

In practice, the most significant feature of the act was its attempt to balance the agencies' desire to respond to children's needs with legal mechanisms that protected parental rights. Children's aid societies were required to help children while at the same time supporting the autonomy and integrity of the family.

the Children's Residential Services Act and the Children's Mental Health Act. The intent of the Child and Family Services Act was to consolidate the separate streams of programs designed to benefit children — child welfare, young offenders and services to those who were developmentally handicapped and those who needed treatment. Acknowledging the importance of prevention and support services, it added the new program stream called "community support."

The legislation also extended the rights of children in care — in many ways making mandatory the good-practice standards already in place at Metro CAS — including the prohibition of corporal punishment; the right to adequate nutrition, clothing, medical and dental care, education and recreation; the right to private communication with family and child advocates; the right to express views about placements and to be involved in a plan of care; and the right to complaints procedures.

Residential Placement Advisory Committees were set up to review the appropriateness of placements of children in larger residential settings and to respond to requests for review by children and parents. The Office of Child and Family Advocacy was established as an avenue for complaints from children and families when the procedures of individual agencies did not bring them satisfactory results.

In practice, however, the most significant feature of the act was its attempt to balance the agencies' desire to respond to children's needs with legal mechanisms that protected parental rights. Children's aid societies were required to help children while at the same time supporting the autonomy and integrity of the family.

Several factors led to this aspect of the new act. One was the increasing attention to civil and human rights, a development that was reflected in many subtle shifts in social work practice, among them strategies rooted in an ideology that government and its agencies should have limited authority to intervene in family affairs and should give greater respect to the rights of children.

Another influence, particularly within the child welfare community, was the publication of a book by famed child psychoanalyst Anna Freud and her colleagues, *Beyond the Best Interests of the Child*, which advocated that "To safeguard the right of parents to raise their children as they see fit, free of government intrusion, except in cases of neglect and abandonment, is to safeguard each child's need for continuity."

The authors proposed that the least restrictive or detrimental alternative that was appropriate and available in each individual circumstance should be the legal basis for safeguarding a child's growth and development. This principle had far-reaching effects in Ontario, where it was enshrined in the Child And Family Services Act.

In its brief to MCSS during the drafting stage of the new act, Metro CAS had registered its concerns that the legislation would not place the child's rights in the forefront. The brief stated that "It is our opinion that there is an overemphasis on parents' rights and family autonomy but little recognition of children's needs."

The government of Premier Bill Davis ignored this input from the society. In practical terms, the failure to address the agency's recommendations meant that the new act put severe constraints upon the children's aid societies' ability to intervene to respond to child welfare concerns. Workers found that the law often hindered effective and efficient protection of children and prevented them from achieving stable placements for those who required out-of-home care. It took years and the perspective of hindsight for these flaws in the legislation to become truly evident.

The government was applauded, however, for the provisions in the act that recognized the need to provide aboriginal children and families with services that reflected their culture, heritage and traditions. During the 1970s and 1980s, there had been several reviews across Canada of provincial child welfare services to aboriginal children. They found that these young people were overrepresented in the system and that workers were generally unaware of the history and needs of aboriginal children, families and communities. Services were insufficient and poor. Change was clearly needed.

One outcome was the involvement of First Nations bands in the provision of services to aboriginal children, and a decrease in CAS placements of these young people with non-aboriginal families. Aboriginal communities also began to provide services directly to their own members — in Toronto, Native Child and Family Services (NCFS) was established in 1988, with former Metro CAS worker Kenn Richard as executive director. Although not a designated children's aid society, NCFS developed a culturally based approach to servicing native families.

Metro CAS and NCFS would work together more and more closely to provide culturally appropriate services to aboriginal children. Richard comments:

"It is our opinion that there is an overemphasis on parents' rights and family autonomy but little recognition of children's needs."
— *Excerpt from Metro CAS's critique of the proposed Child and Family Services Act*

Workers found that the act often hindered effective and efficient protection of children and prevented them from achieving stable placements for those who required out-of-home care.

The government was applauded, however, for the provisions in the act that recognized the need to provide aboriginal children and families with services that reflected their culture, heritage and traditions.

Traditionally, CAS had not asked questions about ethnicity and background. Unless a family was obviously aboriginal, there was no recognition that it might be important to ask. There was no consciousness about aboriginal issues or that we should be doing things differently.

What changed was that the aboriginal community started asking questions, and because of that there was an increase in people self-identifying as aboriginal. Then the 1984 Child and Family Services Act strengthened the provision of services to aboriginal children and families, and Metro CAS started to become more accountable for the aboriginal families on its caseloads.

Paralleling the passage of the Child and Family Services Act was the implementation in 1984 of a federal Young Offenders Act. It replaced the Juvenile Delinquents Act of 1908, which, as was noted in Chapter 2, treated young offenders not as criminals but as children in need of protection. The new act dramatically changed this approach to focus on the consequences for the young offender of his or her misbehaviour. This change relieved the CAS of its century-long responsibility for young people in trouble with the law. Although it saved the Metro society money, the resulting surplus had to be redirected to fund the additional administrative and legal responsibilities required in court proceedings under the Child and Family Services Act.

A CAS Foundation to prevent child abuse

In the aftermath of the Ellis and Popen tragedies, Metro CAS embarked on a number of child abuse prevention projects which were funded and supported by a new charitable foundation established by the agency.

When they were founded in the late Victorian era, the CAS of Toronto and its sister agency, the Infants' Home and Infirmary, were totally dependent upon the charity and goodwill of the community. Gradually, through the intervening years, their day-to-day operations came to be funded to an increasing extent by the provin-

Joyce James and Alec Duncan pose as the couple who can make a difference by fostering. This full-page ad appeared in the *Telegram* in 1979.

cial and municipal governments. By the late 1970s, however, with public money growing tighter, it became clear that funding for prevention programs would have to be found outside Metro CAS's annual operating budget.

In 1979, therefore, the society's board of directors decided that the gifts and bequests from private donors that had been accumulated over the years should be administered by its own Children's Aid Society of Metropolitan Toronto Foundation. The foundation would administer these funds and raise others from non-government sources to develop programs designed to prevent child abuse.

To ensure the overall health of the society, and to enable it to develop innovative projects, Metro CAS transferred to the foundation those properties in which the province had no financial interest. (The society feared that MCSS was planning to expropriate these buildings.) The move was acclaimed as a coup by the board and staff, but it probably contributed to a deterioration of the society's relationship with the province. Queen's Park's official reaction later became evident when a legislative amendment prohibited any further transfers or assignments of assets acquired by agencies with the financial assistance of the province.

Under the leadership of Sue Bochner, a visionary and a successful fundraiser, projects funded by the foundation enabled the agency to test new treatment approaches, to evaluate existing programs and to initiate public education proposals in the area of prevention. Some of the projects that received funding in the foundation's first ten years included Creating Together, Jessie's, the Mother Goose Program and the High Risk Infant Program.

Projects funded by the CAS Foundation enabled the agency to test new treatment approaches, to evaluate existing programs and to initiate public education proposals in the area of prevention.

Creating Together, a drop-in program in Parkdale, provided a warm environment where parents and their preschool children could play and learn together and where children could develop through activities, crafts and play materials. Because of low incomes, high unemployment and substandard, crowded housing, the pressures on these parents and children were immense. The program aimed to help families cope by developing strategies that identified and supported high-risk families before crises developed.

Creating Together, a drop-in program in Parkdale, provided a warm environment where parents and their preschool children could play and learn together and where children could develop through activities, crafts and play materials.

Jessie's was, and is, a unique service for teenage mothers planning to keep their babies. It opened in the fall of 1981, thanks to the vision of June Callwood,

Jessie's was, and is, a unique service for teenage mothers planning to keep their babies. It opened in the fall of 1981, thanks to the vision of June Callwood.

a concerned social activist and well-known writer and broadcaster. The program provides teen mothers with counselling, day care, health, education and other resources and supports an increasing number of teen mothers who plan to keep their babies.

The Mother Goose Program helped the many CAS clients who were parents of young children and did not know how to communicate with their youngsters, perhaps because they had never had satisfactory communication with their own parents. Initiated and led by Barrie Dickson — who, besides being a CAS worker was also a published children's author — the program offered parents "an avenue toward imaginative communication" with their children through storytelling.

The Mother Goose Program offered parents and children "an avenue towards imaginative communication" through storytelling.

The High Risk Infant Program

The High Risk Infant Program was one of the most innovative initiatives of the foundation, one which has long since become an ongoing core-funded part of the agency's efforts to protect high-risk infants without removing them from the care of their parents. It was started in 1982 by one of the society's nurse practitioners, Marilyn Pearson. She describes how the program came about:

> A young mother kept taking her infant to Sick Kids Hospital, saying there was something wrong. The hospital could find nothing amiss, so it kept sending the child back home. I decided to go out to investigate. I found a young mother who had been abused and rejected as a child. Her baby, George, was healthy and normal, although given to irritable crying fits, but his mother simply had no idea of how to look after him. So I kept visiting because I was concerned for George's safety and wanted to help the mother cope. When George was about nine months old, the mother called me and said bluntly: "You'd better come and take him because I think I'm going to kill him."

"When George was about nine months old, the mother called me and said bluntly: "You'd better come and take him because I think I'm going to kill him."

— Marilyn Pearson

George came into the society's care and never went back to his mother, but the experience convinced Pearson of the need to become intensely involved with high-risk families to try to resolve problems before they became so acute. Before long, she was receiving dozens of calls and had a caseload full of high-risk infants, most of them less than three months old. A new program was born. It started out in Toronto East and Toronto West branches with funding from the CAS Foundation and was eventually extended across Metro. Pearson says:

> It destroyed the myth of the typical high-risk mother. She is not necessarily a teenage single parent. In fact, the majority of high risk mothers CAS serves are between twenty and thirty years old, with the next biggest percentage between fifteen and twenty and a smaller number between thirty and forty-five. Most have a partner, although not always the biological parent. Predictably, poverty is a major factor. Bad housing, isolation and stress all play a part, as does, often, a history of sexual and physical abuse.

The nurse practitioners who ran the program offered these mothers a supportive hand — and ear — as well as ongoing medical and practical advice. They visited the mothers and their babies frequently — daily and on weekends, if necessary — to assess the infants' growth, development and health, to assess the mothers' parenting capacity, and to teach parenting skills.

While not all cases were a success, most were. One example was the twenty-three-year-old mother who lived with her partner in a cellar in a downtown rooming house. There were open drains in the floor. The baby had a crib, but his mother kept him in her bed at night because she was afraid of the rats that emerged from the drains. She had no working refrigerator and could not afford formula. Pearson visited the family on a daily basis, fully expecting she would eventually have to apprehend the child. However, as she recalls:

> We got the mom a new fridge and paid for formula and had to bail her out of trouble a few more times, but she turned out to be a

The high risk infant nurse practitioners visited mothers and their babies frequently — daily and on weekends, if necessary — to assess the infants' growth, development and health, to assess the mothers' parenting capacity, and to teach parenting skills.

great mother. She had a second child, and both youngsters did well. She became very good with the kids. She just needed to have someone show her where to look for help.

Sexual abuse

Until the early 1980s, the prevailing view had been that children were more likely to be sexually abused by strangers than by members of their own family, and that the numbers of such sexually abused children were relatively few.

It was only in the early 1980s that Canadians began to appreciate that more children were victims of sexual abuse than had been previously suspected. Until this time, the prevailing view had been that children were more likely to be sexually abused by strangers than by members of their own family, and that the numbers of such sexually abused children were relatively few.

At Metro CAS, where nobody denied that sexual abuse was a very real and complex problem, understanding of the issues and how to deal with them was limited.

Through a series of outspoken presentations to agency staff, Alexander Zaphiris, a professor of social work at the University of Houston, helped to breach the wall of silence that surrounded incest. He emphasized that most instances of child sexual abuse occurred in the family home, that the father or another close relative was usually the perpetrator and that, although more girls than boys were victims, a significant number of boys often suffered the experience of being sexually abused by family members.

"Sometime during their lives, about one in two females and one in three males have been victims of one or more unwanted sexual acts. About four in five had first been committed against these persons when they were children or youths."
— The Badgley Report, 1984

(Subsequently, in 1984, the report of the federal Committee on Sexual Offences Against Children and Youth — the Badgley Report — estimated that "sometime during their lives, about one in two females and one in three males have been victims of one or more unwanted sexual acts. About four in five had first been committed against these persons when they were children or youths.")

In 1981, Metropolitan Toronto chairman Paul Godfrey established a Special Committee on Child Abuse. Under the professional leadership of former Metro CAS community worker Lorna Grant, the committee decided to focus specifically on sexual abuse. Its approach was to develop a coordinated community program to address the sexual abuse of children, similar to one that had been pioneered in California by Henry Giaretto.

The achievement of the Special Committee and of the agencies represented on it — which ranged from children's aid societies and school boards to the police and Crown attorneys — was truly remarkable. It put in place a joint CAS–police protocol for the investigation of every case of child sexual abuse. Each organization designated sexual abuse specialists, all of whom took the same training together. Crisis support groups were developed for children and adults involved in the painful experience of disclosure, and a creative prevention play was performed in schools to educate children about the problem.

Marcellina Mian, at that time the director of the Suspected Child Abuse and Neglect Program at Toronto's Hospital for Sick Children, recalls:

> In 1982, a group of us from Toronto, including Lorna Grant, Joan Davis from Metro CAS and me, went to Henry Giaretto's program in San Jose, California, for training on sexual abuse. This was a time when little was known about how much of an issue this would be for our community, but we were prepared to take steps to address it.
>
> We learned that children should be believed when they make a disclosure of abuse but that that belief cannot be blind. We learned about false allegations and false recantations. We learned about the role of custody and access disputes in allegations of sexual abuse and we learned about recurrent and ongoing allegations of abuse and the difficulties that these can create for all systems involved.
>
> We also found out that not paying attention to physical abuse and neglect while concentrating on sexual abuse can have devastating consequences, and that some of the techniques we learned in the investigations of sexual abuse, such as interviewing other siblings, can be very useful in the investigation of other forms of maltreatment.
>
> On our return, we worked to develop a protocol for an integrated response to the sexual abuse of children. Metro CAS was very much involved in that and, to this day, we have worked together on so many cases and so many issues.

"In 1982, a group of us from Toronto, including Lorna Grant, Joan Davis from Metro CAS and me, went to Henry Giaretto's program in San Jose, California for training on sexual abuse. This was a time when little was known about how much of an issue this would be for our community but we were prepared to take steps to address it."

— Marcellina Mian

The Toronto Street Youth Program was the first phase of a three-part treatment program for adolescents under sixteen years of age who were involved in — or were at risk of becoming involved in — prostitution.

"The girls are given clean pyjamas, fluffy slippers, food and, yes, teddy bears! Not all respond to this homely approach but most react like the children they are — to the caring staff, the good meals and the evening movies."

— Carol Yaworski

These developments improved the community's response to child sexual abuse, and Metro CAS found itself better able to protect children from sexual abuse, investigate allegations of child sexual abuse and introduce more programs to treat those young people who had the misfortune to be sexually abused. The increase in the agency's workload brought about by the new approaches was significant. Workers, nevertheless, realized that the changes gave hope to thousands of the city's children and undertook the various tasks involved with enthusiasm.

The establishment in 1985 of the Toronto Street Youth Program addressed another aspect of the sexual exploitation of children. Funded by a designated grant from MCSS, it was designed as the first phase of a three-part treatment program for adolescents under sixteen years of age who were involved in — or were at risk of becoming involved in — prostitution. The police or children's aid workers would refer young people to a short-term reception centre and safe place located at Metro CAS's Moberly House. Agency staff would then provide them with emergency medical care, crisis counselling and close supervision to prevent them from running away.

If a youth needed intensive support, she — the program served females for the most part — was transferred to a second-phase stabilization program run by Cassata, a private, not-for-profit youth agency. At Cassata, the youth would be offered counselling, life skills training and educational programs. The third phase was intensive, community-based counselling offered by Central Toronto Youth Services.

Between them, these three components aimed to offer a safe, alternative environment to the dangers of the street. Carol Yaworski, who was the initial supervisor of the Moberly House phase of the program, wrote:

Without exception, these youth are runaways, running from social problems, inadequate parenting or physical abuse. They are usually both troubled and scared when the police bring them in. The girls are given clean pyjamas, fluffy slippers, food and, yes, teddy bears! Not all respond to this homely approach but most react like the children they are — to the caring staff, the good meals and the evening movies. Moberly's eight staff members feel that they are meeting the needs of their young clients and providing the basis of the good parenting they sorely need. Many phone or visit later. Even those who return to the street know that they can return to Moberly if they need a safe haven.

Adoption

As outlined in the previous chapter, after 1969 the numbers of children placed for adoption declined dramatically as the result of changing societal values toward single, unmarried mothers. The picture changed again in the 1980s because, in this era, many of the newborns needing adoption came to the agency after a difficult birth or with a family history of mental illness or prenatal drug and alcohol abuse.

One such child, among many others whose story had a happy adoption ending, was Baby Holly. Just before Christmas 1982, she was found, only hours old, lying naked in a pool of water under a transport truck.

When the CAS and the Infants' Home were founded in Toronto in the late nineteenth century, foundlings — babies found abandoned at birth — were relatively common. By the 1980s, however, infants abandoned in this way were very rare due to the support services provided by the society and other agencies, particularly to young pregnant women. This is doubtless the reason why there was a tremendous response from the public and the media to Baby Holly's plight, as described in the agency journal *Our Children*:

> Letters, gifts, money and offers to adopt or foster her poured into the agency and to the Hospital for Sick Children where Holly, as the nurses named her, spent the first three weeks of her life. Feeling that Holly was too identifying a name executive director Doug Barr renamed her and she was placed with Linda and Don, foster parents who eventually adopted her.
>
> "Holly's first seven months were tough," says Linda. "She was a sick, frightened little girl. She would gulp her bottle as if starving

Just before Christmas 1982, Baby Holly was found, only hours old, lying naked in a pool of water under a transport truck.

and then vomit it all back. She cried hysterically for hours, slept for a few minutes, woke and cried again."

When she was about seven months old, Holly turned the corner and never looked back. Now, as she approaches her first birthday, she is a happy, outgoing little girl with sparkling black eyes and dark glossy ringlets. She can climb stairs and she's learning to talk. She loves her brother Ian and they play well together with lots of hugging and kissing. "She's a very special little girl," says Linda, "and we want to assure all those who took her into their hearts that she is much adored."

The agency intensified its efforts to find families for children from the ethnic and racial communities to which they belonged. This was particularly challenging for adoption workers because adoption was an alien concept in some of these communities.

By the 1980s, most of the children Metro CAS placed for adoption were older or had special needs, often because of a physical or developmental handicap. Another change was the increasing number of children of colour who became available for adoption. The agency intensified its efforts to find families for these children from the ethnic and racial communities to which they belonged. This was particularly challenging for adoption workers because adoption was an alien concept in some of these communities.

In the meantime, subsidies, which were first allowed after the passing of the Child Welfare Act of 1978, brought the warmth and security of an adoptive family to youngsters whose needs made adoption prohibitively expensive.

The changing times, however, required more progressive adoption legislation to meet the needs of children and the families who wished to care for them. Much of the society's policy advocacy in the early 1980s focused on this goal, particularly where the hundreds of former adoptees asking for information about their past were concerned. It also became apparent there was a need to provide supportive post-adoptive services to adopting parents, particularly those who had adopted older children or those with special needs.

These issues raised important ethical and philosophical questions. What responsibility did an agency that planned an adoption have? What did the agency owe to the adoptee who felt he or she had not been consulted on this arrangement of their life? To the birth parent to whom confidentiality and anonymity had been promised? To the adoptive parents, who were also promised confidentiality and anonymity, as well as a guarantee that the child would be "theirs"?

The Child and Family Services Act of 1984 resolved these issues. Although the 1978 Child Welfare Act had established a voluntary disclosure registry that released information when both a birth parent and an adult adoptee consented, Metro CAS's promotion of a more comprehensive system resulted in the establishment under the new act of an Adoption Disclosure Register. Birth families and adoptees who so wished could have their names logged in this registry, at which point the registrar would search for and make contact with the other parties to determine if they, too, wished to have their identities disclosed. If so, children's aid societies were then authorized to make the information available, provide counselling and arrange a meeting, should the parties wish one.

Despite the legislative mandate given to CAS to perform adoption disclosure work, the activity was permissive rather than mandatory. As Metro CAS and other societies struggled with meeting the need, funding became the underlying issue. Adults were the target group for these services, and MCSS was reluctant to pay for adult services with child welfare dollars, particularly during an economic recession.

Another change to adoption law and practice, also brought about by the Child and Family Services Act, had a significant impact on the work of Metro CAS. Historically, many adoptions had been made privately, without the involvement of a children's aid society. For example, a family doctor might place a child of a patient with the family of another patient. The new act, however, prohibited anyone other than a children's aid society or a licensed adoption agency from placing children for adoption. This gave rise to the development of private adoption agencies, which were required to be charitable corporations.

These new agencies, which rapidly proliferated, were better able than the children's aid societies to provide prospective adoptive parents with the healthy infants and toddlers for which so many of them were looking. Because relatively few such children were available in Canada, the private agencies increasingly looked for them overseas.

This development in adoption practice began in the late 1980s and gathered momentum over the decade that followed. Adopting a child from overseas was seen

Metro CAS's promotion of a comprehensive adoptive disclosure system resulted in the establishment of an Adoption Disclosure Register for both birth families and adoptees who wished to have their names recorded.

by many potential adoptive parents as a way of avoiding the long delays in securing a child placement through CASs and other domestic adoption agencies. Media coverage of children living in poor or war-torn countries around the world caused many people to consider adopting internationally, in the belief that they were saving a child's life. The numbers of completed international adoptions, however, varied in relation to the political situations in the countries involved.

The development of both private agencies and international adoption left CASs with the increasingly difficult task of finding adoption homes for children who were harder to place — those who were older, had special needs or were living with disabilities. Because of this, in 1988 Metro CAS was able to complete only 101 adoptions, a dramatic decline from the more than 1,000 adoptions the agency completed annually just two decades earlier.

The development of both private agencies and international adoption left CASs with the increasingly difficult task of finding adoption homes for children who were harder to place — those who were older, had special needs or were living with disabilities.

The changing role of foster parents

The changes in the adoption landscape were mirrored in the agency's foster care program. In the past, foster parents had provided love and physical care for children but were involved very little in the evaluation of, and planning for, these children. In the 1980s, foster parents began to be accepted as equal partners with agency staff, and their responsibilities grew accordingly. Enhanced training programs were introduced, as were specialized boarding rates for families caring for children with special needs.

Foster parents now participated in case planning conferences, administered specific programs for the treatment of physical and emotional disorders, taught birth parents about child care and helped to formulate agency policies and practices. The Foster Parent Association supported these new roles through its strong leadership, with substantial encouragement and backing from the society.

Mandy, Jeff and Tina were three children with special needs being cared for in foster family homes.

Mandy, aged five months, was born prematurely and had a congenital abnormality that needed surgical repair. Her mother was a troubled teenage ward of the

Sports celebrities lend their profiles to a Metro CAS foster care recruitment campaign.

society who had caused disturbances in the foster family's community and had threatened to abduct the child. Despite this background, she was determined to have her baby returned to her and visited the child in the foster home three times a week. The foster mother taught Mandy's mother basic baby care and spent time and effort building a trusting relationship with her.

Jeff was the fifteen-year-old son of a single parent and had been in care for about six months. He had a history of petty theft, aggressive and bullying behaviour, truancy and nightly bed-wetting. He was hostile toward his birth mother, abused her regularly and eventually refused to talk to her at all. After he was admitted to foster family care, the bedwetting soon stopped and he began to attend school regularly. His foster father played an important role in this process. He encouraged Jeff to renew contact with his mother and, with his help, Jeff eventually returned home to her.

Seven-year-old Tara had been in a foster home for most of her life. She was developmentally handicapped, could walk only short distances and was not fully toilet trained. She also needed facial and cranial surgery. The foster mother regularly took her to the Hospital for Sick Children to consult with the medical staff about her needs. Although her potential was considered to be limited, she responded well to her foster parents' care.

Mandy, aged five months, was born prematurely and had a congenital abnormality that needed surgical repair. Her mother was a troubled teenage ward of the society who had caused disturbances in the foster family's community and had threatened to abduct the child. Despite this background, she was determined to have her baby returned to her and visited the child in the foster home three times a week. The foster mother taught Mandy's mother basic baby care and spent time and effort building a trusting relationship with her.

Advocacy

One distinguishing feature of the agency in this era was a continuing effort to examine community problems and issues that were pertinent to the society's work and to address them by devoting time, energy and resources to advocacy and community action. The society did this even in the face of expanding demands, declining revenues and ever-closer government scrutiny. Much of this work was undertaken by community development workers, with the support of the Social Issues Committee of the board of directors.

Their work ranged from addressing neighbourhood concerns to providing input into proposed changes to provincial and federal legislation that would affect the welfare of children. The predominant concerns were the need for safe, afford-

Open house held to reach out to the public

able family housing, accessible child care for low-income parents, adequate social assistance and the provision of sufficient funding for the agency's operations.

Multiculturalism

As outlined in previous chapters, Toronto had seen profound changes in the size and composition of its population since the Second World War. These changes were reflected during the 1980s in Metro CAS caseloads, in which families of aboriginal, Middle Eastern, East Asian, South Asian, African, Caribbean and other backgrounds were increasingly represented.

Concern about how the society should respond to the needs of these families, as well as about the adequacy of the agency's services to communities of new Canadians, led to the establishment in 1978 of an agency Multicultural Task Force. Assisted by a U.S. consulting firm, Resources for Change, the task force comprised agency staff and board members as well as representatives of diverse ethnic and racial communities.

Leland Gudge was the staff member designated to assist the work of the task force. He recalls:

"We had some serious work to do in the agency. We had to address not only what seemed to many of us as the inability of the organization to respond in a culturally sensitive way but also had to interpret the concept of a child welfare system to communities for whom the idea was totally alien."

— Leland Gudge

We had some serious work to do in the agency. We had to address not only what seemed to many of us as the inability of the organization to respond in a culturally sensitive way, but we also had to interpret the concept of a child welfare system to communities for whom the idea was totally alien.

Doug Barr and Grenville da Costa, the only person of colour on the board at the time, decided to undertake an assessment of how to tackle these issues, with the help of an American consultancy firm. Hiring a U.S. consultant was controversial but I think it was a safe position for the board at the time, bringing someone in from outside of the city and the country.

We had some mighty struggles with various ethnic organizations, aiming to put some teeth and focus to the recommendations while making sure they were doable. The final recommendations were very different from the direction the consultants were leading us. We ended up with a very comprehensive report that looked at systemic change rather than just issues of race relations, which was how the Americans saw it.

Because the work of the task force was so comprehensive and time-consuming, its recommendations were not tabled until 1983. They committed the society to providing services that were free of racial and ethnic bias and delivered by staff, foster parents and volunteers who were knowledgeable about ethnic and racial differences. The agency immediately set about implementing the proposals.

Janet Haddock, responsible at the time for the multicultural training programs, recalls:

> We were aware that there were many aspects of the organization that needed to change in order for us to improve our services to a diverse — the term in those days was "multicultural" — community. We couldn't just say, "Okay, we're going to do training" or "We're going to offer brochures in various languages." We had to make a paradigm shift. Doug Barr likened the time and effort needed to shift the direction of the agency to changing the direction of an ocean liner.
>
> It required a different way of thinking and a recognition that previously we had done everything from a majority value base and that we needed to recognize that there were a lot of ways of looking at the world and that, accordingly, we had to change the way we operated.

Bruce Rivers, then the manager of the society's residential care programs, recalls going to the training sessions:

> We were asked to explore our awareness and the reaction among many in the agency was, "How could they ask us to do this when we harbour no malice or prejudice toward our brothers and sisters,

"We couldn't just say, okay, we're going to do training or we're going to offer brochures in various languages. We had to make a paradigm shift. Doug Barr likened the time and effort needed to shift the direction of the agency to changing the direction of an ocean liner."

— Janet Haddock

no matter what the colour of their skin?" However, we needed to get in touch with an understanding of racism and how that had become institutionalized, not just in our agency but also throughout society. Our organization broke ground in Canada by taking hold of that issue, embracing it, making it public and committing to a plan to combat it.

Cultural interpreters were trained to ensure that when workers and clients did not share a common language they could communicate in a way that was understood across cultural as well as language barriers.

The society began to undertake more meaningful partnerships with some of Metro Toronto's ethnic-based community organizations. Cultural interpreters were trained to ensure that when workers and clients did not share a common language they could communicate in a way that was understood across cultural as well as language barriers. Multicultural workers with ethnic and cultural backgrounds similar to those of the clients the agency was serving were hired in each branch.

The Pape Alternate Care Program, operated from a homely house in a residential neighbourhood and was enthusiastically supported by the African-Canadian community, which had not previously seen the CAS as a viable source of help with resolving family problems.

An alternate care program specifically designed for children of Caribbean background was established in the east end of Toronto. The Pape Alternate Care Program, as it became known, operated from a homely house in a residential neighbourhood and was enthusiastically supported by the African-Canadian community, which had not previously seen the CAS as a viable source of help with resolving family problems.

Meanwhile, Jewish Family and Child Service (JF&CS) had for many years been lobbying to become the children's aid society for Toronto's Jewish community. It took almost fifteen years of negotiation, conversation and, for JF&CS, frustration, before that agency was fully recognized as a children's aid society in 1980. (Until then, Metro CAS was heavily involved in overseeing JF&CS's child welfare work.)

In a report published in 1967, Jerome Diamond, then executive director of JF&CS, wrote:

> At present, agency policy is for Metro CAS to investigate charges of neglect [in Jewish families]. Then referral to JF&CS for intensive casework is made, where deemed suitable, after a conference with both agencies. [If the child needs to be admitted to care,] all the paperwork is done by our own agency. It goes to the Ministry

who then direct the placement to the Metro CAS, who handle the legal step of court work.

According to current JF&CS executive director Gordie Wolfe, during those fifteen years, "Metro CAS made it possible for JF&CS to serve Jewish families who required child protection services, to maintain children in Jewish foster homes and to preserve the religious traditions that were so important to the agency and which were the driving force behind its struggle to become a children's aid society."

Accountability

Although the dynamics of multiculturalism were a major focus of activity in the 1980s, the society was also increasingly concerned with responding to ongoing demands for accountability toward clients, governments, local communities, staff and foster parents. There was a clear need for more openness, public participation, grievance procedures and mechanisms for standardized program evaluation.

These needs began to be addressed through a series of internal reviews and the work of an evaluation and planning department led by Steve Raiken. The department's responsibilities included developing a system of strategic planning, performance evaluation and a computerized information system (enhanced in 1984 with the purchase of an advanced IBM System 38 mainframe computer). Later, in 1987, the society's antiquated and separate telephone systems were unified and modernized to provide more effective communications among the agency's twenty locations and with outside callers. At about the same time, the first word processing equipment was introduced.

The demands for accountability, however, needed to be carefully balanced with quality services to children and adequate support to the staff, foster parents and volunteers who delivered those services. This challenge became particularly acute when the agency hired a consultant, Neville d'Eca, to develop effective management skills, based on business principles, among supervisors and managers. Many front-line staff thought that a businesslike orientation detracted from supervisors' ability to act as

In 1987, the society's antiquated and separate telephone systems were unified and modernized to provide more effective communications among the agency's twenty locations and with outside callers. At about the same time, the first word processing equipment was introduced.

Governance and management of the society took on a more business-like approach. Annual service plans and periodic long-range plans were developed, allowing the society to develop more systematic methods of determining its programming and funding needs.

Comprehensive policy and procedure manuals were written to guide board members, service staff, administrative staff, foster parents, volunteers and the Emergency After Hours Service on personnel, orientation and training issues.

A salary classification system was introduced that compensated staff not only on their training and experience but also the complexity of the tasks they were required to undertake.

To ensure that the society kept its operations in tune with changing times, major adjustments were made to its service delivery system. Greater attention was paid to client rights, a client complaint procedure was instituted, all resource functions (foster parent recruitment, home studies, child placement, residential programs and adoption) were centralized, the senior management position of director of service delivery was established, and the role of branch directors was redefined.

consultants and teachers in the social work tradition. They feared it would lead to a lessening of morale, greater on-the-job stress and increased staff turnover.

Doug Barr was clear, however, that "In a climate of increased public accountability for the services we provide, the society has chosen to take the initiative and anticipate what needs to be done before problems arise." Annual service plans and periodic long-range plans were developed, allowing the society to develop more systematic methods of determining its programming and funding needs.

These plans were complemented by MCSS's introduction of Exceptional Circumstance Reviews that tried to respond to the twin truths that, on the one hand, children's aid societies could not close down their intake process, yet on the other, the government needed to control costs. The reviews attempted to determine which cost increases were unavoidable and which could be contained.

Comprehensive policy and procedure manuals were written to guide board members, service staff, administrative staff, foster parents, volunteers and the Emergency After Hours Service on personnel, orientation and training issues.

The agency instituted minimum hiring criteria for front-line workers, as well as pre-employment police checks and an updated, more systematic performance appraisal system. A salary classification system was introduced that compensated staff not only on their training and experience but also the complexity of the tasks they were required to undertake. Efforts were made to keep salaries competitive — in 1984, front-line workers earned $30,000 a year on average — so that the agency did not lose staff to organizations where the pay was better. An employee assistance program was developed to provide support to staff involved in work-related crises.

To ensure that the society kept its operations in tune with changing times, major adjustments were made to its service delivery system. Greater attention was paid to client rights, a client complaint procedure was instituted, all resource functions (foster parent recruitment, home studies, child placement, residential programs and adoption) were centralized, the senior management position of director of service delivery was established, and the role of branch directors was redefined.

Service delivery was streamlined by amalgamating Toronto East and Toronto West branches into a single central branch, known as Toronto Branch, which retained the four district offices at 8 Spadina Road, 1678 Bloor Street West, 15

Huntley Street and 741 Broadview Avenue. Etobicoke Branch relocated to a former school building at 70 Chartwell Avenue, while it and the two other suburban branches, North York and Scarborough, all maintained sub-offices in locations where demand for services was high.

Doug Barr's view was that the society needed to base children's services on whether a child was likely to be returned home to his or her family or be made a Crown ward. Accordingly, the agency developed better and earlier permanency planning for those children in its care who were not retuning to their birth families. Improved training for foster parents was provided to help them look after the many young people who were increasingly difficult to care for. Family support functions were strengthened through a Child Care in the Community program, while the agency built up its alternate care programs.

In the 1980s, Metro CAS had five alternate care programs and five child care in the community programs. Both made use of child and youth workers and both worked primarily with children who were living at home with their families. Child Care in the Community workers went into the homes of families to work with them on an individual basis, with the focus frequently upon child management training for parents of children under twelve years of age. Alternate care workers provided group services and some individual counselling to teenagers and their families.

Child Care in the Community workers went into the homes of families to work with them on an individual basis, with the focus frequently upon child management training for parents of children under twelve years of age.

The agency was considered a leader in recognizing the skill set these workers needed to draw upon. Jackie Fargnoli, the director of residential services, describes how this came about:

> When I joined Metro CAS in 1976, the field of child and youth work was still in its infancy, with the majority of what were then called child care workers being young, well-intentioned people who were committed to the care of children and youth. However, they tended to have no formal training or relevant academic credentials, although many were recent university graduates. They entered the field with no "hands-on" experience to prepare them for the challenge of emotionally charged, volatile, aggressive and vulnerable children and youth.

Behaviour management and daily care of young people through the 1960s and 1970s was generally directed and mandated by psychiatrists, social workers and psychotherapists through written "handling orders" carried out by the child care workers. Indeed, the field was also viewed by many as a temporary work experience and a "stepping stone" to other professions such as social work.

Recognizing the need for intensive formal training and "hands-on" experience prior to working with these vulnerable children, the community college system expanded its curriculum from various night courses and extension programs to full-time accredited programs, resulting in the graduation and certification of qualified and professional child and youth workers.

Starting in the late 1970s, Metro CAS began to shift its hiring criteria to recruit graduates of child and youth worker programs. With recognition of the expertise brought by these professionals and as a result of program development, the agency developed career opportunities and diversity of job tasks specific to child and youth workers. What once was considered just a stepping stone position became an established and recognized professional community.

"With recognition of the expertise brought by child and youth workers and as a result of program development, the agency developed career opportunities and diversity of job tasks specific to these professionals. What once was considered just a stepping stone position became an established and recognized professional community."

— Jackie Fargnoli

In-house training was upgraded and, under the direction of Connie Barbour, the director of Toronto Branch, Metro CAS made a major contribution to the literature with an impressive 450-page *Child Welfare Source Book of Knowledge and Practice*. Another book, *Preparing for Practice*, on the basics of child protection, was edited by Nancy Falconer, the supervisor of a demonstration project to determine whether pre-work training would improve the skills and the eventual retention rate of family service staff. Falconer recalls:

Preparing for Practice came about after the demonstration project was discontinued because of a hiring freeze. Health and Welfare Canada, which had funded the project, said we needed to have something come from the experiment and thought that a training manual would be useful.

I hired Karen Swift to help research and write it with me, and early in the project we both felt a dry manual wouldn't be very well read or used. We had just six months to turn it out and that included such things as designing the format, finding a printer and getting approval from Health and Welfare Canada. It was a race and my chapters were written on my very first experience with a computer.

Although the pre-work training concept was revived a decade and a half later, logistical problems in 1983 prevented its systematic introduction across the agency. One lasting outcome, however — and one that ran contrary to Falconer's fear — was the popularity of *Preparing for Practice*. It was an immediate best-seller and has been in demand ever since.

Meanwhile, in August 1980, MCSS undertook a comprehensive review of the agency's operations as part of its plan to more closely monitor the work of children's aid societies. Its interim report contained 168 recommendations, many of them viewed by the society's management as carping and counterproductive.

Executive director Doug Barr was assertive in his response, emphasizing the society's uniqueness and its recognition across North America as an acknowledged leader in the field of child welfare. In his view, the legislative mandate was being fulfilled and the citizens of Metro Toronto were being well served. If MCSS did not appreciate this, other agencies in the community did. Crown ward reviews showed the excellence of the agency's care of children in need of protection. Its public relations work was the best in the province. Other children's aid societies were interested in its process for planning and budgeting.

Barr's approach appeared to have a positive effect, as the ministry's final report was constructive and consistent with the directions already being taken — or being considered — by the agency.

Cost cutting

In this era, communication between MCSS and Metro CAS over funding was often less than amicable, and it deteriorated as the board became distressed by what it saw as gross underfunding. This was exacerbated by MCSS's request in 1982 that the society reduce its base budget of $38 million by $3 million over three years. Mary Louise Clements, the board's president that year, did not mince words in her reply to the ministry: "In general, the board finds your proposals of reduction to be ill-timed and irresponsible and your background information inaccurate and inconclusive."

Her successor, David Fuller, continued the dialogue with an approach that was as diplomatic as possible under the circumstances. By this time, however, it was publicly recognized that relations between the agency and its primary funder were neither harmonious nor effectively collaborative.

To manage in these difficult circumstances, tough budgetary decisions had to be made, including staff reductions (among them the elimination of most department head positions at the branches), early retirement incentives, leaving vacant administrative jobs open, a teen admission policy that limited the number of adolescents in care in favour of meeting their needs in the community, and the closure of York Cottage, the society's staff-operated treatment home for emotionally troubled children.

Although the society placed in other types of care those children in York Cottage who could not return to their families, there was little government funding available to build good community supports and other alternatives to institutional care. The problem was exacerbated by cutbacks in children's mental health services, tight municipal land use controls that made it difficult to open new group homes, and the closing of training schools for young offenders.

The society's Lloyd S. Richardson (LSR) program was transformed from one based in a thirty-two-bed residence to one that supported children living in smaller homes in the community. Between 1987 and 1990, the LSR beds were transferred in stages to 24 Gablehurst Crescent, a small, staff-operated group home, and to a number of what were known as "mixed modality" foster homes. There, child and youth workers worked daily with the foster children and supported the foster parents. The program remained unified, however, under a manager and a team of workers who had access to clinical consultation, community resources and school classrooms. According to former program manager Joanne Maltby:

> Some of the most challenging of the children did much better than we anticipated once they moved into foster care, where they benefited from a normal family experience. Some even lived with LSR program staff who became foster parents.

As the recession of the early 1980s deepened, staff and foster parents had to cope not only with tighter government funding and more rigorous standards but also with more complicated caseloads. Tension from job insecurity and stress escalated among the almost 700 staff members as well as among the more than 500 foster care providers. One senior manager recalls an instance of how this stress played itself out:

> There was a situation where an angry staff member poured a waste paper bin full of water over her supervisor's head. The supervisor was chairing a meeting at the time. The staff member quit soon after. To lighten the mood, branch director Joan Wilson sent out a memo to all staff stating that, henceforth, all waste paper bins must have a hole drilled in the bottom to prevent the repetition of such incidents.

The stress experienced by staff led to one situation where an angry staff member poured a waste paper bin full of water over her supervisor's head. The supervisor was chairing a meeting at the time. The staff member quit soon after. To lighten the mood, branch director Joan Wilson sent out a memo to all staff stating that, henceforth, all waste paper bins must have a hole drilled in the bottom to prevent the repetition of such incidents.

Doug Barr resigns

In the summer of 1984, Doug Barr resigned as the agency's executive director to become chief executive officer of the Canadian Cancer Society. In a farewell message, he wrote:

> How does one break off an intimate relationship of some seventeen years? With a mix of feelings, frankly. For, as I look back on three summers as a student working in protection and children's servic-

es, two years on the board as chairman of the social issues committee, over six years as your executive director and all the years in between, I am filled with feelings of nostalgia, admiration and confidence. Nostalgia for the many challenges encountered and overcome, admiration for the depth of talent and commitment among staff, foster parents and volunteers and confidence in the society's ability to positively and creatively meet the future.

"The last half dozen years in child welfare have required incredible versatility and adaptability on the part of us all. We have seen services to children wax and wane as public priorities. We have witnessed the effect on families and agencies alike of a severe recession. We have experienced a heightened sense of accountability to the public for the services we provide. These have not been easy times."

— Doug Barr

The last half dozen years in child welfare have required incredible versatility and adaptability on the part of us all. We have seen services to children wax and wane as public priorities. We have witnessed the effect on families and agencies alike of a severe recession. We have experienced a heightened sense of accountability to the public for the services we provide. These have not been easy times.

But let it be said of Metro CAS that during this difficult period we did not hide our heads in the sand but, rather, viewed each crisis as an opportunity rather than as a danger. Under restraint, we revitalized and reformed.

Those who had worked with Barr during his years as executive director were sorry to see him leave, and regretted the loss to the agency of his intelligence, hard work and commitment to children. Some also thought, however, that his combative relationship with provincial officials over funding, and his adversarial opposition to government policies that he believed harmed the well-being of children, had jeopardized the society's financial backing and its credibility with the province, the agency's principal funder.

At a time when resources were diminishing, the provincial government tended to view Metro CAS as well funded compared to the other children's aid societies in the province. The society, in turn, thought the province underestimated the difficulty of meeting the unique needs of a large, diverse and complex urban community.

At a time when resources were diminishing, MCSS tended to view Metro CAS as well funded compared to the other children's aid societies in the province. The society, in turn, thought the province underestimated the difficulty of meeting the unique needs of a large, diverse and complex urban community. Barr often fought these battles with the government though "an open, honest and assertive relationship" with the media, which he understood and used skilfully, and via a speaker's bureau that he established. Barr believed that "telling it like it is" would change for the better what he perceived as the government's and the public's distorted image of child welfare. As he wrote:

> Where we feel coverage of CAS issues has been biased, we have attempted to set the record straight, with positive results. Where the coverage has been accurate, we have communicated our appreciation. It is a relationship that requires constant tending but one that can produce a more enlightened public, a child-focused society that is not always on the defensive and a staff that can hold up its head proudly in public.

He believed that the agency was ultimately accountable not to the government but to the public. According to one senior manager, it was for this reason that:

> When he got into budget battles with the ministry he tended to do an end run around them. So he went to the public, saying he was just attempting to take care of the children.
>
> Eventually, the politicians said that enough was enough. I can still remember the famous night when Bob McDonald, the deputy minister, came to a board meeting and just read the riot act, said that the agency would reduce its budget, thanks very much, goodnight. There was not a discussion or any negotiation. This was what was going to happen.

Despite the agency's seemingly constant state of war with MCSS, the board and staff for the most part supported Barr's leadership of the society and his efforts to maintain "progress under restraint" in an era of cost containment and increased accountability. As another senior manager at the time recalled:

> There were open debates as to which direction the society should be taking on various matters. I recall some very spirited meetings

"It is a relationship that requires constant tending but one that can produce a more enlightened public, a child-focussed society that is not always on the defensive and a staff that can hold up its head proudly in public."

— Doug Barr on Metro CAS's relationship with the media

over in the basement of the church next to the Charles Street offices where the board and entire management team were holding public meetings with staff and concerned members of the community around the decisions that were being taken to address the agency's financial situation.

Mel Finlay

The political, financial and social forces described above were foremost in the minds of the society's board of directors as they considered whom they should appoint to succeed Doug Barr as the agency's executive director.

They knew that whoever took on the job would have to work with a provincial government that was less equipped than ever to support new and expanding child welfare and other social needs. For the sake of the agency's financial and political viability in this changed environment, they wanted a leader who would seek a lower profile than Barr, one more willing to toe the line on the government's increasing demands for accountability.

They chose Mel Finlay, who for many years had worked in social service policy development for the government of Alberta. He had taken on a significant role in the development of a regionalized structure for the delivery of social and community health services in that province and, at the time of his appointment to Metro CAS, was the local director for those programs in the Calgary region.

This background, along with Finlay's expertise as a negotiator and with the media, was attractive to the society's board. They thought that his experience working at the heart of government would foster a less tumultuous relationship with MCSS and enable the agency to comply more readily with the province's expectations. As Finlay recalls:

> My challenge as executive director was to rationalize the delivery
> of child welfare programs that were funded by a government that

had adopted a more businesslike approach to the management of social services and that was demanding more accountability from those it paid to deliver mandated services.

Staff, meanwhile, were looking for more resources, smaller workloads and better salaries. MCSS was clear, however, that budget increases would be pegged at the rate of inflation — or less — despite growing caseloads, children with increasingly complex needs, and the mounting costs of maintaining the agency's many properties. At the same time, the province ordered the society to eliminate its budget deficit of more than $1 million.

The agency would be forced to make some hard choices and respond creatively to the changing times. That this would be a challenge was epitomized by the steady deterioration of the rapport between the society's executive staff and its front-line employees. There were some who felt that Finlay appeared not to value or make use of the knowledge and skills of the agency's staff in conceptualizing child welfare practice in a large, complex urban community. Finlay does not disagree with that sentiment:

> I am not a social worker and I thought that those in the forefront of service delivery were much more capable than I would have been in that role. My job was to ensure the agency had sufficient dollars to deliver effectively the services we were mandated to provide. To do this, I attempted to create a climate in which we could look at how we were delivering those services and ask whether it was the most effective way. Because I posed these issues, I think I was seen as a threat.
>
> It certainly put the middle managers in a real bind. While I was requiring of them a greater level of participation in the [decisions] we needed to make to help us adjust to the new fiscal and accountability realities, they also fully comprehended the pressures that front-line staff were under in trying to do the best job they could with minimal resources.

The agency would be forced to make some hard choices and respond creatively to the changing times. That this would be a challenge was epitomized by the steady deterioration of the rapport between the society's executive staff and its front-line employees.

Unfortunately, however, you cannot turn a ship around overnight, even if there is agreement on what needs to be done. But there was no agreement on what we had to do. Yet, I had to plan ahead to manage the changes that were being required of us.

Finlay managed the changes mainly by cutting staff and programs. The result was a proposal in 1986 to eliminate eighty-six staff positions, a plan that garnered swift criticism from MCSS and the community (much of it organized by the agency's community work staff) because most of the cuts were to be made from front-line services rather than from support programs or administrative areas. Finlay, however, recalls that:

> With the kind of dollars we needed to cut [to meet government expectations], the savings had to come from a reduction in programs and program staff. There was no attempt to preserve management positions. It was just not possible to maintain the status quo. We needed to make changes in our expensive residential programs while championing the foster care program as a cost-effective solution for looking after children who needed to live away from home.

"With the kind of dollars we needed to cut [to meet government expectations], the savings had to come from a reduction in programs and program staff. There was no attempt to preserve management positions. It was just not possible to maintain the status quo. We needed to make changes in our expensive residential programs while championing the foster care program as a cost-effective solution for looking after children who needed to live away from home."
— Mel Finlay

The unionized staff go on strike

The lack of funding, increased workloads and a perception that management was authoritarian and defensive led to mounting stresses among those on the front line.

During contract negotiations in 1986 between the society and Local 2316 of the Canadian Union of Public Employees (CUPE), union leaders believed that its members' interests were not a major concern of the agency's administration. They felt that, because important issues were being trivialized and disrespected, it would be impossible for normal collective bargaining to take place. Kenn Richard, the chair of the union's negotiating committee, went as far as to say in a letter to John Sweeney, the minister of community and social services, that "[some union members] feel that the society, most specifically Mel Finlay, is deliberately provoking a strike situation as a cost-saving measure to provide quick resolution to the current financial problems facing the agency."

Finlay denied this allegation, saying it would have been inappropriate for the agency to save money on the backs of workers, even if it had been possible. The union's negotiating team nonetheless requested that the minister recoup what it described as "unethical" savings that would be realized through salaries that would go unpaid as a result of a possible strike. The government of Premier David Peterson did later respond by temporarily withholding those funds.

Negotiations eventually broke down, resulting in a fourteen-day strike in July 1986. It became quickly evident that many of the supervisory staff who maintained emergency services to children and families in need were very sympathetic to the striking front-line workers, as were some board members. For example, supervisors regularly passed refreshments out through agency windows to picketers, and one board member offered strikers coffee and doughnuts purchased on the way to a board meeting.

The impact of the strike was significant. Clearly, the union had argued its case convincingly. Its members achieved a salary increase of 3.2 percent — raising the average compensation of a front-line worker to $33,000 — almost a full percentage point higher than the final offer management had made prior to the walkout.

Mel Finlay resigns

Despite the settlement of the strike, staff morale continued at low ebb. Many of the union's issues remained unresolved and there continued to be mistrust between the parties. At the same time, Finlay thought that the board no longer endorsed the direction in which he was taking the agency, and so in February 1988 he decided to resign his position as executive director.

Finlay had, by his own admission, "ruffled feathers" in the difficult job of repairing relationships with the province while trying to change the way the society delivered services in an era of diminishing resources. He recalls:

Supervisors regularly passed refreshments out through agency windows to picketers, and one board member offered strikers coffee and dough-nuts purchased on the way to a board meeting.

Finlay had, by his own admission, "ruffled feathers" in the difficult job of repairing relationships with the province while trying to change the way the society delivered services in an era of diminishing resources.

It had become clearer just what the costs were in attempting to change the direction of a 100-year-old agency. People were clearly upset at what was happening, so there was a pulling back from that. Also, I didn't fully appreciate the way in which the board and the executive committee had changed over the three years of my contract as executive director. We were dealing with a different attitude and agenda at the end of my term than the ones in place when I was hired.

As Finlay's predecessor Doug Barr had also discovered, it was difficult for the agency, after "the golden years" described in Chapter 6, to adjust to the new realities of government fiscal restraint and demands for accountability.

Finlay went on to work in the business world as a consultant, and subsequently became a Baptist minister. For several months after his resignation, the board decided that — rather than appoint an interim director while it sought out a successor — its own executive committee would run the agency directly, supported by senior staff members Jim Thompson, the director of service delivery, and Larry Harrison, the director of administrative services. In reality, Thompson and Harrison effectively assumed the executive director's role, reporting weekly to the executive committee at early-morning meetings.

Foster parent slowdown

One of the major challenges Thompson, Harrison and the executive committee faced was a work slowdown by foster parents, which arose out of the foster parents' distress at the low boarding rates the province set. According to Wilma Wrabko, the president of the agency's Foster Parent Association, they believed "The significant difference in payments to private foster care and day care providers as compared to [Metro CAS's] foster parents is inequitable and unacceptable."

Foster parents were also distraught because they felt a lack of recognition of the work they did to carry out their essential tasks.

In June 1988, the association informed the executive committee that, because of this dissatisfaction, their members would conduct a work slowdown, during which regular foster parents would refuse new placements of children in their homes unless they received significant per diem increases, plus expenses for each child. Foster parents in special programs, who already received more, would also work to rule and refuse new placements.

The slowdown lasted throughout July 1988 and was effective in achieving most of the association's goals. The society negotiated successfully with the government, and the rates at which foster parents were reimbursed for caring for each child increased by about 10 percent. The slowdown also achieved greater acknowledgment of the agency's, indeed the province's, dependence on foster parents. As the provincial cabinet minister John Sweeney said, "We simply can't attach a dollar value to the selfless and challenging work done by so many foster parents throughout the province."

Foster parents deserved the sense of increased appreciation they gained that summer. Although fewer in number — by a third — than they had been just a decade and a half earlier, their commitment remained astonishing. Many loyal foster parents displayed great tenacity and skill in caring for a growing number of young people who presented grave challenges. They performed amazing feats despite low rates of compensation and little recognition of the effects fostering had on their own families.

One such foster parent was Susan Oley, who became part of the agency's developmental care program that offered a family alternative to institutionalization for children with developmental handicaps. Oley recalls:

> In 1987, we were introduced to Rico, a tiny, curly-headed boy of seven years. He was in need of a home with a family with whom he could stay until he was able to live independently. Rico was born with spina bifida and was paralyzed from the waist down. He looked fragile and his needs were numerous, but his eyes were lively and appealing.
>
> Rico had a severe stutter, especially when he was nervous. When he came to us, he weighed only 24 pounds [11 kg], so small

During the slowdown, regular foster parents would refuse new placements of children in their homes unless they received significant per diem increases, plus expenses for each child. Foster parents in special programs, who already received more, would also work to rule and refuse new placements.

"We simply can't attach a dollar value to the selfless and challenging work done by so many foster parents throughout the province."
— John Sweeney

that he could sit on the edge of the kitchen counter to help me prepare meals. I remember all his anxiety of the first few months, his worries about eating, not knowing how to play and whether we would ask him to leave.

Thirteen years later, we are filled with memories of a little boy who is now almost twenty years old. There have been many trials and tribulations. I'll never forget all the time we have spent promoting Rico independence, helping him to dress and care for his hygiene, to transfer in and out of his wheel chair and to develop a group of friends. I'll always remember his compassion and understanding toward other children who came to stay with us.

Rico's only wish was to be with his natural family. He wanted so much to become independent, thinking that this was the only reason he didn't live with them. In 1992, Rico's hard work paid off and he went to Florida to spend Christmas with his family. He continues to visit them yearly and is proud of his brother and sister, but has now decided that his life is in Toronto and visiting them is enough.

Now Rico seems happy, has a girlfriend and is participating in a co-op work program. He still has many new challenges ahead of him, but I don't think he is afraid any more. He has control of his future and his choices. He also knows that whatever he does, he will always be a part of our family.

Oley subsequently received an outstanding achievement award from the Ontario Association of Children's Aid Societies for her work with developmentally handicapped children .

Pape Adolescent Resource Centre

At the end of 1985, the society had 1,640 children in care. Almost 800 of these were living in the society's 400 foster homes, while the remainder were looked after in agency group homes or outside institutions. As they reached their mid-teens, these young people needed help with the transition most of them would shortly be making from agency care to legal, financial and social independence.

To meet this need, the Pape Adolescent Resource Centre (PARC) opened in 1986 as a collaborative project between Metro CAS, the Catholic CAS and MCSS. Housed in the building recently vacated by the Pape Alternate Care Program described above, PARC was designed as a transitional program for youth fifteen years and older who were in the process of leaving, or had already left, the care of the Toronto children's aid societies. Services were to include counselling on independent living skills, employment, housing, literacy, sexuality and substance and alcohol abuse.

By encouraging and supporting personal and emotional growth and providing a variety of tailored supports to meet the different needs of many agency wards and former wards, PARC quickly became one of the society's highest-profile and most successful programs. More than fifteen years later, it remains a central component of the agency's services to youth.

By encouraging and supporting personal and emotional growth and providing a variety of tailored supports to meet the different needs of many agency wards and former wards, PARC quickly became one of the society's highest-profile and most successful programs.

Innovation and leadership

Notwithstanding the challenges of the 1980s, Metro CAS continued to innovate and provide leadership in the child welfare field at a difficult time in its history. Every year, the society made a difference in the lives of over 9,000 families and more than 17,000 children, of whom roughly 2,600 annually were offered quality care by foster parents and other providers. For every child in the society's care, however, agency staff provided services to another seven in their own homes, working hard to protect them and to support their families. Around 1,000 volunteers remained as committed as ever, providing more than 20,000 hours of service each month.

Despite the difficulties in finding the necessary resources from a barely adequate annual budget of $51 million, the society established new programs that took a broader view of how a child welfare agency should respond to the needs of young

Despite the difficulties in finding the necessary resources from a barely adequate annual budget of $51 million, the society established new programs that took a broader view of how a child welfare agency should respond to the needs of young people at the end of the twentieth century.

people at the end of the twentieth century. Many of these programs were support-ed by the CAS Foundation, which raised more than $300,000 annually to fund projects ranging from parental skills training and incest victim support to youth employment programs.

Metro CAS believed that it was well equipped to enter the fast approaching 1990s, which it would do under a new executive director.

CHAPTER 8

Recession and Reform, 1989–1998

Toronto in the 1990s

An economic recession, federal and provincial changes to the social safety net and municipal unification transformed Toronto in this era.

On January 1, 1998, the amalgamation of Metropolitan Toronto's seven municipal governments created a new City of Toronto. This change did not significantly affect the governance of Metro CAS, which since 1957 had served all of the territory in the new city's jurisdiction, although on July 1, 1998 the society did reflect the change by reverting to its former name, the Children's Aid Society of Toronto.

(Because these changes did not occur until 1998, at the very end of the period covered by this book, and to avoid confusion to the reader, the terms Metro Toronto and Metro CAS will be used throughout this chapter.)

At the time of municipal amalgamation, Metro Toronto was home to 2.4 million people, just over half the population (4.6 million) of the Toronto census metropolitan area. More than a million residents of Metropolitan Toronto, or 47 percent of the population, were born outside Canada, accounting for one in four of the nation's immigrants. Between 1991 and 1996, more than 300,000 foreign-born newcomers settled in Metro, of whom 20 percent were children and 10 percent were refugees. The main sources of these immigrants were Sri Lanka, China, the Philippines and Hong Kong. This influx of newcomers has contributed to Toronto's standing as one of the most culturally diverse cities in the world.

At the time of municipal amalgamation, more than a million residents of Metropolitan Toronto, or 47 percent of the population, were born outside Canada, accounting for one in four of the nation's immigrants.

Almost 60 percent (more than 5,300) of the families served annually by Metro CAS were led by lone parents.

The trends established over the two previous decades toward common law unions, delayed marriages and divorce or separation when such relationships no longer satisfied one or both partners continued into the 1990s. The fertility rate, which had also been declining during this time, reached its lowest-ever level in 1997, as mothers gave birth on average to only 1.6 children each.

The number of single-parent-led families in Metro Toronto, however, grew by 23 percent, from approximately 95,000 in 1991 to more than 117,000 in 1996; however, almost 60 percent (more than 5,300) of the families served annually by Metro CAS were led by lone parents. By the late 1990s, Ontarians living in same-sex unions gained unprecedented social acceptance, as well as legal rights comparable to those of heterosexual common law partners.

A number of economic forces came to bear during this decade. There was a prolonged recession that lasted from 1990 until 1995, as well as the increasing pace of business globalization and a wave of corporate restructuring designed to meet the challenges of the free trade agreement between Canada, the United States and Mexico. All of this placed great pressure on families. Large numbers of people were put out of work as many employers either closed down their businesses or relocated elsewhere. This was particularly so in business sectors that employed low-skilled or unskilled staff, a segment of the economy where clients of CASs were most likely to be represented. Even when the economy recovered in the mid-1990s, relatively few of the newly available jobs were full-time. For many people, self-employment became an increasingly important source of income.

As unemployment climbed, so did the costs to governments as tax revenues decreased and payments of unemployment and social assistance benefits grew. Both the federal and provincial governments ran higher budgetary deficits and felt considerable pressure to cut spending wherever they could. This pressure came from economists, as well as ordinary Canadians who were becoming increasingly concerned about how governments could meet their obligations without bankrupting their treasuries.

In 1993, the government of Premier Bob Rae responded to these concerns with a public policy initiative known as the "Social Contract." It was an attempt to avoid public-sector layoffs by cutting back the salaries of civil servants and employees of government-funded agencies such as CASs. Its principal tool was the imposition of compulsory unpaid holidays — up to twelve days a year, quickly dubbed "Rae Days" — in return for job security. At the same time, public agencies were subjected to budget cuts through the imposition of an expenditure control plan. The Social Contract was vehemently opposed by the labour movement, which saw it as implying the workers' consent when there was none and felt that it wrongfully forced the reopening of negotiated collective agreements.

The federal government, meanwhile, cut spending on unemployment insurance (which it renamed employment insurance) by 40 percent, introduced a cap on the costs it shared with Ontario under the Canada Assistance Plan, and eventually replaced that plan with a less generous one, the Canada Health and Social Transfer. These events brought sizeable cuts in federal support for health and social programs, leaving the provincial government to cope as best it could.

Against this background, the provincial election of 1995 ushered in a new government, led by Premier Mike Harris, with a mandate to introduce a "common sense revolution" that promised voters large savings in their income taxes and significant cuts in government spending. The resulting sea change in the role of government in Ontario emphasized accountability, reduced layers of administration, services that were consumer-driven and organizations that were more autonomous and self-reliant.

Despite the previous two governments' efforts to increase welfare rates as a social and economic investment in people — as recommended in 1988 by the Social Assistance Review Committee — by 1995 most recipients were still living below the poverty line. Undeterred by this scenario, one of the new government's first acts was to reduce by almost 22 percent the amount it paid to those living on social assistance, while at the same time tightening the eligibility criteria. Since almost 60 percent of the clients of Metro CAS depended on this program for their family income, the changes caused them a disproportionate degree of hardship.

While the caseloads of social assistance workers may have dropped as a result of the new eligibility requirements, poverty rates did not. In 1996, a total of 200,000 Metro households, almost 25 percent, had incomes of less than $20,000 a year — more than $8,000 below the poverty line for a three-person family.

The Social Contract's principal means of avoiding layoffs in the civil service was the imposition of compulsory unpaid holidays — up to twelve days a year, quickly dubbed "Rae Days" — in return for job security.

One of the new government's first acts was to reduce by almost 22 percent the amount it paid to those living on social assistance, while at the same time tightening the eligibility criteria. Since almost 60 percent of the clients of Metro CAS depended on this program for their family income, the changes caused them a disproportionate degree of hardship.

By 1999, it was estimated that 37 percent of children under the age of twelve living in Metro Toronto, and more than three-quarters of the children served by Metro CAS, were poor.

In past years, those who relied on shelters had primarily been single men, but the Golden Report revealed that youth under eighteen years of age and families with children were now the fastest-growing groups of users of emergency accommodation.

By 1999, it was estimated that 37 percent of children under the age of twelve living in Metro Toronto, and more than three-quarters of the children served by Metro CAS, were poor. Food bank use soared because many parents were using more and more of their food allowances to pay for shelter. Even so, most still found it difficult to find or keep suitable housing, while poverty also created mounting health, social and educational problems for their children.

Homeless people became increasingly visible on the streets, the result of poverty and a decline in the stock of affordable housing, conditions that were worsened by the elimination of government subsidies for apartments where rents were geared to tenants' income. In 1999, a municipal task force chaired by Anne Golden, the president of the United Way of Greater Toronto, tabled its report, *Taking Responsibility for Homelessness: An Action Plan for Toronto* (also known as the Golden Report). It found that, on an average night, more than 3,000 people sought refuge in shelters — and even more during periods of cold weather. Traditionally, those who relied on shelters had primarily been single men, but the Golden Report revealed that youth under eighteen years of age and families with children were now the fastest-growing groups of users of emergency accommodation.

Meanwhile, the Harris government required Metro CAS and other social service agencies to reduce their base budgets by 5 percent; some organizations had to absorb even larger cuts, while funding for others was eliminated entirely, forcing them to reduce their services drastically, to amalgamate or to close their doors.

Family breakdown, social problems and community dislocation were direct consequences of these policy changes. Increasingly, families were left to their own devices and were exposed to the vagaries of the market economy. This erosion of the welfare state seemed to have wiped out the effects of more than fifty years of progressive social reform aimed at improving the lives of Torontonians and other Ontarians.

Bruce Rivers

Jim Patterson, who was board president in 1988, recalls the priorities the board set in seeking a new chief executive:

We wanted someone who really understood Ontario child welfare, who had their roots in the system, for whom running the agency would be a passion and not just a job. He or she had to be capable, able to work with staff, foster parents, the government, the press, with everyone regardless of their political stripe, regardless of whether they were union people or senior managers. We got that person when we hired Bruce Rivers.

In September 1988, Bruce Rivers assumed responsibility for directing what, by that time, had become the largest board-operated child welfare agency in North America. Metro CAS had an annual budget of more than $50 million, a staff of 700, four hundred foster homes and 1,000 volunteers. Rivers had worked almost exclusively at Metro CAS since earning his MSW degree in 1976, first as a front-line worker and then in a series of management positions of increasing responsibility. For the three years before he became the society's executive director, he had been the director of service at Metro's Catholic CAS.

The board's appointment of Rivers to the top job at Metro CAS was strongly supported by the agency's staff and by foster parents, with whom he had earned significant credibility during his years as a worker and manager. They recognized him as a good administrator, found him personable and approachable and knew he was a person who cared about people and who put the needs of children first.

The board's appointment of Bruce Rivers to the top job at Metro CAS was strongly supported by the agency's staff and by foster parents, with whom he had earned significant credibility during his years as a worker and manager.

Metro CAS in the Nineties

As described in Chapter 7, a number of events during the 1980s caused the relationship between Metro CAS and MCSS, the agency's principal funder, to deteriorate. At the same time, there had been much debate within the society about the direction the agency should be taking, both to meet the needs of children and families and to provide staff with necessary resources and good working conditions, in lean economic times. One of Bruce Rivers' first initiatives as executive director — with the support of the board under presidents Barry Brace and

The validation the society received from a pair of reviews of its work demonstrated that the agency was able to weather difficult times, such as those it had experienced during the recent past, while maintaining high standards.

With its faith renewed in its historical values of sound management, innovative programming and dedicated staff, foster parents and volunteers, the society went about developing a vision to guide its operations over the succeeding five years.

Chris Stringer   was to address these issues by developing a vision for Metro CAS in the 1990s.

In 1989, a review of the society's operations had been jointly undertaken with MCSS, and it outlined the agency's strengths while identifying areas that required further work. Meanwhile, the society had received a certificate of accreditation from the Council on Accreditation, a body sponsored by 540 North American family service agencies. This endorsement confirmed that the agency was conducting its operations effectively and managing its funds wisely. The validation the society received from these two reviews demonstrated that the agency was able to weather difficult times, such as those it had experienced during the recent past, while maintaining high standards.

With its faith renewed in its historical values of sound management, innovative programming and dedicated staff, foster parents and volunteers, the society went about developing a vision to guide its operations over the succeeding five years. The process was based on building consensus among children in care, families served by the agency, staff, foster parents, volunteers, board members, funders and community organizations.

The outcome was the long-range plan of 1990, which comprised new mission and values statements as well as five long-range goals that were to be used as a framework for both strategic planning and day-to-day activities. At the same time, a new code of ethics to govern the actions of board members, staff, foster parents and volunteers was introduced.

The new mission statement committed the society to protecting children from emotional, sexual and physical harm by working with individual children and their families in the community; providing a high standard and continuity of substitute parental care and relationships for those children who cannot remain at home; and developing, in partnership with others, prevention programs that encourage healthy and positive relationships among children and families in the community. All this was to be undertaken in a climate of dignity, integrity and respect for individual differences.

The values statement addressed the primacy of the child's needs above all other considerations; continuity of care for children in both service and placement; supportive teamwork and partnership, recognizing the contribution of all who provide and support service to children and families; and leadership and advocacy in developing solutions to child welfare issues.

The five long-range goals included clarifying the society's prevention and preventive roles; developing and implementing strategies that supported a positive work environment; responding to complex issues that affected service delivery, notably more proactive race relations; resolving funding issues; and developing effective relations between the society, governments and the broader community.

Board members, management and front-line staff, foster parents and volunteers all worked hard to implement the new mission and values statements and the long-range goals. Some examples of their achievements are described below.

Funding and service challenges of the early 1990s

At the beginning of the 1990s, as the economic climate worsened, Metro CAS became increasingly concerned about the erosion of its capacity to serve children and families adequately. Despite an accumulated deficit of almost $2.5 million, demands for the agency to expand its services were increasing due to the recession and the growing complexity and urgency of the problems experienced by many families.

Despite an accumulated deficit of almost $2.5 million, demands for the agency to expand its services were increasing due to the recession and the growing complexity and urgency of the problems experienced by many families.

Eighty-three percent of those served by the society lived at or below the poverty line, an indicator of the stress that economic disadvantage placed on family life, compromising parenting ability and increasing the risk to children. A lack of adequate housing was a factor in 18 percent of the situations that led to the admission of a child to the agency's care. While frequent cocaine use was reported in less than one percent of Metro Toronto's population, approximately 12 percent of families who came to the society's attention were harmed in some way by the abuse of this drug. Violence in the community, and within families, was growing steadily, with child abuse a feature in the lives of more than one-third of the families receiving agency services.

Workers were becoming concerned not only about the conditions under which many of their clients had to live but also about their own high caseloads and their personal safety in the community. A typical worker handled a caseload of twenty-six to thirty, while some were responsible for even more. Threatened and actual assaults to workers as they went about their day-to-day tasks were not uncommon. These issues would often leave staff anxious and overwhelmed, causing them to suffer personal stress and increasing the risk of burnout and high employee turnover. At the same time, the increasing size and diversity of Metro Toronto's many racial, ethnic and cultural communities added to the pressure for knowledgeable workers and specific programming to meet their specialized needs.

The agency embarked on an advocacy campaign based on the belief that services to children and families needed to receive first call on government resources.

In the face of these challenges, the board and staff worked to make the best use of limited resources, although not without concern that program reductions in response to financial restraint would affect the scope of services the society was able to offer. Concurrent with these efforts, therefore, the agency embarked on an advocacy campaign — organized by Sharron Richards, its child welfare advocate — based on the belief that services to children and families needed to receive first call on government resources.

Politicians and MCSS staff were lobbied, not only by executive director Bruce Rivers and board president Bob Witterick, but also by Steve Lowden, a board member of the CAS Foundation; Askari Hussein, a youth in care; foster parent Sheila Dowdall; and Gina Gignac, the president of CUPE Local 2316, representing the society's unionized employees. They spoke of the challenges they faced daily — poverty, homelessness, substance abuse, family violence, child abuse — and the increased difficulty and expense of finding suitable placements for children in the agency's care, one-third of whom had to be placed in beds outside Metro Toronto because suitable homes could not be found for them in the city.

They also proposed solutions that, through a more creative and flexible use of funding, would allow for both an expansion of foster care as well as a greater emphasis on early intervention and family preservation programs. Such programs would enable children to remain with their families while the agency worked with them to solve their problems.

The campaign was a novel one for a social service organization at that time in that it involved key government, political and business leaders. Although it did not result in the provision of additional resources, it did lead to the development of a new funding formula that offered CASs across the province the chance to refocus their programs to better meet the needs of the children and families they were serving.

Not long afterward, however, the society was subjected to the government's expenditure control plan under the so-called Social Contract described at the beginning of this chapter. Under this plan the agency was required to cut its annual spending — which then amounted to more than $70 million — by $1.5 million a year over three years. The theme was not new, but coming on the heels of several years of fiscal restraint, the level of desperation it created in the face of increasing service needs was considerable.

The society was, however, able to weather the tough times through exceptional leadership and the collective dedication of its committed board members, staff, foster parents and volunteers.

Tony Quan, the society's director of finance and administration, and his team of accountants battled incredibly long odds to balance the agency's budget while providing staff with information about the organization's financial situation. This contrasted sharply with previous eras, as Sybil Smith recalls:

> Staff today are very much aware of issues with the province, with the agency's budget, because Bruce [Rivers], Carolyn [Buck] and Tony [Quan] made sure that there was a flow of information and consultation with staff about these issues. This contrasts sharply with thirty years ago, when we as workers came in and did our jobs as best we could, in good times or bad, but without the slightest idea of what the challenges were in running the agency or what the budget was or how the money was spent.

Despite the difficult financial challenges of the 1990s, the board and senior managers of the society encouraged innovation and creativity and strategized with the agency's funders on how best to provide long-term benefits for the children and families the organization serves. According to associate executive director Carolyn Buck, "This is why the society stands out as a child welfare flagship."

Despite the difficult financial challenges of the 1990s, the society's board and senior managers encouraged innovation and creativity and strategized with its funders on how best to provide long-term benefits for children and families.

Early intervention and prevention

Four innovative examples of the early intervention and prevention programs started at this time are Family Builders, Babies Best Start, the Family Resource Centre and day treatment programs.

Modelled on the American Behavioral Sciences Institute's Homebuilders Program and undertaken in partnership with the Catholic CAS, Family Builders was a crisis intervention project and family preservation program aimed at preventing children from being removed from their families and placed in CAS care. It helped parents resolve crises, assess problems and explore options.

For each family in the program, society workers delivered an intensive, short-term, home- and community-based crisis intervention and family education service over a four- to six-week period, for up to twenty hours a week. Families set their own goals and, by building on their strengths, workers helped them achieve those goals. Each worker typically delivered services to two families at a time, and was available twenty-four hours a day, seven days a week for emergencies.

As an example of the program's work, its former manager, Joan Davis, recalls the comments of one mother and her son:

> The child perceived the goals to be worked on as "bed time and me and my brother going places." He wrote that "we learned a lot, like not to fight and to go to bed at the right time." His perception of what he did differently was, "I go to bed at ten and I don't fight and get mad." His mother's ideas about the most useful things the family worked on were "how to handle and discipline the children together and make my husband a gentleman." Skills she learned and said she would continue to use were "being firm with the kids, listening to my husband and not fighting with him or screaming very often."

Babies Best Start, set up with a grant from the CAS Foundation but subsequently funded through grants from Human Resources Development Canada, focused on early intervention and community involvement to support vulnerable

Family Builders was a crisis intervention project and family preservation program aimed at preventing children from being removed from their families and placed in CAS care.

Babies Best Start focused on early intervention and community involvement to support vulnerable children under five years of age and their mothers.

children under five years of age and their mothers. Supervised by society nurse practitioner Brenda Pickup, the program was, and is, based on volunteer home visitors who, because of their own abilities as parents, were able to pass on these skills to other mothers. The peer approach worked because it brought together women of similar backgrounds, language and culture.

Khadija Ahmed, a home visitor and an immigrant from Somalia, recalled her concern over help that many migrants from North Africa, particularly Somalia and Ethiopia, desperately needed to adjust to a new culture, language and climate: "Back home, a child is wrapped in a blanket when he has a fever. They don't know about medicines that help to bring the fever down."

Mahes Parameswaran remembered how, in Sri Lanka, oil was rubbed on a baby's skin and then the child was left out in the sun during the morning hours. "We had to tell new families to Canada that Canadian doctors tell us that this is not good for the baby," she said.

The home visitors took an initial forty-two hours of training before being assigned as volunteers. They then continued to meet every two weeks for instruction on nutrition, heath, infant development, behaviour and discipline. During this time, the women would also gather to discuss any problems or difficulties they may have had reaching out to a particular mother or family. Pickup was available for consultation and support. She adds:

> Since its founding, the program, now sponsored by Aisling Discoveries Child and Family Centre, has reached over 2,000 parents and their children. Today, it employs forty-five women, all community parents, speaking over thirty different languages and actively supports 500 families, mostly newcomers to Canada.

Another prevention program was the Family Resource Centre, which offered a place for children in the short-term care of the society to visit with their parents in a home-like setting. These mothers and fathers, in turn, were supported by the centre's staff to learn positive parenting techniques. Former program coordinator Sue Hansford recalls:

The Family Resource Centre offered a place for children in the short-term care of the society to visit with their parents in a home-like setting. These mothers and fathers, in turn, were supported by the centre's staff to learn positive parenting techniques.

A number of young mothers participated in regular visits at the centre, anywhere from three to five days per week. It provided an excellent opportunity for us to assess their parenting skills and capabilities along with providing ongoing support and teaching assistance.

A number of parents who attended the centre were working to combat addiction to drugs or alcohol, which hindered their ability to care for their children on a regular and predictable basis. Hansford remembers the visits of one such mother:

> She visited her infant regularly at the centre before we felt comfortable allowing visits in the family home. She told us that it was helpful to have someone to turn to, someone who would listen about her addiction problems. Having help with infant care was a relief to her and she appreciated the assistance she received in learning how to care for her baby.

In the 1990s the agency established two day treatment programs, aimed at preventing the admission of children to residential or foster care and to help children who had spent time in such care to rejoin their families.

As an outgrowth of the alternate care programs described earlier in this book, in the 1990s the agency established two day treatment programs. Located in former admission-assessment residences, they offered children and their families a combination of individual counselling and group programming along with an on-site classroom. The primary goal was to prevent the need to admit children to residential or foster care and to help those children who had spent time in such care to rejoin their families. The program was also designed to help prevent foster care placements from breaking down.

Primary prevention through community development

The society's community work program maintained its commitment to primary prevention initiatives that reduced the incidence of child abuse and neglect. It did this through identifying issues, advocacy and by helping communities develop local services for children and families.

The newly flexible funding formula allowed the society's community work program, which celebrated its thirtieth anniversary in 1998, to maintain its commitment to primary prevention initiatives that reduced the incidence of child abuse and neglect. It did this through identifying issues, advocacy and by helping communities develop local support services for children and families. The program also addressed the social and economic inequalities that placed children, families and communities at risk. Much of this work was supported by the social and child welfare policy committee of the board of directors, which continued the society's long tradition of activism on social policy issues that affect the lives of the agency's clients.

One of these communities was Swansea Mews, a 150-unit public housing project located in the city's west end. Built in the 1970s, the project was designed to avoid both the dense concentrations of low-income families that were prevalent in housing projects elsewhere in the city and the related challenges that could develop from such concentration.

Over the years, Metro CAS community workers had provided support to the Swansea Mews community, by organizing the tenants, fundraising and addressing issues such as racism, financial deficits and lack of resources. Community worker Ken Sosa remembers some of the programs he helped organize:

> The Youth Counselling Project was one of the Swansea Mews community's great successes. As a result of the project, there was a reduction in vandalism and youth in conflict with the law. There was an increase in the number of children and youth who participated in dramatic arts, entrepreneurial activities and city-wide recreational competitions. Another project was the development of a basketball program and a "just for girls" program. All of these community activities were designed to help children and youth develop self-confidence and feel part of a community that cared about their well-being and supported their development.

Throughout the 1990s, another of the society's community workers, Ann Fitzpatrick, worked full-time to try to increase support for affordable housing for agency clients, including youth leaving the society's care. Another worker, Colin Hughes, devoted his full-time attention to issues related to child poverty. In this capacity, he was the Metro Toronto coordinator for Campaign 2000, the advocacy organization formed after the 1989 House of Commons resolution, mentioned

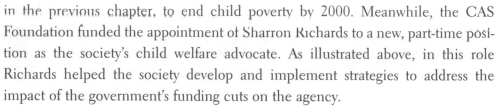

in the previous chapter, to end child poverty by 2000. Meanwhile, the CAS Foundation funded the appointment of Sharron Richards to a new, part-time position as the society's child welfare advocate. As illustrated above, in this role Richards helped the society develop and implement strategies to address the impact of the government's funding cuts on the agency.

The community work program has had a significant impact on the growth of community life in Toronto. Many creative projects to support immigrant and refugee children and their families, and low-income children and families, arose from the work of the society's community workers.

The community work program has had a significant impact on the growth of community life in Toronto. Many creative projects to support immigrant and refugee children and their families, and low-income children and families, arose from the work of the society's community workers. They include the Somali Women and Children's Support Network, multiservice agencies such as the Jane-Finch Family and Child Centre and LAMP — the Lakeshore Area Multiservice Program — and community programs like Creating Together, described in Chapter 7.

Community partnerships

Without the support and cooperation of external service providers such as those described above and elsewhere in this book, the society's task of protecting children from emotional, physical and sexual harm would have been next to impossible. The story of the psychiatrist Dr. Paul Steinhauer illustrates the effects of these partnerships.

During a thirty-eight-year career that ended only with his untimely death in 2000, Steinhauer treated children at his own medical practice, was on staff at Toronto's Hospital for Sick Children and was a tireless lobbyist for the rights and welfare of children.

Steinhauer's passion contributed significantly to child welfare practice. He was an insightful board member of the CAS of Toronto. And as a caring foster parent, he researched the needs of children in care and consulted widely with child welfare workers about how best to meet the needs of the children on their caseloads.

Of particular significance, however, was his work in developing tools to assess families and parenting capacity to help workers gather information about all aspects of a family's life. Family service supervisor Lin Brough describes the tools as: "A detailed map of patterns within a family that allow workers to predict a par-

Dr. Paul Steinhauer

ent's ability to nurture children. They ensure that assessments are comprehensive and allow workers to be objective in their view of families."

Steinhauer's death left a wide gap in research and advocacy for children in Ontario. The legacy of his work, however, will benefit children for years to come.

Of particular significance was Paul Steinhauer's work in developing tools to assess families and parenting capacity to help workers gather information about all aspects of a family's life.

Young people at risk: homeless and runaway youth

As was highlighted at the beginning of this chapter, during the 1990s young people were among those most at risk of becoming homeless. Forty-six percent of shelter users in Metro Toronto were children and their parents, while many thousands of teenagers and young adults survived as best they could on the city's streets. Many were under sixteen years old, and were often runaways from CAS care.

There were many reasons these young people found themselves in this situation, including family neglect, conflict and rejection as well as physical and sexual abuse. To them, street life seemed safer than life with their families, most of whom had had a long history of unsuccessful involvement with CAS workers and other professionals. To meet their survival needs, however, these street-involved youth were forced into illegal or undesirable sources of income, making them prime targets for exploitation. Threats to their health and safety were characteristic of the lives they led.

There were many reasons why young people became homeless, including family neglect, conflict and rejection as well as physical and sexual abuse.

Society staff were challenged to respond to the needs of these young people, many of whom, because of their experiences, found it hard to trust adults, particularly child welfare workers and others in positions of authority. As one participant in a Metro CAS focus group said:

> Fourteen different CAS placements have a devastating effect on kids like me. Once you go through it you feel not cared about, and you think, what the f— —, why not live on the street — the people on the street care, my family doesn't.

In 1985, the society had established the Toronto Street Youth Program, described in the previous chapter, for youth engaged in prostitution, one of the survival techniques adopted by some street-involved youth. While this program was able to meet the needs of many such young people, it was unsuitable for the majority of homeless and runaway youth who were not drawn into the sex trade.

While older homeless youth could depend on the shelter system, it was not an option for youth under the age of sixteen who refused to be admitted to or stay in traditional CAS care. For them, the society tried to set up a designated emergency shelter to which a young person could be admitted on his or her own request without the need for parental permission or the order of a judge.

While older homeless youth could depend on the shelter system, it was not an option for youth under the age of sixteen who refused to be admitted to or stay in traditional CAS care. For them, the society tried to set up a designated emergency shelter to which a young person could be admitted on his or her own request without the need for parental permission or the order of a judge. However, the legal obstacles to open such a shelter proved insurmountable.

Outreach and drop-in services seemed to provide a more workable solution, which is why, in 1994, Metro CAS agreed to cooperate with community agencies that worked with the older population of street-involved youth to provide protective services to runaways under sixteen years old. Research had shown that these youth were more likely to trust a worker from one of those agencies rather than one from the CAS. Jason's story, told in the agency newspaper *Communicate* — which had replaced the journal *Our Children* in 1989 — illustrates the success of this approach:

> Fourteen-year old Jason regularly "bounced" between his mother's home, CAS care and the street. He is difficult to work with because he routinely misses appointments with his worker. He was on the run for two months, living on the streets and surviving by his wits.
>
> Recently robbed and beaten, he refused to report this to the police for fear they would return him to the CAS. He told a nurse at the street health clinic, where he went to seek treatment for his injuries, that he planned to go to Vancouver for the winter. The nurse tried to help him consider more constructive alternatives. Jason trusted her because his peers had told him that she would not immediately pick up the phone to call the CAS.
>
> A week later, Jason returned to the clinic and asked the nurse to negotiate his return to his mother's place. Jason spent the winter safely at home rather than on the streets of Vancouver.

Young people at risk: lesbian, gay and bisexual youth

Research had shown that a disproportionate number of homeless and runaway youth were lesbian, gay or bisexual. Despite the more permissive climate of Metro Toronto at the end of the twentieth century, the effects upon these young people of growing up lesbian or gay were devastating. Not only did they have to survive the turmoil of adolescence, but they also had to develop a positive identity in the face of the overwhelming potential for discrimination. Like their non-gay peers, they too learned the myths and stereotypes about homosexuality that were still prevalent in society. They risked rejection from loved ones while trying to find a place in the world that, at best, gave no guidance, and at worst, said it did not want them because they were sick, immoral or sinful.

The negative stereotyping of lesbian and gay people took its toll on these youths' self-esteem. Unlike other minority youth, they often discovered that home or CAS foster care was no refuge from prejudice or discrimination. They quickly learned to survive in hostile environments by hiding or denying their true identities. This invisibility came at great cost to their well-being and social development: lesbian and gay youth tended to leave home and school prematurely and were up to five times more likely than their peers to attempt suicide.

Diane, a seventeen-year-old Crown ward, described her all-too-common experience:

> I wrote this poem to my best friend at school, which was my way of letting her know that I loved her. My teacher found it and told my worker. The staff at the group home told me that I mustn't talk about these things, even though the other girls talked about boys all the time. I was told my issues were unimportant and were not to be discussed. I really think that by silencing me they thought it would go away. I got really angry when my worker kept asking me if I was sure I was a lesbian, like I had to justify who I am.

This poster is displayed at all CAS of Toronto branches. Created by a young artist, it represents the agency's commitment to a gay-positive environment.

Lesbian and gay youth tended to leave home and school prematurely and were up to five times more likely than their peers to attempt suicide.

The agency established the Lesbian, Gay and Bisexual Youth Project. It worked to identify systemic barriers within the agency that prevented it from meeting the needs of these youth and to recommend practice, policy and administrative changes.

In the early 1990s, the society acknowledged that it needed to do a better job of meeting the needs of young people like Diane. With the help of a grant from the CAS Foundation and a steering committee led by John McCullagh and comprising staff, foster parents, community organizations and youth, the agency established the Lesbian, Gay and Bisexual Youth Project. It worked to identify systemic barriers within the agency that prevented it from meeting the needs of these youth and to recommend practice, policy and administrative changes.

In 1995, the society's board approved more than thirty recommendations made in the committee's groundbreaking report, *We Are Your Children Too*, and Metro CAS was recognized as the North American leader in the provision of accessible child welfare services to lesbian, gay and bisexual youth. Among other things, it led to the development of best-practice standards and specialized training for staff, foster parents and volunteers, the opening of a dedicated LIFE house for lesbian, gay and bisexual youth, and a greater sense of inclusion in the agency's programs and services for these youth.

As one youth commented, the agency's new openness made him feel safe to come out as a gay person: "You need to feel that someone still cares for you, that your life [as a gay person] can be normal and that it's okay to be afraid that it may not be."

In 1998, three years after the board adopted the recommendations contained in *We Are Your Children Too*, it passed a sexuality policy that promoted healthy sexuality and sexual expression among the agency's children and youth. The policy was launched at a forum where Sue Johansen, a popular television and radio host of programs for young adults on issues related to sexuality, spoke to about 150 youth, staff and foster parents about the kind of sex education young people wanted. An early outcome of the policy was a youth relationships project that educated young people about violence toward women and helped them to develop beneficial relationship skills. It was featured in a television documentary broadcast by the Life Network.

Child welfare practice in a diverse community

As illustrated by Metro CAS's commitment to inclusiveness in its services to lesbian, gay and bisexual clients, the agency in this era strove constantly to meet the challenge that diversity posed in serving to the many different communities in Metro Toronto. Executive director Bruce Rivers defined this challenge in terms of equity and access:

> As an organization, we are committed to the proactive develop-
> ment of programs designed to address racism, immigration, con-
> nection to family and adjustment to Canada.

As the earlier chapters of this book illustrate, the agency did not arrive at this position overnight. It started in the 1970s with an in-depth internal assessment by the society's board and staff, after which the agency reached out to various communities with in hopes of convincing them that their input would be valuable and acted upon.

According to Angela King, the supervisor of a community-based service team in Toronto West Branch and an expert in the provision of culturally sensitive child welfare services:

> The outcome was a policy and an action plan that covered every
> aspect of service. This has grown and developed over the years so that
> now we have a code of ethics that values the inherent worth of each
> individual and which includes a commitment to the removal of all
> barriers to equal opportunity. We also have a policy that ensures that
> all who receive or provide agency services are free from discrimina-
> tion and harassment. All staff, foster parents and volunteers are
> offered the opportunity to learn about and to understand other cul-
> tures and issues associated with racism. The objective is to ensure that
> culturally competent practices are integrated into our work.

"The objective is to ensure that culturally competent practices are integrated into our work."
— Angela King

This attempt to be more representative of the communities the society served was reflected in the composition of the board of directors, staff, foster parents and

The agency's services became more accessible to minority communities and went beyond serving clients in their own languages to establishing links with those communities.

volunteers. The agency's services became more accessible to minority communities and went beyond serving clients in their own languages to establishing links with those communities. The society to built bridges by cooperating closely with such groups such as the Vietnamese Association, the Afgan Women's Organization, Chinese Family Life Services and many others. According to King, "The key to success is learning to share power with communities by involving them in our work and by getting their input into policy development."

One example of this approach was the agency's effort to build partnerships with the Muslim community. A Muslim outreach group, consisting of community representatives, CAS staff and foster parents, was established in 1993, when the society's statistics indicated it was working with almost 300 Muslim families. Many were new immigrants or refugees struggling to adapt to a new country and culture. The children of these families often wanted to participate in activities and coeducational programs that stood in sharp contrast to what traditionally would have been acceptable in Muslim communities. Family conflict often arose as a result, and CAS workers sometimes had to get involved.

While these CAS workers had to fulfil their legislated responsibilities to protect children from abuse and neglect, providing service that was both helpful and respectful of Muslim beliefs was equally as important. The outreach group developed training workshops — which included presentations on Islam and Muslim culture as well as panel discussions on working with Muslim families — for agency staff and foster parents. Community members, in turn, participated in workshops on child welfare issues from a cultural perspective.

The process of building partnerships with Metro Toronto's many racial, ethnic and cultural communities led eventually to the launch in 1998 of the Bridging Diversity Project. With the help of the CAS Foundation, the project was intended to help the society engage various ethnic, racial and cultural groups in a two-way learning process about child protection. It was hoped that, in addition to increasing knowledge of the values, customs, religion and culture of Metro's many and diverse communities, the project would generate a broader base from which to recruit staff, foster parents and volunteers.

Growing up in care

Looking after Crown wards, children and youth who are in the permanent care of the agency represents a significant responsibility for Metro CAS. In the 1990s, their numbers represented about 40 percent of the approximately 2,500 young people in the society's care.

The agency believed that it was important to recognize these young people's achievements, which were often made in the face of significant challenges. That is why in 1996 the society held, at a downtown hotel, its first annual recognition night for those who were turning twenty-one years of age and had been in the agency's long-term care. Some travelled long distances to attend, and many brought guests who included birth parents, foster parents, siblings, partners and co-workers.

The atmosphere was that of a family gathering for a special event. There were greetings from board president Marjorie Perkins, a buffet dinner, recognition of youth by Margaret Leitenberger, the director of long-term care, and a special acknowledgment by executive director Bruce Rivers of those youth who were pursuing postsecondary education.

The growth and progress the young people had made despite the challenges of being in care was a common theme throughout the speeches. Each youth received a certificate of recognition. Those in attendance were moved as they watched the youths walk up to the stage with their heads held high to receive their certificates.

One of the youth being recognized commented:

> This evening made me feel good about being part of the CAS organization and I would like to thank all staff for their continuous efforts to help the youth of Toronto. The recognition that I received tonight has given me motivation to move on to many more great achievements. Thanks to all the staff for providing me with the necessary support and services when I needed them.

Increasingly, many of these young people began to speak publicly about their experiences in care. One example is the 1993 broadcast on TV Ontario of a video

SPEAK OUT

An Anthology of Stories by
Youth in Care

Edited and with an Introduction by
Michael Fay

In 1996 the society held its first annual recognition night for those who were turning twenty-one years of age and had been in the agency's long-term care.

"Thanks to all the staff for providing me with the necessary support and services when I needed them."
— Youth graduate

adaptation of *Speak Out*, a 170-page anthology of stories written by thirty youth from PARC, the agency program that helps its adolescent wards make a successful transition to independence.

The anthology had been published with the help of the CAS Foundation four years earlier. It was full of compelling stories by young people in the agency's care about such issues that had affected them as child abuse, poverty, neglect and family misfortune. Mark's story was not untypical:

> The time it happened was mid-'85 and I was 15. My mother was put in the hospital and I was left with the apartment. At the same time, I felt mixed up, like if I was part of a juggling act. What am I going to do with my life at 15? What's going to happen? Is my mother going to make it? What am I going to do with the apartment?
>
> My mother had bought a few things even though she didn't have enough money in the bank to pay for them. So I looked at them … and I looked at the apartment and something came over me about destroying the things that she'd bought. I was [upset] about what was going on and I took my anger and frustration out on the apartment and on what my mother had bought.
>
> And then, somehow, I brought myself to a standstill, went into my bedroom to calm down, relax, cry a little and get myself together, take myself out of the apartment and leave. Four months later, my mother died.

On another occasion, a group of PARC youth met with Premier Rae to discuss the needs of youth who had experienced the child welfare system. They told him of their concerns that children in care were often passed from one worker to another, and from one foster home to another, without involving them in the decision-making process. Rae supported their concerns, which were among those the society addressed in a new model of service, known as Continuity of Care and Relationships and Integration.

Continuity of Care

The Continuity of Care service model was introduced across the society in 1994. It owed much to the insight, leadership and vision of Carolyn Buck, then the agency's director of services. In a powerful speech to staff, Buck explained the thinking that led to the change:

> Our service delivery system was designed at a time when foster homes were plentiful, community programs were fewer, staffing was hierarchal and stable, clients were less diverse and powerless to speak for themselves and the authority wielded by the agency was virtually unchallenged.
>
> The world has changed dramatically … and the issues facing Toronto's children and families are [now] different and more complex than those of the past. While we have grappled with the consequences of these issues and have succeeded in sporadic or local responses to them, with the exception of addressing the issue of sexual abuse most of our new programs are not universal and therefore equal access has become a serious problem.
>
> Our programs vary from branch to branch, often with a differing philosophical basis and differing methods of service delivery. It is not a given, therefore, that a client in one part of the city would receive equivalent service in another part of the city. We have also tended to respond to issues by creating a new rule or set of procedures. The result is the disempowerment of both our professional staff and our clients.

The new model, the result of an extensive and participatory planning process that involved staff, foster parents, volunteers and adult clients and children in care, sought to involve children and families in the service decisions that affected them. Foster parents were to be equal members of the service team, and their role would

The new service model, which was the result of an extensive and participatory planning process that involved staff, foster parents, volunteers and adult clients and children in care, sought to involve children and families in the service decisions that affected them.

expand to include significant therapeutic work, not only with the child but also with his or her family.

Under the new model, the society's programs were to be coordinated internally and complemented by those of external service providers. Given the complexity of the problems faced by the children and families with whom the agency worked, teamwork would be a major component of the new approach to service delivery; an isolated approach was no longer relevant nor cost-effective.

The agency undertook a massive restructuring that involved new job descriptions, new teams and new office locations for most staff; community-based service teams were established, as was a specialized branch for children in the agency's long-term care. A higher profile was to be given to the agency's clinical, research and prevention efforts.

A foster care resources branch was established to develop, maintain, train and support foster families in their work.

The society's foster care programs were an integral part of this reorganization. A foster care resources branch was established to develop, maintain, train and support foster families in their work. Homefinding and assessment would be delivered by an integrated team of staff, foster parents and volunteers. Foster care support workers would directly support foster homes but would not be responsible for the children in the homes; the children would be served by their own worker, who would follow them if they had to move to another foster home or a residential placement. Foster homes and their support workers would be clustered by region and would meet regularly for training, information sharing and mutual assistance.

At the same time as the agency introduced this new service model, the board of directors engaged in an in-depth evaluation of the society's governance structure, and decided to reduce the number of board members from twenty-six to nineteen and the number of board committees from twelve to five. The Board established a critical success factor reporting system to focus on outcome and achievement related to the Society's long-range goals.

Fostering for Metro CAS

During the 1990s, the number of families who fostered children in the society's care fluctuated widely (and in 1991 reached a low of 352), as homes constantly closed and new ones opened in their place. At the same time, there was an increase in the number of children placed in foster homes. In 1988, for example, foster parents looked after 895 children; by 1994, those numbers had increased to 1,097.

According to Peter Hagerdoorn, for many years the assistant manager of foster care for the society, there were many reasons why foster care recruitment was a challenge in the final years of the twentieth century:

> Mainly it was economic. Housing in Toronto was expensive and starter homes were often beyond the reach of those young families that used to make good beginning foster parents. We also lost many prospective foster parents to day care and privately operated homes because we couldn't compete with their rates. Compounding these difficulties was the fact that children in foster care needed increasingly specialized services and we required foster parents with increasingly specialized skills to care for them. People who used to open their homes because they had "room for one more" now found that that was not enough.

The Continuity of Care restructuring process described above, which led to a greater emphasis on strengthening the level of support provided to foster families, was one way the agency tried to address this problem. Another was an effort between Metro CAS, Catholic CAS, Jewish Family and Child Service and the CASs in the outlying regions of Simcoe, Durham, Halton, York and Peel to work together to redesign the way foster care services were to be provided. The idea was to develop and manage foster care on a regional basis and erase the distinction that traditionally had been made between "our" foster homes and "their" foster homes and "our" children and "their" children.

Joe and Wilma Wrabko receive the Child Welfare League of Canada's Foster Parents Leadership Award from Sandra Scarth, then the league's executive director.

"People who used to open their homes because they had "room for one more" now found that that was not enough."
— Peter Hagerdoorn on the challenge of foster care recruitment

*The Looking After Children system was developed
in Britain to assess and meet the needs of children
in out-of-home care.*

At the same time, the society participated in a pilot of the Looking After Children system developed in Britain to assess and meet the needs of children in out-of-home care. This program aimed to encourage greater collaboration among child welfare staff, foster parents and other care providers to put the concept of good parenting into practice in areas such as health, education, identity, family and social relationships, emotional and behavioural development and self-care skills.

Despite the increased emphasis on professionalism, however, the factors that motivated families in the 1990s to welcome foster children into their homes had changed little from the impulses that drove those whom Vera Moberly had recruited for the Infants' Home eighty years before. For Betty Luff's family, it was the love of children.

> That's why we started fostering, and because we love kids we felt we could do something to help families by providing a temporary home for their children. Little did we know fostering would become a way of life for us. We find fostering rewarding and challenging. It is never easy when you are saying goodbye. Our reward is knowing a family is back together or an adopting family has someone special to share their lives with.

For Imelda Ayres it was because:

> We had one child in school and were not planning to have any more children. My husband had a good job so I didn't really have to go to work. I had a fair amount of spare time, and I like small children, so we thought we should try fostering and see if we could make some contribution to society, especially small children in need of love and care.

The motivation for Sharon Beck, vice president of the society's Foster Parent Association (FPA) during the 1990s, was to make a difference in the lives of children who come into her home.

I really enjoy watching premature and failure-to-thrive babies begin to develop. It's also very rewarding to see children who are behaviourally out of control come around. But fostering is not without its challenges and heartaches, separation being one of the most difficult. When a young child returns home or is adopted by a permanent family, it places everyone in the family on an emotional roller coaster. Foster parenting also requires more than just parenting. Individuals are called upon to work with a great many staff from across the agency and often with a foster child's birth family. We attend meetings and assist in planning the care of children for whom we are responsible.

Wilma Wrabko became a legend among those who fostered children for Metro CAS. Not only was she the long-time president of the FPA but, along with her husband Joe, she also found time to care for more than 100 children in a fostering career than spanned thirty-five years. One of those children was Jackie, who was placed with the Wrabkos when she was nineteen months old, straight from the Hospital for Sick Children. Twenty-four years later, she is still part of their family. As Wrabko explains:

> Jackie was diagnosed as developmentally delayed and possibly autistic. She spent her time in hospital lying in the fetal position and she never made eye contact with her caregivers. Medical people at that time worried that the child had made a decision not to survive.
>
> However, survive she did. She began to respond to the care and stimulation we provided. We taught her sign language, but eventually she learned to speak. There was no turning back. She succeeded in school. She developed the capacity to form enduring relationships. With support, she had developed her personal self-care and self-management skills, although she will always need guidance in those areas. She is skilled in the use of a computer.

Sharon Beck and her family.

"Fostering is not without its challenges and heartaches, separation being one of the most difficult."

— Sharon Beck

We are grateful for the help we have received in caring for Jackie over the years. But most importantly, we are proud of the gains she has made and continues to make. As we like to say, "Foster Care works!"

Adoption in the 1990s

During the 1990s, Metro CAS completed an average of about seventy-five adoptions a year. While most were infants or older children with special needs, and several were children adopted by their long-term foster parents, newborns placed for adoption in this era usually came to the society's attention through its Pregnancy and Aftercare (PAC) Program.

This voluntary counselling and referral service helped expectant parents to make decisions about a pregnancy. Without coercion or attempting to influence the outcome, PAC workers would assist them to decide whether or not they would parent the child, place the child for adoption or terminate the pregnancy, after which they would help the parents follow through with the decisions they had made.

Adoption practices in this era moved more and more toward openness, with the birth parents encouraged to become involved in the selection of an adoptive family for their child.

Adoption practices in this era moved more and more toward openness, with the birth parents encouraged to become involved in the selection of an adoptive family for their child. While the identities of both the birth and adoptive parents were protected, birth parents increasingly began to attend the adoption placement conference and to participate in the process of selection.

As knowledge about the needs of adoptees grew, there was a growing acceptance of the importance of providing them with information about their birth family and the circumstances of their adoption. Life books (a record of an adopted child's life that uses words, photos and graphics and that contains the child's artwork and other memorabilia), letters, exchanges of photos, and so on, all became commonplace.

Life books (a record of an adopted child's life that uses words, photos and graphics and that contains the child's artwork and other memorabilia), letters, exchanges of photos, and so on, all became commonplace.

The Continuity of Care model of teamwork and cooperation extended to work between foster parents and adoptive parents. All but one of Linda and her husband's four children were in foster care prior to their adoption. In a tribute to these foster parents "who cared for our children before they were ours," Linda wrote:

It would have been easy to forget about our children's foster parents. So why didn't we? The answer is quite simple. They are good people. They are our link to our children's past. They once cared for and loved our children as we do now. We gladly offer news of our children's development, accomplishments and milestones to these special people who truly share our joy. It is a foster parent's reward for their labour of love. It is an adoptive parent's way of saying thank you.

As the decade progressed, it became ever more challenging to find suitable foster and adoptive families for the young people in the society's care. To broaden the number of potential homes for children awaiting placements, the society placed more and more of them with single-parent families or with those who were middle-aged — in the past, such applicants would likely have been considered unsuitable to become adoptive or foster parents. In 1994, the agency also invited same-sex couples to apply to become foster parents, taking the position that sexual orientation should not be an obstacle to their being considered as adoptive or foster parents.

Although these decisions about same-sex fostering and adoption were very controversial, they followed two years of study and reflection by a broad-based board and staff committee that considered independent research, reviewed the literature and sought input from external experts. The leadership taken on this issue by the board's president, the prominent businessman Jack Darville, was crucial to the agency's decision to acknowledge that sexual orientation had nothing to do with parental competence, and that gay men and lesbians were as capable as anyone else of being good parents.

Significantly, the society's board made its decision on same-sex adoption on the same day that the provincial legislature voted not to extend the definition of spouse to include same-sex relationships. Although this did not affect the agency's right to place children in approved same-sex foster homes, the vote did mean that it was not yet legal for the society and other adoption agencies to place children with same-sex partners for the purposes of adoption.

The society's advocacy to meet the needs of children by extending the pool of adoptive homes in this way, however, was vindicated five years later, when the gov-

In 1994, the agency invited same-sex couples to apply to become foster parents, taking the position that sexual orientation should not be an obstacle to their being considered as adoptive or foster parents.

Jack Darville, former Board President.

ernment amended Ontario's laws with respect to same-sex couples, changes that included the right to apply to adopt children.

Significantly, the society's board made its decision to support same-sex adoption on the same day that the provincial legislature voted not to extend the definition of spouse to include same-sex relationships.

Volunteering at Metro CAS

Metro CAS began as a volunteer organization, and volunteers have remained a strong component at the society ever since. Joan Berndt joined that illustrious group because:

> I read an appeal on the back of one of the *Our Children* magazines. We had two successful adoptions through the agency and I felt volunteering was a way of thanking the agency. However, I wasn't sure I wanted to work with kids and couldn't drive. As an interior designer, I was unsure about how I could be used. The agency was undaunted, however, and one of my first tasks was helping young moms. I then became a parent aide and then took on other responsibilities with the board of directors.

Joan Berndt, longtime society volunteer.

For Sidney Gordon, "Becoming a volunteer just followed naturally from being retired. The volunteer centre suggested I become a tutor at the CAS. That suggestion has brought me significant satisfaction for many years."

Malcolm McKeil was a young child and youth worker when he started volunteering for the agency: "It provided me with much training and experience that I would have been hard-pressed to get elsewhere. I learned a lot about people, the world and myself through working with the families and staff at CAS."

Before the Second World War, when fewer people drove, volunteers would often chauffeur workers on their regular visits to the homes of clients.

Since the earliest days of the automobile, the society had used volunteer drivers to transport children in care to and from appointments to visit their parents, social workers, doctors and dentists. Before the Second World War, when fewer people drove, these volunteers would also often chauffeur workers on their regular visits to the homes of clients. Organizing the required drives and coordinating them with the available drivers, however, had long been a logistical nightmare.

This is why, in 1991, in a joint initiative with the Catholic CAS, the agency developed an innovative, computer-based transportation management system known as the Children's Aid Amalgamated Transportation System, more commonly referred to by its acronym CAATS.

The challenge facing CAATS was threefold: to combine the volunteer drivers affiliated with both agencies; to change the method for requesting drives from paper to an online computer; and to link each agency's mainframe systems. As CAATS supervisor Enid Freedman remarked, "In those days, computerization was still in its infancy at both Metro and Catholic CASs. For many workers, CAATS was their first experience with a personal computer and to daunting terms such as 'download,' 'network,' 'cursor' and 'field.'"

Although, as with any new technology, CAATS had its share of problems, by 1995 the system was successfully coordinating almost 60,000 drives a year — 65 percent of them on behalf of children in the care of Metro CAS. It made requesting drives for children fast and efficient and lessened the time workers spent on at least one administrative task.

One of the drivers who benefited from this new technology was Valerie Witterick. Over the course of thirty years as a volunteer for Metro CAS, Witterick has been a volunteer driver as well as a special friend to children, a parent aide, a member of numerous committees and president of the board of directors. In 1997, Lieutenant Governor Hilary Weston presented her with Ontario's Volunteer Service Award in recognition of her outstanding voluntary service to the people of Metro Toronto. As former volunteer coordinator Melanie Persaud recalls:

> When one speaks of Valerie Witterick, the word "dynamo" inevitably comes to mind. She is in perpetual motion. Always willing to help at the drop of a hat, she took to wearing a pager so that the clients with whom she worked could reach her when they were in need of support. She embodies the term "community spirit" and it's become a family value. Her husband Bob is an active member with the CAS Foundation and a former board president of the soci-

"For many workers, CAATS was their first experience with a personal computer and to daunting terms such as download, network, cursor and field."
— *Enid Freedman*

Lieutenant Governor Hilary Weston and Valerie Witterick on the cover of the agency newspaper *Communicate*.

ety while her daughter Kathy followed in her mother's footsteps as
a volunteer for the agency.

Looking back to the past and forward to the future

In most respects modern technology came late to Metro CAS. For example, a manual telephone switchboard was still in use until 1987, while by 1991 the agency had deployed only four personal computers.

In 1991, the agency celebrated the 100th anniversary of the founding of the Children's Aid Society of Toronto by J.J. Kelso and his associates. Among the special events that year was a reunion on the shores of Lake Ontario (organized by a committee that included Joan Davis, Jean Fuerd, Jim Clendinning, Mary Hutchings, Sheila McDermott, Ann Parsons, Sharron Richards, Bruce Rivers and Mona Robinson) at which 450 current and former staff, foster parents and volunteers spent an evening of pride, celebration and camaraderie. The guests greeted friends, reminisced, and even met "famous names from the past" — including none other than J.J. himself, brought to life again by former executive director Doug Barr.

The mandate of the agency had not changed in the hundred years since its founding, but by 1996 it was time for Metro CAS to develop a new set of long-range goals that would help define the society's strategic direction for the balance of the century. Board members, staff, foster parents, volunteers and the agency's partners in the community were all consulted in the development of these objectives.

The new goals included ensuring children and families a full range of child welfare services, delivered at the right time and in the right place and with sensitivity to issues of race, ethnicity, culture and religion. Other goals promoted improving the public's understanding of the agency's work, efficient management of its financial resources and effective collaboration with community partners.

Although, as described in Chapter 6, the society had experimented in the 1970s with the use of computer-assisted models to measure agency performance, in most respects modern technology came late to Metro CAS. For example, a manual telephone switchboard was still in use until 1987, while by 1991 the agency had deployed only four personal computers.

Early in his term as executive director, Bruce Rivers recognized the rapid changes technology was bringing to business life, as well as its potential to make the management of not-for-profit social service agencies more efficient. The earlier notion of computers as a mere support system had been surpassed.

In 1993, the society replaced its System 38 mainframe computer with a state-of-the-art IBM AS/400 model that made it possible for the agency to upgrade its financial and accounting systems. By mid-decade, local area networks of personal computers were established, and an e-mail system — with a mailbox for each member of staff — was introduced. Shortly afterward, the society became the first CAS in Ontario to be fully connected to the Internet. This enabled workers to e-mail clients, colleagues and others via the global electronic network, while the agency itself gained a powerful new means of promoting its services though its own Web site.

The most significant development, however, was the agency's introduction, under the leadership of Brian O'Connor, Sam Lee and Corrie Tuyl, of a computerized family service information system and a risk-assessment tool. This simple and elegant technology, developed in-house, helped to influence provincial systems development and revolutionized the way in which our front-line staff managed their work with children and families.

A new direction for the CAS Foundation

The Children's Aid Society of Metropolitan Toronto Foundation, established in 1979 to support child abuse prevention programs not funded by government, had allocated millions of dollars to the society and to programs in the community over the years.

While hundreds of individuals and community groups had been faithful donors to the foundation, it had also formed particularly strong partnerships with the business community. Although some corporations preferred to sustain an individual program or project, many others supported the foundation's work through such special events as the Teddy Bear Affair, a black-tie gala that began in 1986 and became one of the most successful fundraising events in the city.

Teddy Bear Affair.

By the beginning of the period covered by this chapter, the foundation, under its president Sue Bochner, had become a spectacular success. Difficulties, howev-

Staff clown around at Foundation fundraiser.

er, began to emerge in the early 1990s that led to a rift between Metro CAS and the CAS Foundation.

In its early years, the foundation's board had been made up largely of current or former Metro CAS board members, and the relationship between the two organizations was quite informal. A pair of issues brought about an estrangement between the two: the lease of an unsuitable building for the society's North York Branch and the foundation's ambition to take on a more national focus.

In 1990, at the height of a booming real estate market, the foundation sold, for $13 million, the property on Yonge Street in Willowdale that Metro CAS had inherited in 1957 from York CAS and upon which a year later the society had built its North Branch offices. The initial plan was for the foundation to purchase or build new offices to replace those on Yonge Street. However, it proved hard to find an appropriate building or site, which forced staff to move a temporary office in an industrial neighbourhood in Don Mills.

The new location wasn't well suited to the society's work. It was hard to reach, remote from clients and proved to be an unfriendly environment for staff. In lieu of purchasing a new building, the foundation had committed to pay rent for the North York Branch offices, an arrangement that continued throughout the 1990s, although in 1993 the offices were relocated to more suitable premises at 4211 Yonge Street.

The second source of conflict was the foundation's decision to become a national fundraising organization. The society opposed this move, believing that the foundation would then distance itself from its obligations to fund programs supported by Metro CAS and the Metro Toronto community. There were also concerns that the foundation would begin to use the assets that had been transferred to it when it was established in 1979 to fund these national efforts. Despite these concerns of the society, the foundation established a parallel body, the Kidder Foundation, to begin national fundraising.

In an attempt to resolve the issues, the society and the foundation established a joint committee of their boards. When this committee failed to come to an agreement, the society exercised its rights under the foundation's bylaws to move members of the society board onto the foundation board. This prompted the foundation's board to resign en masse and move to establish the independent Invest In Kids Foundation.

Shortly afterward, Sue Bochner left the CAS Foundation and was replaced in an interim capacity by its manager of grants and allocations, Lynne Slotek.

In 1995, there was a newly constituted foundation board, consisting of several former Metro CAS presidents and chaired by Chris Stringer, along with former and current members of the society's board. It appointed Sheilagh Johnson as the foundation's executive director. Johnson brought more than twenty-five years of public relations, administration and development experience to her new job. For the previous decade, she had been the director of public relations for the Catholic CAS and had established that agency's own charitable foundation.

Johnson's mandate was to stabilize the foundation and tie it closer to Metro CAS. In the meantime, corporate and individual donors were concerned about the issues that had triggered the resignation of the former board members. The viability of the foundation's traditionally successful fundraising events came into question, and the large base of volunteers was confused by what was happening.

Johnson moved quickly to address these concerns, to bring focus to the organization and, with the participation of its board of directors, address what the foundation's priorities should be. These would include a clear emphasis on funding the society's programs and a commitment to the educational and recreational needs of children in care.

Many of these children were lagging behind their peers in school, most did not finish high school and even fewer moved on to post-secondary education. The foundation began to direct funds toward tutoring and special educational assistance, and an ambitious program to help young people through college and university was begun. This work was supported by an education advocate, a staff position at the society that was funded by the foundation. By 1998, the foundation was helping more than 100 former Crown wards to attend postsecondary institutions, with several of them pursuing graduate studies in law, medicine, social work and science.

Corporations responded positively to the foundation's focus on education and enrichment and several new partnerships developed. In 1998, CIBC World Markets established a $300,000 Miracle Fund within the foundation "to provide children with the small miracles that make a difference." A Brownie uniform, a bicycle or the chance to go on the school trip were all possible thanks to this new fund. The same

The foundation began to direct funds toward tutoring and special educational assistance, and an ambitious program to help young people through college and university was begun.

By 1998, the foundation was helping more than 100 former Crown wards to attend postsecondary institutions, with several of them pursuing graduate studies in law, medicine, social work and science.

CIBC World Markets established a $300,000 Miracle Fund within the foundation "to provide children with the small miracles that make a difference."

year, Nike P.L.A.Y. Canada, in conjunction with the Raptors Foundation, established a recreation fund. This additional source of income for Metro CAS programs was extremely valuable at a time when government funding priorities left little money for children to participate in sports and after-school activities.

The foundation also began to support the work of PARC, the transitional program for youth leaving CAS care. It did this not only by transferring money to the program but also by enlisting support for the program from the business community and individual donors.

Although the foundation had traditionally not funded the society's core expenditures, by the mid-1990s budgetary restraints had become such that it was being called upon to support programs — including the primary prevention work undertaken by the society's community workers and by its child welfare and education advocates — that in the past had been funded by government.

As the foundation's fundraising efforts became more and more successful (tripling in the years between 1995 and 1999), the issue of allocating funds nationwide arose once again — many of the foundation's new partners wanted their dollars to help disadvantaged children not only in Metro Toronto but also across the country. This time around, the society and the foundation agreed on a mutually acceptable strategy. Working through the Ontario Association of Children's Aid Societies (OACAS) and the Child Welfare League of Canada, the foundation began to support education and prevention programs in Ontario and in several other provinces. In 1988, to reflect this new direction, the foundation changed its name from the Children's Aid Society of Metropolitan Toronto Foundation to the Children's Aid Foundation.

At a time when government funding of many programs had decreased significantly, the foundation proved to be a lifeline to many small Metro CAS programs as well as community groups working to prevent the abuse of children.

At a time when government funding of many programs had decreased significantly, the foundation proved to be a lifeline to many small Metro CAS programs as well as community groups working to prevent the abuse of children. Its role was to walk the fine line between making a difference in the lives of these children without endorsing government efforts to divest themselves of their responsibilities for the well-being of young people and their families.

Child Mortality Task Force

As was described at the beginning of this book, in the early days of child welfare in Toronto the rate of infant mortality was very high, due to the susceptibility of children to life-threatening infections. The rate of mortality in children's institutions such as the Infants' Home was even higher as a result of the epidemics that constantly swept those residences.

The introduction of pasteurization, immunization and antibiotics, and the move away from institutional to boarding home care for children who were unable to live with their birth families, gradually reduced the death rate. Nevertheless, by the 1990s child welfare agencies across the country had once again come under increasing scrutiny as the result of some high-profile child deaths. The public, concerned that the systems established to protect children might have been failing to do so, was demanding answers.

It was for this reason that, in 1996, a Child Mortality Task Force was established by Mary McConville, the executive director of OACAS, and Jim Cairns, the province's deputy chief coroner, along with Bruce Rivers and other leaders in the field. The task force was given the job of developing strategies to reduce the incidence of such deaths, and over a period of fourteen months it worked with MCSS and all fifty-five CASs across Ontario, as well as with experts in the fields of child welfare, social work education and research, medicine and the law.

The task force determined that, although the death rate among children receiving services from a CAS was lower than for children in the general population, it was higher than average among those children known to CASs who died of accidents, suicides, homicides and undetermined causes.

Over the two-year survey period, 100 children receiving services from an Ontario CAS had died. Thirty-one were in a foster home or other residential program, while the remaining sixty-nine had been living in the community with their families and were receiving supervision, support or investigation and assessment services from a CAS. Of the 100, six committed suicide and eleven were murdered, although none of the homicides occurred while a child was in a foster home or other residential program.

The public, concerned that the systems established to protect children might have been failing to do so, was demanding answers.

The task force determined that, although the death rate among children receiving services from a CAS was lower than for children in the general population, it was higher than average among those children known to CASs who died of accidents, suicides, homicides and undetermined causes.

Most of the Toronto Star's *coverage was unbalanced and unfavourable toward CAS workers, despite the fact that Metro CAS had given the newspaper's reporters unprecedented access to workers and foster parents. The daily barrage of criticism demoralized foster parents and staff, leaving some to wonder why they bothered to come to work in the mornings. The negative publicity was particularly devastating to children in care, several of whom expressed worries about their personal safety.*

The task force's recommendations, many of which were co-opted by the Toronto Star *when formulating its own prescriptions, included:*
*   *legislative amendments to better protect children (including a stronger focus on child neglect);*
*   *public education about risks to young children;*
*   *a provincewide interactive database of families and children receiving child protection services; and*
*   *the use by CAS workers of a standardized risk-assessment tool.*

The inquests underscored the complexity of child protection services and the need for a diverse approach to strengthening the capacity of both the child welfare system and local communities to protect children.

The work of the task force was the focus of intense media coverage, most notably in the *Toronto Star,* which tried to parallel the work of the task force through its own investigative reporting on page one. Most of the *Star's* coverage was unbalanced and unfavourable toward CAS workers, despite the fact that Metro CAS had given the newspaper's reporters unprecedented access to workers and foster parents. Although the society and OACAS attempted to make timely, appropriate responses, including a meeting with the paper's editorial board, the daily barrage of criticism demoralized foster parents and staff, leaving some to wonder why they bothered to come to work in the mornings. The negative publicity was particularly devastating to children in care, several of whom expressed worries about their personal safety.

Nevertheless, the task force reports, published in March and July 1997, and the stories in the media did help focus the spotlight on the needs of vulnerable children and the child welfare system's capacity to meet them. Among the task force's recommendations — many of which were co-opted by the *Star* when it formulated its own prescription in its pages — were legislative amendments to better protect children (including a stronger focus on child neglect), public education about risks to young children, a provincewide interactive database of families and children receiving child protection services, and the use by CAS workers of a standardized risk-assessment tool.

The deaths of Shanay Johnson and Jennifer Koval's'kyj-England

In part to ensure that the Child Mortality Task Force's recommendations were supported by MCSS and the field at large, the coroner's office determined that inquests would be held into the deaths of six children known to CASs across the province.

These inquests, held in 1997 and 1998, described in graphic detail the tragedies that can befall children at risk when the child welfare system lacks the necessary tools and system supports to protect them adequately. They underscored the complexity of child protection services and the need for a diverse approach to strengthening the capacity of both the child welfare system and local communities to protect children.

Two of the inquests were into the deaths of Shanay Johnson and Jennifer Koval's'kyj-England, both of whom were known to Metro CAS. They focused on the role of the society and its decision making with respect to both children. In Jennifer's case, the inquest also focused on the lengthy delays in establishing permanent plans for her future and highlighted the inadequacies of the Child and Family Services Act in ensuring that the child's needs were placed ahead of those of the adults in her life.

Shanay Johnson and her two sisters were apprehended by Metro CAS in January 1992, when Shanay was one month old, because their mother, Teresa Johnson, appeared to be under the influence of drugs. The children were eventually made society wards and they remained in the agency's care until June 1993, by which time the workers believed that Teresa had stopped abusing drugs and had sufficiently stabilized her life that her children could be returned to her under a supervision order. The family appeared to be doing well enough for the supervision order to be terminated in September of that year. Just over a month later, however, Shanay died. Her mother pleaded guilty to manslaughter.

Seven-year-old Jennifer Koval's'kyj-England was killed by her stepfather, Ron England, early one morning in April 1996 after she had walked into her grandmother Marion Johnston's bedroom to find him stabbing her. Ron England (Johnston's adopted son) was a diagnosed paranoid schizophrenic who, at the time of the murders, was not taking his medication. Ron gave himself up to the police and the courts subsequently found him not to be criminally responsible because of his mental disorder.

Jennifer had originally been apprehended by the CAS because her mother was unable to care for her adequately. In due course there was a trial that resulted in a court order that placed Jennifer in Ron England's care, under the supervision of Metro CAS. Because there were so many parties involved, the litigation continued and resulted in more than fifty-eight separate child welfare court hearings over the next five years. A final decision about which of a number of family members was to have custody of Jennifer was still pending at her death.

The jurors in the six inquests combined to make more than 400 recommendations to government, service providers and professionals. They echoed those of

Together, the jurors in the Johnson and Koval's'kyj-England inquests, along with those in the four other inquests held elsewhere in the province, made more than 400 recommendations to government, service providers and professionals.

the Child Mortality Task Force and put a human face on the need for changes to the child welfare system. The juries in the Johnson and Koval's'kyj-England inquests endorsed most of the recommendations suggested to them by Metro CAS.

The jurors called for the Child and Family Services Act be updated, for information to be shared more freely among professionals, for improved training of CAS staff, and for the public — and other professionals — to be made more aware of child abuse and neglect. They also recommended that the province make more funds available to enable CASs to fulfil their mandates adequately, that workload standards for CAS staff be developed and that a standardized, provincewide risk-assessment system be introduced. In addition, they proposed that a comprehensive computerized database be developed for CASs across the province.

The media gave blanket coverage to Shanay Johnson's inquest, the first in the series and the only one to be held in downtown Toronto, home base for many print, radio and television reporters. The society, its work, and its board, staff, foster parents and volunteers were thrust onto the evening television newscasts and the front pages of the morning newspapers.

To help workers deal with the stress of testifying at the inquests — and of doing so under the not-always-friendly glare of the media spotlight — the society designed a support plan. During both inquests, staff were not only given access to professional counselling under the agency's employee assistance program but they were also helped by a peer support team.

A peer support team was established in 1997 to help staff deal with such traumatic events as the death of a child or an assault. This groundbreaking initiative was unique for a child welfare agency at the time.

Coordinated by family services supervisor Phillip Howe, the peer support team had been established in 1997 to help staff deal with such traumatic events as the death of a child or an assault. This groundbreaking initiative was unique for a child welfare agency at the time, and has since been adapted by other not-for-profit social service organizations across North America.

In the meantime, executive director Bruce Rivers' approach to the intense scrutiny was to be proactive rather than reactive:

> As a public organization, funded by and accountable to the taxpayer, we have a responsibility, and a real interest, in helping to build a public understanding of the work we do and the challenges we

face. So every contact with the media becomes a strategic opportunity to inform the public about the day-to-day realities of our work.

During the inquests, Rivers and other agency staff, notably chief counsel Kristina Reitmeier and executive assistant Cory Tuyl, gave frequent interviews to newspaper, radio and television reporters, openly acknowledging problems where they existed and identifying solutions. This helped ensure that journalists, and therefore the public, were educated about the complex issues affecting the child welfare system.

According to former board president Marjorie Perkins: "Bruce felt deeply about what happened to those children. He was shaken and grieving. But he was also able to explain and support his staff to describe what happened and what needed to be done to prevent a reoccurrence. There was no defensive shutting down."

Before, during and after the inquests, front-line staff and foster parents talked almost daily to radio and television reporters and newspaper and magazine journalists about how they were working hard to improve the lives of the children and families on their caseloads about the challenges they faced in doing so. Typical was a feature article by Kim Pittaway in *Chatelaine*, in which she wrote about the lives of CAS workers "behind the headlines," exemplified by the work of long-time Metro CAS staff member Diane Ternan:

> After tragedies [such as the death of a child like Shanay Johnson,] front-line social workers typically get most of the blame. Why hadn't they seen that little Matthew was in danger? Why had Sara's father, jailed once for assaulting his first child at age 10 weeks, been allowed near her? But Diane knows from such experience that such cases are rarely as black and white as the grainy front page photo might have you believe. Social workers must deal with the facts as they find them, trust their own eyes, ears — and guts — in assessing the risks facing a child. And even when you follow all the rules, double-check your instincts and investigate every doubt, mistakes can happen.

"But Diane [Ternan] knows from ... experience that [child abuse] cases are rarely as black and white as the grainy front page photo might have you believe."
— Excerpt from "Behind the Headlines" article in Chatelaine

It was this very public examination of the child welfare system that provided the impetus for the provincial government to embark on the necessary reforms that Metro CAS had been recommending for many years.

Although not all the coverage was as positive as Pittaway's, and some of it was painful in the extreme, the society judged its efforts to increase public awareness of the complexities of child welfare work to have been successful. It was this very public examination of the child welfare system that provided the impetus for the provincial government to embark on the necessary reforms that Metro CAS had been recommending for many years.

Child Welfare Reform

Metro CAS carefully studied the recommendations of the inquest jurors and implemented those that that were within its control. At a press conference in May 1998, on the anniversary of the conclusion of the Johnson inquest, executive director Bruce Rivers said, "The Society can reassure the public that, where it is within our power to do so, we have acted to improve our capacity to protect the children and will be accountable in that regard."

Earlier, in an article published in the *Toronto Star* after the inquest into Shanay Johnson's death, Rivers stated that, while CASs were responsible for protecting the community's children, it was necessary to change those things over which societies had no direct control. Among them was the need for updated child welfare legislation:

> A pattern of neglect culminating in death by abuse marked Shanay's life with her mother. Yet neglect does not prompt the same level of scrutiny that occurs with an abused child. This clearly calls for a strengthening of Ontario's child welfare legislation to include neglect … as grounds for bringing a child into the care of the state.

He also urged the province to make legislative changes that would limit the time children could remain in the temporary care of a CAS. Underfunding of the children's services system was another concern:

The financial resources allocated to [Metro CAS's] base budget have been cut by $4.5 million [in the past five years]. This translates into 50 fewer staff at a time when demand remains high, cases are more complex and the social safety net is rapidly disappearing. Our caseloads are in the twenties but when multiplied by family size it means that each worker is dealing with the needs of 70 individual children, youth and adults. We cannot make balancing the budget a greater priority than the welfare of children.

He also pointed out that the alleviation of the poverty that had created the fertile ground in which child abuse and neglect could easily flourish would ease the public's mounting concern over the deaths of children, particularly those known to CASs.

The government's response was to develop a process of change that became known as its Child Welfare Reform agenda, which MCSS carried out in close cooperation with OACAS and CASs across Ontario. To assist in the process, Metro CAS seconded five of its experienced staff — Trudy Blugerman, Felies Einhorn, Hanna Gavendo, John McCullagh and Corrie Tuyl — to MCSS.

As part of the groundwork to its reform of the system, the government commissioned a review of the Child and Family Services Act's protection provisions by a panel of experts. (This panel included two former staff members of Metro CAS: the chair, Judge Mary Jane Hatton, and Dr. Nico Trocmé of the University of Toronto.) It also ordered a review of the relationship between MCSS and CASs where accountability was concerned, and an audit of 3,000 child protection case files to examine compliance with the ministry's expectations.

There followed a series of initiatives that, it was hoped, would make it easier for those working on the front-line of child welfare to protect children adequately. One of the most important of these initiatives was the introduction in 1999 of a new funding framework for CASs: their operating expenses were now to be financed entirely by the provincial government, thus ending the long time involvement of municipal governments in subsidizing child welfare services.

The purpose of the new framework was to ensure that individual societies were funded on a more equitable basis that reflected their workload and service needs

The Child Welfare Reform Agenda included:
- a review of the CFSA by a panel of experts;
- a review of the accountability relationship between MCSS and CASs;
- an audit of 3,000 child protection case files;
- a new funding framework;
- a provincewide risk-assessment model;
- a provincewide child welfare information system.

more realistically. It included the allocation of $170 million over three years in new funding "to allow societies to hire more staff, provide more training and revitalize foster care." In reality, however, this simply restored the 5 percent cut to child welfare agencies the government had made in 1995.

In May 1999, the Ontario legislature unanimously passed the Child and Family Services Amendment Act, which swung the pendulum back to a focus on the rights of children.

In May 1999, the Ontario legislature unanimously passed the Child and Family Services Amendment Act, whose provisions made it clear that the paramount purpose of child welfare legislation was to promote the interests of children. This represented a swing in the child welfare practice pendulum back from a focus on the rights of parents to those of children. In effect, it belatedly recognized the concerns, highlighted in Chapter 7, that had been raised in the early 1980s by Metro CAS — but ignored by the government of the day — about the importance of placing children's rights and needs in the forefront of the legislation.

The Child and Family Services Amendment Act also broadened the grounds on which a child could be found to be in need of protection, specifically including for the first time the concept of neglect and lowering the threshold for earlier action to protect children. It also promoted more decisive planning for children's futures so that permanent arrangements for those in the care of CASs could be made as soon as possible.

Other reforms to the child welfare system included a mandated, provincewide approach to risk assessment; increased training for CAS boards and staff, foster parents and ministry staff; closer ministry monitoring of the work of CASs; and a new database to link all child welfare agencies across the province.

These reforms were to be reviewed regularly — including a statutory review of child welfare legislation every five years — to ensure that the provincial government and CASs persisted in meeting their common goal of protecting children better.

The tragic deaths of Shanay Johnson, Jennifer Koval's'kyj-England and the other children into whose deaths inquests were held brought about the most significant changes in more than a decade to the system established to protect Ontario's children

The tragic deaths of Shanay Johnson, Jennifer Koval's'kyj-England and the other children into whose deaths inquests were held brought about one positive outcome: the most significant changes in more than a decade to the system established to protect Ontario's children. Along with MCSS, OACAS and its sister agencies across the province, Metro CAS worked diligently to implement those changes. That, however, is a story that must await a later history.

When the CAS of Toronto was founded in 1891, it had no paid staff and depended entirely on volunteers to carry out its work of protecting children and providing substitute care for young people who could not live with their families. While this work was funded by charitable donations, they were not enough to prevent the new agency from recording a deficit in its first year.

Ten years later, at the beginning of a new century, the society remained largely reliant on volunteers — board members, fundraisers, children's visitors and foster parents — although by that time it had begun to employ a few salaried staff members. Nevertheless, it still had to manage its work on an inadequate annual budget, which in 1900 was less than $10,000. While the City of Toronto contributed $3,000, the agency was still dependent on private philanthropy, as it would continue to be for decades to come.

A hundred years later, however, by which time the society had become one of the largest board-operated child welfare agencies in North America, it had a core operating budget of $106 million. Most of this was spent on staffing — in 1998, the salary scale for a front-line worker ranged from $38,500 to $51,000 — and on reimbursing foster parents and other providers for their outlay in looking after children in the agency's care. While these costs were now fully funded by the government of Ontario, the agency was able to balance its books only through careful, efficient management of resources.

By the end of the twentieth century, more than 700 staff, assisted by almost 600 volunteers, helped protect almost 24,000 children a year while providing support to more than 10,000 families. For every child admitted to its care, the agency helped six more in their own homes.

Each year in the 1990s, however, more than 2,000 young people were unable to live with their own families. Three hundred and seventy foster families now provide many of these children with safe, stable and caring homes. Others are looked after in a variety of children's residences, while many older youth live independently in the community under the agency's supervision.

Child abuse and neglect, family breakdown, relationship conflicts, poverty, inadequate housing and the challenges of finding sufficient financial and human resources to address them seem as prevalent at the beginning of the twenty-first century as they were at the end of the nineteenth.

Throughout much of the society's history — and that of the Infants' Homes with which it amalgamated more than fifty years ago — the issues it has faced have been consistent: child abuse and neglect, family breakdown, relationship conflicts, poverty, inadequate housing and the challenges of finding sufficient financial and human resources to address them. All of these seem as prevalent at the beginning of the twenty-first century as they were at the end of the nineteenth.

Despite these challenges, the society has achieved many successes over the years in contributing to the well-being of Toronto's children. Not least among them has been the advancement in child welfare practice that resulted from the series of tragic and highly publicized child deaths and related coroners' inquests described in Chapter 8. The reforms that followed — which were comparable to those that occurred in the 1920s, with the introduction of boarding home care, and those that took place in the forty years after the Second World War, when agency services expanded significantly and sweeping changes were made to legislation and practice — have had a major impact on all aspects of the society's work.

Child protection services cannot be provided in isolation from prevention programs that keep children in their own families whenever possible or the provision of alternatives for those young people who are unable to live at home.

As necessary as the reforms of the late 1990s were, they placed the emphasis of child welfare practice on compliance and accountability and focused on the protection side of the child welfare mandate, with little attention being paid to the parenting role of CASs. Child protection services, however, cannot be provided in isolation from prevention programs that keep children in their own families whenever possible or the provision of alternatives for those young people who are unable to live at home. A major challenge for the CAS of Toronto in the new century, therefore, will be to maintain the continuum of support and services it provides for children and their families and to deliver them in the context of flexibility, creativity and sound clinical judgment.

To meet this challenge, the society and its funders will have to continue to develop innovative early intervention and prevention programs, "pushing the envelope" where necessary, to ensure that as many children as possible can remain safely in their own homes. At the same time they must support extended family members and local communities in providing creatively for children who cannot live with their parents. For those children whose needs include being looked after by caregivers other than their family members, the agency will need adequate resources to meet those needs through imaginatively revitalized foster care and adoption programs. It must also be recognized by Queen's Park that the responsibility for looking after the needs of CAS wards does not necessarily end when they reach the age of eighteen or twenty-one.

The government's reform initiatives have brought increased resources, standardized procedures and better opportunities for the development of the knowledge and skills required of child welfare practitioners. Meeting the new MCSS accountability and compliance requirements, however, has led front-line CAS workers and their supervisors to spend less time providing services directly to children and families and more time documenting their activities and performing other administrative tasks. Despite lowered caseloads and a substantial infusion of money for additional staff, workers at the CAS of Toronto currently spend only 20 percent of their time on direct service. Workers have fewer opportunities to reduce risks to children, while the number of young people admitted to the society's care or being brought before a family court judge have increased dramatically.

It takes time to develop helping and trusting relationships with children and families. If service delivery is to be improved and children protected and cared for adequately, workers will need the time and resources to develop relationships with their clients and to reflect thoughtfully about how to get positive results for the children for whom they are responsible. The sooner children receive the support they need, the greater the chance that they will develop into healthy and productive adults.

For these goals to be realized, the community and governments must commit to adequately fund child welfare and other social and health services. There must also be an investment in children and their families to relieve the poverty in which so many of them live. According to Toronto Campaign 2000, one in three of the

The sooner children receive the support they need, the greater the chance that they will develop into healthy and productive adults.

city's children are poor. More and more hungry children are using food banks, while an increasing percentage are homeless or inadequately housed. Meanwhile, the CAS of Toronto and other community agencies have fewer resources to support such families, despite the knowledge that poverty increases risks to children and the likelihood of child welfare involvement.

This book is about the legacy of 125 years of caring for Toronto's children by the board, staff, foster parents and volunteers of the Children's Aid Society of Toronto. Throughout that long history, each new generation of those who have worked and volunteered for the agency have enhanced that heritage. For those who are currently members of the CAS of Toronto community, what does being involved with the society mean?

For one social worker, CAS means that young people have the right to be cared for:

> A fifteen-year-old youth whose parents have died doesn't have to rent a bed in a rooming house and work six hours a day in a fast food place to stay in high school.

"Why do I work for the CAS?" asks another social worker:

> Because, quite simply, there could be no greater privilege and pleasure than to work for the welfare of children. All life is special but new life is very special indeed.

A parent explains that:

> Thanks to my CAS worker, I never felt alone. There is always someone there to listen to me and help me to be the kind of parent I want to be. I couldn't do it alone. The CAS helped us with our problems before they got out of hand. Now we know how to sit down and talk about our problems. They helped us not to give up.

Another parent recalls that:

> I hated the Children's Aid at the time, but looking back I know that
> me and my kids wouldn't even be friends today without the help of
> our CAS worker. It's been hard, but he has kept us on track.

A youth remembers that being in care meant that he had someone to talk to:

> My workers were respectful of the fact that I was a human being,
> not a number on a caseload. When you notice that, it can really
> give your self-esteem a big boost.

Another youth describes how:

> I came into care because I felt I deserved a safe and warm place to
> live. I know that every child deserves peace, happiness and securi-
> ty in their lives and CAS gave me that.

A nine-year-old boy speaks of his adult special friend:

> We go on trips like to Fun City and Wild Water Kingdom. She
> rents videos and we go to the movies. Sometimes we go to her
> house and we play Monopoly and stuff and eat hot dogs and chips
> and stuff. I get to see her once a week and I like that.

The special friend, meanwhile, relates that volunteering for the agency means
a lot to her:

> It's been really challenging. We've weathered storms together and
> have been able to maintain a relationship. That's been very
> rewarding. But you have to learn to be flexible; they're changing all
> the time, those kids, and I've learned a lot from them.

The volunteer services coordinator knows that:

> We really do some excellent work at this agency. I am proud of my colleagues and the effort that they put forward. Being a volunteer coordinator means that I am allowed the privilege to showcase this work. When I'm recruiting new volunteers I tell them what my colleagues are attempting to do and how they can help.

A foster mother remembers how:

> About thirteen years ago, my youngest child was about nine years old and I sadly realized that my baby years were probably over. So I decided to leave my job and foster babies instead. The joy that I've experienced in doing that has certainly changed my life and I look forward to many more years of this rewarding responsibility.

An adoptive mother talks about how she was a single mother with a background similar to many children in care:

> My workers made me feel safe enough to be totally honest with them and they saw the positives in my past. My son and I will be eternally grateful.

Another adoptive family says that:

> The CAS is an indispensable organization that brings happiness to numerous Toronto children and their parents who need their guidance and expertise. Our home is alive with a small child's laughter and love because of them. There's nothing more wonderful. Thank you.

A board member comments that:

> Members of the board endeavour to represent the society in the community and to bring the perspectives of their own experiences to the decisions they make. These are important responsibilities. We take them seriously. And we consider ourselves privileged to serve on the board of an organization as well managed, capable and caring as this one.

A corporate donor says:

> We look carefully at where we donate our money. The Children's Aid Foundation is one charity that is always at the top of our list. We know the excellent work that they do and we are proud to be a part of it.

A former member of the agency's staff who is now retired says that:

> One cannot work at the CAS of Toronto without a lasting effect. I have fond memories of my many years at the agency and the opportunity it afforded me to develop lifelong friendships and professional relationships. I'm lucky in the opportunities the agency gave me to help protect kids from abuse and neglect, to help parents build healthy families and to help provide a safe, nurturing place for children and young adults who couldn't live with their own families.

A staff Alumni Association was formed in 1995 as a means of capturing this kind of commitment among retired and former staff members of the society. Its objectives are to keep them in touch with the agency and with each other and to enable those who wish to do so to continue their contribution to child welfare by working as volunteers on society and foundation projects.

These objectives are being met successfully. Many staff alumni continue to contribute time and energy to assist the agency in its mandate to protect children, and they have also contributed to several projects, including sponsoring this book on the society's history.

That history is a rich one. The legacy of caring and compassion pioneered by J.J. Kelso, Vera Moberly, John MacDonald, Bob Mills and others continues in the work the Children's Aid Society of Toronto at the beginning of a new millennium.

Names by which the Agency Has Been Known

1875–1877	Infants' Home of Toronto	1891–1893	Toronto Children's Aid Society
1877–1942	Infants' Home and Infirmary	1893–1951	Children's Aid Society of Toronto
1942–1951	Infants' Homes of Toronto		

1951–1957	Children's Aid and Infants' Homes of Toronto
1957–1998	Children's Aid Society of Metropolitan Toronto
1998–	Children's Aid Society of Toronto

Presidents and Chief Executive Officers

Infants' Home

Presidents

1875–1900	Charlotte Ridout
1900–1901	Ms. T.W. Dyas
1901–1918	Marion Boultbee
1918–1919	Ms. J. Wright (acting)
1919–1926	Ms. J.D. Tyrrell
1926–1933	Ms. J.K. McMaster
1933–1936	Ms. C. Gurney
1936–1939	Ms. E. Jarvis
1939–1942	Ms. J. Baxter
1942–1946	Winnifred Scott
1946–1949	Margaret Rolph
1949–1951	Helen Bongard

Matrons

1877–1878	Ms. Robinson
1878–1879	Ms. Gwyn

Lady Superintendents

1879–1886	Ms. Gwyn
1886–1892	Ms. Boultbee
1892–1893	Ms. Macdonald
1893–1911	Ms. Jordan
1911–1918	Isobel Wilson
1918–1919	Ms. Hobkirk

General Secretary

1919–1924	Vera Moberly

Executive Secretaries

1924–1945	Vera Moberly
1945–1951	Belle Carver

Children's Aid Society

Presidents

1891–1892	John Joseph Kelso
1892–1921	John Kidson MacDonald
1921–1931	A.R. Auld
1931–1945	C.S. MacDonald
1945–1948	A.F.D. Lace
1948–1950	A.W. Eastmure
1950–1953	J.W. Walker
1953–1955	A.W. Eastmure
1955–1957	J.M. Macintosh
1957–1960	M.F. Newman
1960–1963	Mary Heintzman
1963–1966	E.A. Meredith
1966–1968	R.O. Moore
1968–1970	Alan Watson
1970–1972	Thomas Abel
1972–1974	Charles Tidy
1974–1976	Albert Edwards
1976–1978	Anne Corbett
1978–1980	Peter Tuck
1980–1982	Joan Soloninka
1982–1983	Mary Louise Clements
1983–1984	David Fuller
1984–1985	David Murray
1985–1986	Carol Irwin
1986–1987	Ev Elting
1987–1988	Jim Patterson
1988–1989	Ralph Agard
1989–1990	Barry Brace
1990–1991	Chris Stringer
1991–1992	Bob Witterick
1992–1995	Jack Darville
1995–1996	Joyce Barretto
1997–1998	George Henne
1998–1999	Pam Horton
1999–2000	Valerie Witterick

Secretaries

1891–1893	Stuart Coleman
1893–1894	Rev. J.E. Starr
1894–1906	Stuart Coleman
1906–1923	William Duncan

Managing Directors

1923–1947	Bob Mills
1947–1951	Stuart Sutton

Executive Directors

1951–1954	Stuart Sutton
1954–1973	Lloyd Richardson
1973–1978	Ed Watson
1978–1984	Doug Barr
1984–1988	Mel Finlay
1989–	Bruce Rivers

Administrative Offices and Shelters

Infants' Home

Administrative offices and shelters

1875–1876	11 Caer Howell [Elm] Street
1876–1882	678 Yonge Street
1882–1926	21 St. Mary Street
1926–1951	34 Grosvenor Street

Receiving Centres

1941–1947	38–40 Huntley Street
1947–1951	15 Huntley Street

Children's Aid Society

Administrative offices

1891–1894	32 Church Street
1894–1902	12 Richmond Street East
1902–1924	229 Simcoe Street
1924–1928	80 University Avenue
1928–1953	32 Isabella Street
1953–	33 Charles Street East

Shelters

1891–1894	18 Centre Avenue
1894–1902	135 Adelaide Street East
1902–1928	229 Simcoe Street
1928–1953	33 Charles Street East

Receiving Centre

1951–1974	15 Huntley Street

APPENDIX 4

Bibliography and a Note on Sources

Advisory Committee on Child Welfare (1964). *Report*. Toronto: Ministry of Social and Family Services.

Aitken, Gail (1983). *Criteria of Adoptability in Ontario, 1945–1965: The Circumstances, Processes and Effects of Policy Change*. Unpublished Ph.D. thesis, University of Toronto.

Aitken, Gail (1987). Critical Compromises in Ontario's Child Welfare Policy. In Ismael, Jacqueline S. (ed.). *The Canadian Welfare State: Evolution and Transition*. Edmonton: University of Alberta Press.

Allen, Judge H. Ward (1982). *Judicial Inquiry into the Case of Kim Anne Popen by the Children's Aid Society of the City of Sarnia and the County of Lambton*. Toronto: Queen's Printer for Ontario.

ARA Consulting Group (1998). *Child Welfare Accountability Review*. Toronto: Ministry of Community and Social Services.

Baker, Maureen (1996). *Families: Changing Trends in Canada*. Toronto: McGraw-Hill.

Bullen, John (1986). Hidden Workers: Child Labour and the Family Economy in Late Nineteenth Century Urban Canada. *Labour/Le Travail*, No. 18.

Bullen, John (1988). J.J. Kelso and the "New" Child Savers: The Genesis of the Children's Aid Movement in Ontario. Windsor, Ontario: Paper presented at the Canadian Historical Association Annual Meeting, University of Windsor.

Child Mortality Task Force (1997). *Final Report*. Toronto: Ontario Association of Children's Aid Societies and the Office of the Chief Coroner of Ontario.

Children's Aid Society of Metropolitan Toronto. *Service Plans 1990–1998.* Unpublished.

Children's Aid Society of Metropolitan Toronto (1990). *Metro CAS in the 1990s.* Unpublished.

Children's Aid Society of Metropolitan Toronto (1996). *Long Range Plan 1996–1999.* Unpublished.

Children's Aid Society of Toronto (1999). *Long Range Plan 2000–2003.* Unpublished.

Committee on Child Care and Adoption Services (1951). *Report to the Minister.* Toronto: Department of Public Welfare.

Clement, Dan (1999). *Toronto at a Turning Point.* Toronto: United Way of Greater Toronto.

Dawson, Ross (1982). "Sexual Abuse of Children: A Training Program for Children's Aid Society Staff Providing Services to Sexually Abused Children and Their Families." Unpublished.

Department of the Provincial Treasurer, Bureau of Statistical Research (1947). *A Conspectus of the Province of Ontario, Canada.* Toronto: King's Printer.

Directors of Service of Ontario's Children's Aid Societies (2001). *A Critical Analysis of the Evolution of Reform: The Unintended Consequences of Child Welfare Reform on Clinical Practice.* Unpublished.

Falconer, Nancy (1983). *Preparing for Practice.* Toronto: Children's Aid Society of Metropolitan Toronto.

Garber, Ralph (1978). *Report of the Task Force on Child Abuse.* Toronto: Queen's Printer for Ontario.

Glazebrook, G.P. de T. (1971). *The Story of Toronto.* Toronto: University of Toronto Press.

Goldstein, Joseph, Freud, Anna and Solnit, Albert (1973). *Beyond the Best Interests of the Child.* Toronto: Macmillan Canada.

Hanson, Hugh (1974). *Report on Selected Issues and Relationships by the Task Force on Children's Support Services, Vol. 5.* Toronto: Queen's Printer for Ontario.

Hoen, Beth, Wild, Philippa and Bales, Vicki (1996). *A History of the Roles assumed by the Ministry of Community and Social Services in the Provision of Child Welfare Services.* Unpublished.

Jolliffe, Russell (1952). *The History of the Children's Aid Society of Toronto 1891–1947*. Unpublished MSW thesis, University of Toronto.

Jones, Andrew and Rutman, Leonard (1981). *In the Children's Aid: J.J. Kelso and Child Welfare in Ontario*. Toronto: University of Toronto Press.

Kealey, Gregory S. (1987). Labour and Working Class History in Canada: Prospects in the 1980s. *Labour/Le Travail*, No. 19.

Kirk, H. David (1981). *Adoptive Kinship: A Modern Institution in Need of Reform*. Toronto: Butterworth.

Latimer, Elspeth A. (1953). *Methods of Child Care as Reflected in the Infants' Home of Toronto, 1875–1920*. Unpublished MSW thesis, University of Toronto.

Lemon, Eleanor (1975). Vera Moberly. *Our Children*, Vol. 12, No. 1. Toronto: Children's Aid Society of Metropolitan Toronto.

Lemon, Eleanor (1975). J.J. Kelso, the Children's Advocate. *Our Children*, Vol. 12, No. 2. Toronto: Children's Aid Society of Metropolitan Toronto.

Lemon, Eleanor (1975). Robert Mills. *Our Children*, Vol. 12, No. 2. Toronto: Children's Aid Society of Metropolitan Toronto.

Mayor's Homelessness Action Task Force (1999). *Taking Responsibility for Homelessness: An Action Plan for Toronto*. Toronto: City of Toronto.

McCullagh, John (1995). *We Are Your Children Too: Accessible Child Welfare Services for Lesbian, Gay and Bisexual Youth*. Toronto: Children's Aid Society of Metropolitan Toronto.

McLean, Catherine (1975). John Kidson MacDonald. *Our Children*, Vol. 12, No. 3. Toronto: Children's Aid Society of Metropolitan Toronto.

Milan, Anne (2000). One Hundred Years of Families. *Canadian Social Trends*, No. 56. Ottawa: Statistics Canada.

Ministry of Community and Social Services Staff (1983). *Three Decades of Change: The Evolution of Residential Care and Community Alternatives in Children's Services*. Toronto: Ministry of Community and Social Services.

Morrison, Terrence (1971). *The Child and Urban Social Reform in Late Nineteenth Century Ontario*. Unpublished Ph.D. thesis, University of Toronto.

Panel of Experts on Child Protection (1998). *Protecting Vulnerable Children*. Toronto: Ministry of Community and Social Services.

Piva, Michael (1979). *The Condition of the Working Class in Toronto, 1900–1921.* Ottawa: University of Ottawa Press.

Rooke, Patricia T. and Schnell, R.L. (1983). *Discarding the Asylum: From Child Rescue to the Welfare State in English Canada.* Lanham, Maryland: University Press of America.

Silverman, Peter (1978). *Who Speaks for the Children? The Plight of the Battered Child.* Toronto: Musson Book Company.

Spettigue, C. Owen (1958). *An Historical Review of Ontario Legislation on Child Welfare.* Toronto: Department of Public Welfare.

Strange, Carolyn (1995). *Toronto's Girl Problem: The Perils and Pleasures of the City, 1880–1930.* Toronto: University of Toronto Press.

Sutherland, Neil (1976). *Children in English Canadian Society: Framing the Twentieth Century Consensus.* Toronto: University of Toronto Press.

Task Force on Adoption and Foster Care (1970). *Report.* Toronto: Ministry of Community and Social Services.

Toronto Campaign 2000 (2000). *Report Card on Child Poverty in Toronto.* Toronto: Campaign 2000.

Urwick, Currie and Partners (1970). *Study of the Managerial Effectiveness of Children's Aid Societies in Ontario.* Unpublished.

Valverde, Mariana (1991). *The Age of Light, Soap and Water: Moral Reform in English Canada, 1885–1925.* Toronto: McClelland and Stewart.

White, Randall (1985). *Ontario, 1610–1985: A Political and Economic History.* Toronto: Dundurn Press.

Williams, Clifford J. (1984). *Decades of Service: A History of the Ontario Ministry of Community and Social Services 1930–1980.* Toronto: Ministry of Community and Social Services.

Besides the manuscripts listed above, and the personal testimonies of those credited on the acknowledgments page, a major reference source used in the writing of this book was the historical material on the Children's Aid Society of Toronto and the Infants' Home and Infirmary housed in the archives of the City of Toronto.

This archival material includes annual reports, board and committee minutes, financial records, complaint books, operational records, policies and position papers, theses, fundraising appeals, public relations brochures, newspaper clippings, correspondence, agency reviews and provincial government papers.

The agency journal, *Our Children*, published between 1964 and 1987, and its successor, *Communicate*, which commenced publication in 1991, were major reference sources on the events of the last four decades of the twentieth century. Many of the articles these journals contain were written anonymously, and excerpts from several of them are reproduced verbatim as part of the text of this book.

The photographs reproduced throughout the book, except those credited below, are from the archives of the Children's Aid Society of Toronto. The author wishes to thank the copyright owners of the following photographs for permission to reproduce them:

Chapter 1, page 28. Reproduced with permission of City of Toronto Archives, SC1, Item 142.

Chapter 2, page 45. Reproduced with permission of City of Toronto Archives, SC1, Series B, 1896 Annual Report, Back Cover.

Chapter 2, page 45. Reproduced with permission of City of Toronto Archives, SC1, Series B, 1903 Annual Report, Page 1.

Chapter 2, page 47. Reproduced with permission of City of Toronto Archives, SC1, Series B, 1908 Annual Report, Page 26.

Chapter 2, page 50. Reproduced with permission of City of Toronto Archives, SC1, Series B, 1910 Annual Report, Page 21.

Chapter 2, page 60. Reproduced with permission of City of Toronto Archives, SC1, Series B, 1896 Annual Report, Page 55.

Chapter 3, page 76. Reproduced printed with permission of City of Toronto Archives, SC1, Item 2.

Chapter 3, page 84. Reproduced with permission of City of Toronto Archives, SC1, Series B, 1924 Annual Report, Page 5.

Chapter 4, page 97. Reproduced with permission of City of Toronto Archives, SC1, Item 134.

Chapter 4, page 104. Reproduced with permission of City of Toronto Archives, SC1, Series G, File 1, Item 1.

Chapter 5, page 114. Reproduced with permission of City of Toronto Archives, SC1, Series B, 1951 Annual Report, Page 7.

Chapter 8, page 254. Reproduced with permission of *The Globe and Mail*.

INDEX